The Macroeconomics of the Arab States of the Gulf

The Macroeconomics of the Arab States of the Gulf

Raphael Espinoza, Ghada Fayad,
and Ananthakrishnan Prasad

OXFORD
UNIVERSITY PRESS

OXFORD
UNIVERSITY PRESS

Great Clarendon Street, Oxford, OX2 6DP,
United Kingdom

Oxford University Press is a department of the University of Oxford.
It furthers the University's objective of excellence in research, scholarship,
and education by publishing worldwide. Oxford is a registered trade mark of
Oxford University Press in the UK and in certain other countries

First Edition published in 2013

Impression: 1

Published in the United States of America by Oxford University Press
198 Madison Avenue, New York, NY 10016, United States of America

British Library Cataloguing in Publication Data
Data available

Library of Congress Control Number: 2013943976

ISBN 978–0–19–968379–6

Printed and bound in Great Britain by
CPI Group (UK) Ltd, Croydon, CR0 4YY

Foreword

The Gulf Cooperation Council (GCC) countries have made immense progress in developing their economies over the past ten years. While the prosperity of the region is undeniably linked to developments in the oil and gas sectors, it was prudent policymaking emphasizing domestic investments that led to the region's rapid growth and increased economic diversity. The importance of the GCC has now expanded beyond oil and gas markets into other sectors: it is a major market for migrant workers, a source of remittances, a financial center, and a hub for international trade and business services. That is why this book not only examines the region's management of macroeconomic cycles, but also analyzes issues around labor markets, immigration, diversification, and market efficiency.

Some of the region's challenges are clear. Commodity exporters such as the GCC often run the risk of overreliance on their natural resources, eventually resulting in a "resource curse". This can originate in inefficiencies in government, or the mismanagement of volatile national income.

Despite these challenges, the region has so far managed to use its oil wealth to provide services for its citizens and to attract the foreign workers and capital needed for the infrastructure developments that will lead to quality-of-life improvements.

Indeed, the GCC countries entered the global crisis from a position of strength. GCC governments had the policy tools and options available to them when they were needed to support domestic demand, provide liquidity support, and recapitalize banks. While the economic impact of most of these measures was intuitively understood by GCC policymakers, by and large only a few such decisions were based on rigorous data analyses. Going forward, ensuring that these policies are implemented for maximum benefit will require the kind of deeper analytical inquiry this book provides.

Fiscal and monetary policies are important aspects of that inquiry in the GCC. With pegged exchange rate regimes, monetary policy is constrained by financial integration, and fiscal instruments become the policymakers' main method of adjustment. But because these countries now rely heavily on foreign workers and imports, fiscal multipliers may be weak. An important empirical question thus becomes determining the impact of fiscal and monetary policies on economic activity. It is questions such as these that this book attempts to answer. A fuller understanding of the interplay of these policy choices is vital to the work of the region's policymakers who are shaping the economic futures of these countries' citizens for years to come.

The global crisis revealed the region's strengths and weaknesses, making this a particularly appropriate time to analyze the GCC region's macroeconomic situation. Such analysis relies on the expertise of this book's authors but also on the spirit of trust and cooperation that has been cultivated between the International Monetary Fund and its member countries' authorities. To date, this is the only book available on the macroeconomics of the GCC countries, providing original insights into the functioning of the GCC markets and the policy challenges ahead.

This book, like other IMF work in the region, is part of an ongoing research agenda that recognizes the area's important contributions to global economic and financial stability. Maintaining and building on that stability are important steps toward broadening equality and fostering prosperity.

Christine Lagarde
Managing Director
International Monetary Fund

Acknowledgments

This book is the product of several years of research undertaken at the International Monetary Fund, as well as research time spent at the Oxford Centre for the Analysis of Resource-Rich Economies. We are grateful to both these institutions and in particular to Messrs Masood Ahmed, Tim Callen, Sandy Donaldson, Alfred Kammer, David Robinson, Abdelhak Senhadji, Rick Van der Ploeg, and Anthony Venables for providing the supporting environment and resources that enabled us to complete this book.

We also benefitted enormously from the comments from five anonymous referees, Christopher Adam, Zsofia Arvai, Alberto Behar, Samya Beidas-Strom, Kevin Carey, Reda Cherif, May Khamis, Prakash Loungani, Tobias Rasmussen, David Robinson, Abdelhak Senhadji, Niklas Westelius, Oral Williams, as well as colleagues and seminar participants at the Mediterranean Research Conferences, 2010 and 2011, the GCC Banking Conference, 2011, and the Qatar Capital Markets Conference, Qatar 2012, and at Oxford University and the IMF.

We are also grateful to Chifundo Moya, Arthur Ribeiro, and Renas Sidahmed for their excellent research and editorial assistance. Special thanks go to Adam Swallow, the Economics and Finance Academic Editor at Oxford University Press, and the Assistant Editor Aimee Wright for supporting this project at a very early stage. Our book could not have seen the light without the continuing support of our families and loved ones, to whom our final thanks go.

The views expressed in this book are those of the authors and do not necessarily represent those of the IMF or IMF policy.

R. Espinoza
G. Fayad
A. Prasad

Contents

List of Figures	xiii
List of Tables	xv
List of Abbreviations	xvii
1. Introductory Chapter	1
1.1 Introduction	1
1.2 Structural Characteristics	4
1.3 Macroeconomic Policy During the Crisis	7
References	11
2. The Determinants of Long-Term Growth in the GCC Countries	13
2.1 Introduction	13
2.2 Economic Data	16
2.3 Diversification and the Drivers of Long-Term Growth	20
2.3.1 Diversification	20
2.3.2 The Stock of Capital	21
2.3.3 Human Capital	24
2.4 A Growth-Accounting Exercise	25
2.5 Total Factor Productivity and Country Characteristics	29
2.5.1 Type of Capital	29
2.5.2 Institutions and the Empirical Growth Literature	30
Initial Income per Capita and Convergence	31
Size of the Government	33
Inflation and Macroeconomic Stability	33
Volatility and Growth	34
Openness to Trade	35
Institutions	35
References	37
3. The Macroeconomic Impact of Migration	40
3.1 Introduction	40
3.2 Background on GCC Labor Markets	42

3.2.1 Immigration and Remittances 42
Immigrants' Rights 42
Composition of Foreign Workforce 43
Remittances 44
3.2.2 Labor Market Segmentation and Wage Disparities 45
3.2.3 Unemployment 47
3.2.4 Nationalization 49
3.3 Diversification in the GCC 50
3.4 Simple Theoretical Model 51
3.5 Estimation 56
3.6 Results 59
3.7 Conclusion 61
Technical Appendix 62
References 63

4. Government Spending, Subsidies, and Economic Efficiency 65
4.1 Introduction 65
4.2 Government Spending and the GCC Development Strategy 67
4.2.1 Public Investment 67
4.2.2 Support to the Corporate Sector and Subsidies 70
4.3 An Inverse Ramsey Model 73
4.4 Distortions in Labor Markets 78
4.5 Conclusion 83
References 84

5. Fiscal Policy for Macroeconomic Stability 86
5.1 Introduction 86
5.2 Background 88
5.3 The Empirical Literature on Fiscal Multipliers 90
5.4 Econometric Estimates of Fiscal Multipliers 92
5.4.1 Panel Model 93
5.4.2 Fiscal Policy and Economic Cycles 95
5.5 Contribution of Fiscal Policy to Economic Cycles 102
5.6 Conclusion 108
References 110

6. Monetary Policy with a Fixed Exchange Rate Regime 112
6.1 Introduction 112

6.2 Experience with Inflation in the GCC Countries 113
6.3 Behavior of GCC Monetary Policy vis-à-vis the United States 115
6.4 Interest Rate Pass-Through 116
6.5 Monetary Transmission in the GCC—A Panel VAR Approach 121
6.5.1 Data 123
6.5.2 Annual Data Panel VAR 123
6.5.3 Quarterly Data Panel VAR 131
6.6 Summary and Policy Implications 134
References 134

7. Nonperforming Loans and Financial Stability 136
7.1 Introduction 136
7.2 Determinants of Nonperforming Loans 139
7.3 A Panel Model for GCC Banks 141
7.4 Concluding on the Systemic Importance of Credit Risk 145
Appendix 148
References 149

8. Financial Markets in the GCC Countries 151
8.1 Introduction 151
8.2 Background on GCC Stock Markets 152
8.2.1 GCC stock Markets' Integration: Global and Regional Spillovers 154
8.3 Banking System 155
8.4 Econometric Methods 160
8.4.1 Conditional Value at Risk (Co-VaR) Methodology 160
8.4.2 Distress Dependence Methodology 161
8.5 Results 162
8.5.1 International Spillovers 162
8.5.2 Local Spillovers within and Between UAE and Saudi Arabia 163
8.6 Conclusion 167
References 167

9. The Importance of the GCC for the Wider Region 168
9.1 Economic Openness and Spillovers 168

9.1.1 The Importance of Migration and Remittances 169
9.1.2 International Trade 170
9.1.3 Complementarity between Migration and FDI 172
9.1.4 Foreign Aid 174
9.2 Concluding on the Importance of the GCC 176
References 178

Index 181

List of Figures

1.1	GCC: Proved reserves and projected depletion of oil and gas, selected years	5
1.2	Sachs and Warner's (2001) natural resource curse	6
2.1	World rankings of income per capita (2009)	19
2.2	Oil production and per capita income in the region (1990–2005)	20
2.3	Total factor productivity relative to the US (total GDP and non-oil GDP) (logarithmic scale, 2008)	27
2.4	Contributions to the annual percentage change in GDP per worker (1990–2009)	28
2.5	Imports of capital, by type (darker color for increasingly R&D-intensive capital)	30
2.6	Contributions to TFP (1991–2009), in difference from median non-oil-exporting country	32
3.1	Remittance outflows in percent of GDP, average 2000–10	45
3.2	Saudi to non-Saudi monthly wages in the private sector by education, 2009 (ratio)	47
3.3	Wage ratios by sector and nationality in Bahrain, 2002–10	48
3.4	Youth and total unemployment rates (in percent, latest available date)	48
3.5	Share of non-oil exports in total exports (in percent)	51
3.6	Share of petrochemical exports in total non-oil exports (in percent)	52
4.1	Budgetary spending, by outlay	66
4.2	Investment/non-oil GDP and oil GDP/non-oil GDP (1980–2009)	69
4.3	Total Factor Productivity and the Public Investment Management Index	69
4.4	Subsidies and size of the oil sector	74
4.5	Subsidies and welfare losses	77
4.6	Equilibrium in the labor market	81
5.1	Non-oil real GDP growth and real growth in total government expenditure	94
5.2	Fiscal multiplier (impact of total government spending on non-oil GDP)	101
5.3	Impact of world growth on non-oil growth in the GCC	102
5.4	Pro-cyclicality of fiscal policy: Response of government spending to non-oil GDP shocks, in percent deviation from baseline	103

5.5 Saudi Arabia (non-oil GDP growth on LHS scale, contributions on the RHS) 105
5.6 UAE (non-oil GDP growth on LHS scale, contributions on the RHS) 106
5.7 Kuwait (data post-1996 is from IMF; data pre-1996 is from UN). Dummies for estimation in 1991 and 1992 107
5.8 Qatar (non-oil GDP growth on LHS scale, contributions on the RHS) 107
5.9 Oman (non-oil GDP growth on LHS scale, contributions on the RHS) 108
5.10 Bahrain (non-oil GDP growth on LHS scale, contributions on the RHS) 109
6.1 CPI inflation, in percentage points 113
6.2 Interbank and retail interest rates (in percent) 118
6.3 Dynamic adjustment of deposit and lending rates to shocks in the interbank rates 119
6.4 Annual data panel VAR 124
6.5 Quarterly data panel VAR 128
6.6 Robustness to VAR specification and composition 132
7.1 NPL ratio and economic activity in the GCC 138
7.2 Bank heterogeneity and the business cycle 139
7.3 Logit transformation of the NPL ratio 142
7.4 Dynamics of NPLs with maintained macroeconomic shocks 145
7.5 Feedback effect—panel VAR impulse response functions 146
8.1 GCC: Market indices, January 2007–March 2012 156
8.2 Expected default frequencies of local UAE banks, 2008–10 159
8.3 Expected default frequencies of Saudi banks, 2008–10 159
8.4 International spillovers to UAE banks: Effect of distress in Europe and the United States, 2008–10 162
8.5 International spillovers to Saudi Arabian banks: Effect of distress in Europe and the United States, 2008–10 163
8.6 Bank stability index of local banks, 2008–10 165
8.7 Intra-regional spillovers between UAE and Saudi Arabian banks, 2008–10 166
9.1 Remittances from the GCC in 2010 170
9.2 Geographical distribution of GCC merchandise trade, 2000–10 171
9.3 Merchandise trade with the GCC, 2011 171
9.4 GCC outward FDI, 1985–2009 173
9.5 GCC aid outflows by source country, 2002–10 174
9.6 Arab aid through development funds, 2002–10 175
9.7 Sectoral distribution of Arab aid through development funds, 2002–10 176

List of Tables

1.1 GCC selected economic indicators, 1981–90 average, 1991–2000 average, 2001–10 average 3

2.1 Nominal GDP and annual growth rate of real GDP and real GDP per worker (1990 to 2009) 14

2.2 Employment and population in the GCC, in millions 16

2.3 Nominal value added by sectors, in percent of nominal non-oil GDP 22

2.4 Investment and growth in the stock of capital 24

2.5 Growth accounting of GDP per capita, (contributions, in percentage points, 1990–2009) 28

3.1 Share of high-skilled migrants by region in 2000 44

3.2 Government views and policies on immigration, 2009 44

3.3 Public-sector employment as a share of total employment of nationals in the GCC 46

3.4 Effect of remittance outflows on the REER, 1980–2009 60

4.1 Subsidies and opportunity costs/implicit subsidies, 2010 71

5.1 Standard deviation of GDP growth per capita in percent, 1976–2007 87

5.2 Characteristics of GCC economies and government expenditure 89

5.3 Data sources 93

5.4 GCC panel fiscal multipliers—dependent variable: non-oil real GDP growth 96

5.5 GCC panel fiscal multipliers, controlling for inflation and oil prices 98

5.6 Elasticity of spending to a permanent increase in oil price in the VARs 101

5.7 Non-oil GDP growth: Forecast Error Variance Decomposition two years ahead 104

6.1 Cointegration vector 120

6.2 Forecast Error Variance Contribution 121

6.3 Correlation matrix of innovations 123

6.4 OLS estimates of the annual VAR 126

7.1 Summary statistics on nonperforming loans, 1995–2008 137

7.2	Macroeconomic and firm-specific determinants of NPLs	144
7.3	Bankscope coverage in the GCC	148
8.1	Foreign investment ceiling for listed stocks in the GCC markets	153
8.2	Market capitalization losses	155
8.3	Correlations of stock market indices with S&P 500	155
8.4	Stock market volatilities	157
8.5	GCC: Loans, deposits, and foreign assets and liabilities, 2011	157
8.6	Co-VaR estimates for UAE banks, 2008–10	164
8.7	Co-VaR estimates for Saudi Arabian banks, 2008–10	165
9.1	Growth spillover model	177

List of Abbreviations

AIC	Akaike Information Criterion
BIC	Bayesian Information Criterion
BSI	Bank Stability Index
Co-VaR	Conditional Value at Risk
CPI	Consumer Price Index
CPIA	Country Policy and Institutional Assessment
ECM	Error Correction Model
EDF	Expected Default Frequency
FE	fixed effects
FEVD	Forecast Error Variance Decomposition
FFR	Fed Funds Rate
FSI	financial soundness indicator
GCC	Gulf Cooperation Council
HDI	Human Development Index
ICRG	International Country Risk Guide
IEA	International Energy Agency
IRF	impulse response function
IV	instrumental variable
JPoD	Joint Probability of Default
LR	likelihood ratio
LHS	Left-hand side
MENA	Middle East and North Africa
NPL	nonperforming loan
PIMI	Public Investment Management Index
PMG	pooled mean group
POLS	pooled ordinary least squares
PPP	Purchasing Power Parity
PWT	Penn Word Tables
RE	random effects
REDF	Real Estate Development Fund
REER	real effective exchange rate
RHS	Right-hand side
SBC	Schwarz Bayesian Criterion
TFP	Total Factor Productivity
VAR	Vector Auto-Regression
VIX	Volatility Index

1

Introductory Chapter

1.1 Introduction

The countries of the Gulf Cooperation Council (GCC) have gone through considerable changes in the last decade, spurred by high oil prices and ambitious diversification plans.[1] The changes have affected literally all sectors of the economy. Large-scale immigration has provided the labor force while capital inflows and financial development have leveraged oil wealth to finance diversification. Regional integration plans are advancing although it is not clear yet what the prospects are for monetary union.

As the GCC economies modernize, macroeconomic policies will gain importance. And with the increasing sophistication of their market economies, policymakers and analysts will need to further their understanding of the macroeconomic structure and of the linkages that are now at work in the region. The aim of this book is to provide original insights into the functioning of the GCC macroeconomy and the policy challenges ahead, and is based on quantitative assessments of the structure of the economy and of the key macroeconomic relationships. Econometric models can now be estimated in the GCC because the structural break that took place in the late 1970s is more than thirty years ago. A major drawback for statistical analysis remains, however, the absence of quarterly data for the national accounts. Analyses can benefit nevertheless from the cross-sectional dimension: panel models are often appropriate because the GCC is a fairly homogenous group. This is one reason why the focus of the book is on the GCC as opposed to a larger group

[1] The GCC comprises six member countries, namely, Bahrain, Kuwait, Oman, Saudi Arabia, Qatar, and the United Arab Emirates.

of Middle-Eastern oil producers, though many of the issues covered in the different chapters would also be relevant for the broader region.

The second reason why we focus on the GCC is that this group of countries has been advancing economic union. In May 1981, the rulers of the six GCC states reached an agreement, formulated in the GCC Charter, that the objectives of the GCC include strengthening ties between peoples, formulating similar regulations in various economic and administrative areas, and fostering scientific and technical progress. The creation of a monetary union has also been an important objective of the GCC that was stated soon after its foundation in 1981.

The GCC economic agreement of 1981 was revised in 2001, setting a timetable to establish a customs union and peg currencies to the US dollar by January 1, 2003. The Common External Tariff was established in 2003, and the common market, giving citizens the same rights and entitlements in each country, started on January 1, 2008. Convergence criteria for a monetary union, to be achieved by 2005, have also been discussed since 2001, and the initial plan was to introduce the single currency by 2010 (Al-Jasser and Al-Hamidy 2003).

The convergence criteria[2] established ceilings and floors on: inflation rates (the weighted average of inflation rates in all members plus two percentage points); short-term interest rates (the average of the lowest three among members' three-month interbank rates plus two percentage points); foreign exchange reserves (at least four months of imports); fiscal deficits (not to exceed 3 percent of GDP);[3] and public debt to GDP ratios (not to exceed 60 percent). The GCC countries have made a lot of progress and have achieved the convergence criteria on nearly all fronts. Table 1.1 shows the relevant economic indicators for the GCC on average. In addition, GCC countries officially pegged their currencies to the US dollar in 2002–3.[4]

There are both costs and benefits to regional integration, which are well documented and quantified in the literature (see, for example, McCallum 1995 and Frankel and Rose 2002). The most straightforward argument in favor of common markets and currency unions is that countries that lower tariffs and that share currencies trade larger volumes of goods within the union because transaction costs are substantially reduced. International trade

[2] The convergence criteria have been agreed and are under discussion, but are not yet formally adopted.

[3] The ceiling would be higher if oil prices fall below $25 per barrel.

[4] The GCC currencies have been formally pegged to the US dollar for a long time and have been very stable over the years. The Bahraini Dinar, Qatari Riyal, Saudi Riyal, and the UAE Dirham were officially pegged to the Special Drawing Rights exchange rate, but in practice have moved with the US dollar since the 1980s (Al-Jasser and Al-Hamidy 2003). The Omani Riyal has been formally pegged to the US dollar since the 1970s. The Kuwaiti dinar was linked to a special basket of currencies, but since the US dollar was assigned a very large weight in the basket, its exchange rate vis-à-vis the dollar has remained broadly stable over time.

Table 1.1. GCC selected economic indicators, 1981–90 average, 1991–2000 average, 2001–10 average

	1981–90 average	1991–2000 average	2001–10 average
Nominal GDP (USD billions)	184.3	274.2	721.1
Real GDP growth (PPP GDP weighted average)	0.6	4.2	5.0
Non-oil real GDP growth (PPP GDP weighted average)		4.6	6.6
GDP per capita (USD)	10206.0	18092.0	20756.0
Oil production (mbpd)	11.0	13.5	15.0
Oil exports (mbpd)	8.2	10.7	14.6
CPI (period average, percent change)	1.2	1.6	3.5
Fiscal balance (USD billions)	–7.8	0.9	89.7
Fiscal balance (percent of GDP, PPP GDP weighted average)	–6.3	5.4	11.6
Gross public debt (percent of GDP, PPP GDP weighted average)	13.2	56.8	32.1
Current account balance (percent of GDP, PPP GDP weighted average)	5.1	–4.8	15.8
Current account balance (USD billions)	12.0	–2.4	121.6
Gross official reserves (USD billions)	102.2	66.1	280.1
Population (millions)	18.9	25.9	35.6

Source: Authors' calculations

theory also suggests that a reduction of transaction costs induces a more efficient allocation of resources by encouraging countries to engage in specialization in industries in which they have a comparative advantage. Closely related to this argument is that common markets and currency unions encourage financial integration. The idea is similar: reducing transaction costs encourages greater intra-regional holdings of assets in money markets as well as in equity and bond markets. This is advantageous because risk-sharing within the region allows residents of one country to insure against domestic shocks by holding assets in neighboring countries. Financial integration is also thought to facilitate greater investment in physical capital within a region by allowing borrowers to make use of savings in neighboring countries (see, for instance, Agénor 2003).

A currency union is particularly important for financial integration because foreign exchange rate risk is the biggest risk taken in international financial transactions. In addition, currency union arrangements are good for controlling inflation: pegging currencies to another country that is pursuing a credible anti-inflationary monetary regime is a strong way to anchor inflation expectations. However, as member countries' central banks lose independence in setting monetary policies, currency unions are fragile when facing asymmetric growth and inflation shocks. A contractionary monetary policy may be appropriate for one country but highly inappropriate for another union member. Mundell (1961) famously highlighted four criteria to judge the benefits of monetary union: (1) the extent of regional trade; (2) the synchronization of economic cycles; (3) the degree of labor mobility; and (4) the extent of risk-sharing.

Rutledge (2009) covers these aspects in detail, discussing the history and key developments to date and considering the appropriateness of GCC monetary union. Our book therefore does not cover these issues directly. In addition, topics related to the level of the exchange rate and to intergenerational equity are not discussed here either, as exchange rate issues have been covered in Cobham and Dibeh's edited volume (2009) and in IMF (2008), and there is a recent literature on the optimal spending/savings of resource windfalls under uncertainty (Cherif and Hasanov 2012), capital scarcity (van der Ploeg and Venables 2011), or absorptive capacity constraints (Araujo, Li, Poplawski-Ribeiro, and Zanna 2012; van der Ploeg 2012). This book is about long-term growth and structural issues and short-term macroeconomic stabilization policies.

The book can be divided into two groups of studies, and we follow this structure in this introductory chapter. The first part of the book discusses structural characteristics: the determinants of long-term growth (Chapter 2); the macroeconomic importance of the foreign labor force (Chapter 3); and the prevalence of government spending in the economy (Chapter 4). The second part discusses short-term macroeconomic policy: the effect of fiscal and monetary policies (Chapters 5 and 6); the determinants and consequences of financial instability (Chapter 7); and the performance of the financial sector during the crisis (Chapter 8). This first chapter provides some background on the region and introduces the other book chapters before concluding on the importance of the GCC for its neighbors.

1.2 Structural Characteristics

The GCC countries occupy 2 percent of world total land area and host about 36 million inhabitants (less than 1 percent of total world population; 2009 data). Non-nationals comprise on average about one-third of total GCC population, and they account for two-thirds or more of the labor force. The total GDP of the six GCC member countries in 2006 was $713 billion, with a weighted average per capita income of $20,000 (Table 1.1). Social indicators point to a high standard of living: life expectancy has increased to seventy-four years and the literacy rate exceeds 70 percent. Infant mortality is less than half the world average, and primary school enrollment is 90 percent of the school-age population.

Oil and gas dominate the GCC economies (Figure 1.1). Oil contributes to about one-third to total GDP and three-fourths to annual government

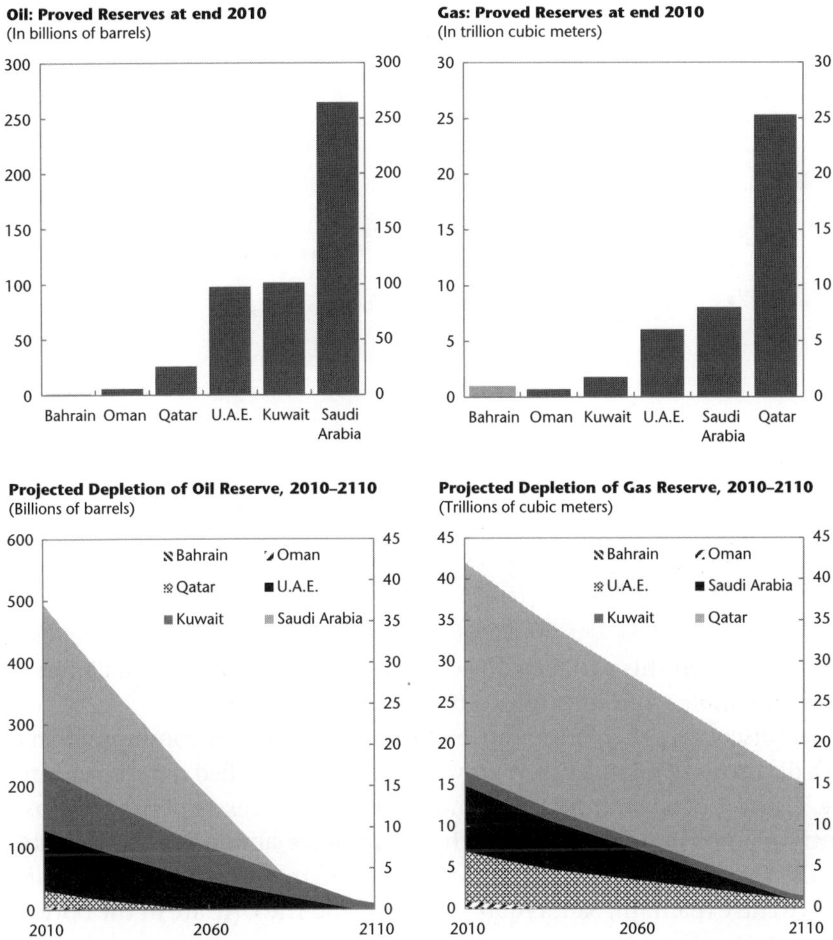

Figure 1.1. GCC: Proved reserves and projected depletion of oil and gas, selected years
Source: BP and authors' calculations

revenues and exports.[5] The global importance of GCC countries stems from their jointly accounting for over 40 percent of global oil reserves and close to one-quarter of global natural gas reserves. Saudi Arabia, Kuwait, and the UAE are major oil producers and exporters, while Qatar has the third largest gas reserves in the world and is currently the largest liquefied natural gas exporter. These four countries have around 50 to 100 years of reserves at current production levels. Notwithstanding that, oil and gas endowments differ greatly between countries: in particular oil reserves are small in Bahrain

[5] Even in Bahrain and Oman, where oil resources are not small, oil represents a dominant share of exports and fiscal revenues.

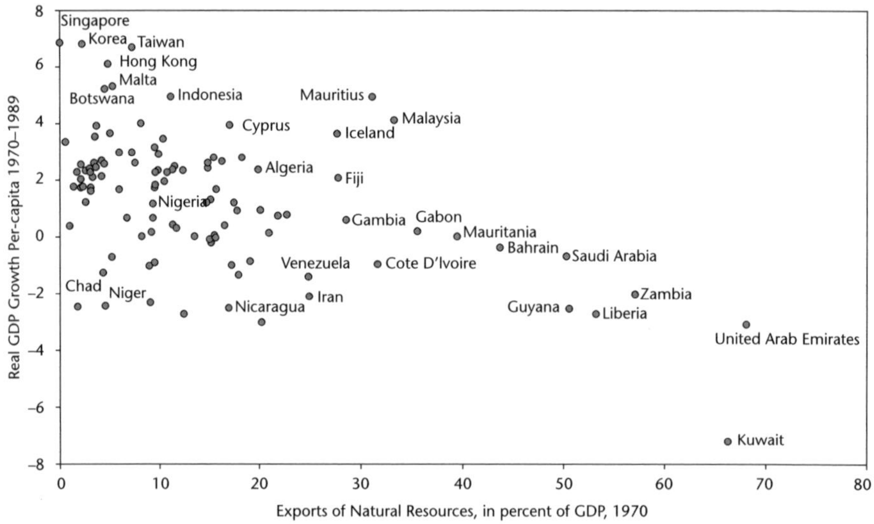

Figure 1.2. Sachs and Warner's (2001) natural resource curse
Source: Sachs and Warner (2001)

and Oman. Given this variance, the Gulf countries will face the challenge of diversifying their economies over different time horizons.

When discussing the performance of oil producers, it is common to start with a diagnosis of relatively low growth and of the so-called natural resource curse. Figure 1.2, taken from Sachs and Warner (2001), exemplifies the cross-country relationship between growth and resource abundance, and in this plot, the GCC countries would seem to feature extreme forms of the natural resource curse (Bahrain, Saudi Arabia, Kuwait, and the UAE are in the bottom right corner).

However, there have been progressive improvements in macroeconomic performance of GCC countries over the last decades and the updated data does not confirm the dismal performance that could be expected from a reading of Figure 1.2. We discuss in detail the long-term growth performance of the GCC in Chapter 2 and show that although productivity growth has been disappointing in the region, GDP growth has not been weak and we do not think the resource curse diagnosis is applicable to the GCC.

Oil producers typically have difficulties diversifying exports and the "Dutch disease" has been pointed at as a possible explanation for low growth in resource-rich countries. Revenues from exports appreciate the real exchange rate (because demand for domestic goods increases as the government and the private sector become wealthier), and this can affect the competitiveness of those very export industries that matter for long-term growth (manufacturing, hi-tech industries, etc.—see Sachs and Warner 1999). Chapter 3 discusses why the real exchange rates of the GCC have not appreciated dramatically, looking at the importance of foreign workers and their remittances in relieving the pressure on domestic markets and the real exchange rate.

A second reason why growth may be disappointing for commodity exporters is that economic incentives are distorted by rent-seeking and by wealthy governments that can afford to heavily intervene in markets. Since the crash in oil prices in 1998–9, GCC countries have undertaken a number of structural reforms and improved their business climate and international competitiveness. The restructuring and privatization of utilities and related services have also received some attention. Chapter 4 shows nonetheless that there remain many distortions in these economies, in particular subsidies that affect incentives and market efficiency. Subsidies may be justified from a distributive point of view, but the chapter argues that subsidy policies in the GCC countries need to be more carefully calibrated.

1.3 Macroeconomic Policy During the Crisis

The global financial crisis affected the GCC countries mainly through (i) the sharp fall in oil prices and a cutback in oil production, (ii) a sharp fall in asset prices, and (iii) the drying up of external funding. Global deleveraging, heightened risk aversion, and reversal of speculative inflows attracted by expectations of revaluation of local currencies dried up international credit markets and increased substantially refinancing costs. The co-movement in these stress factors was accentuated by country-specific factors (such as cross linkages in the financial and corporate sectors in Kuwait and significant external leverage in Dubai).

The direct exposure of GCC countries' financial systems to the US subprime market was however relatively low.[6] As a result, the direct financial transmission of the global crisis appears to have been limited. However, high oil prices and easy liquidity conditions had fueled high bank credit growth, of over 30 percent in the two years preceding the crisis, and encouraged banks and other financial institutions (particularly investment and real estate companies) to increase their leverage and investments in stock markets. This led to an unprecedented increase in asset prices and overheating of the economy. The onset of the global financial crisis and the fall in oil prices triggered a vicious cycle of a steep fall in asset prices, reduced liquidity, and credit constraints.

[6] However, investment companies (non-deposit-taking financial institutions) in Bahrain and Kuwait had significant exposures in international real estate assets, including subprime assets.

With global demand falling and lower oil prices, lower exports and government revenues drove down the fiscal and current account surpluses of the GCC in 2009. In addition, GCC countries are estimated to have lost about $350 billion in valuation of their sovereign wealth fund assets (Setser and Ziemba 2009). Despite these losses, GCC authorities reacted to the crisis by maintaining or even increasing government spending in 2009–10, in line with the G20 push for countercyclical fiscal policies. The resulting stimulus proved useful in shielding the region from a deep recession. Indeed, Chapter 5 estimates the size of fiscal multipliers in the region and finds that one dollar of spending increases GDP by 0.2–0.4 dollars in the short term.

The immediate impact of the global crisis on the financial system was felt in interbank liquidity and manifested in increased interest rates. Reversal of speculative short-term wholesale funds linked to the exchange rate speculation resulted in significant liquidity pressures, increasing the need for central bank medium-term liquidity injections and placement of government deposits with commercial banks. There were temporary sharp spikes in short-term interest rates, necessitating central bank measures to reduce policy rates. In the post-September 2008 period, sporadic events such as the announcement of losses by a commercial bank due to customer-related derivative transactions (in Kuwait) and the difficulties in refinancing by banks in Abu Dhabi created some risk aversion among private depositors.[7] The authorities responded forcefully to stabilize the interbank market and restore liquidity. All central banks except Qatar (where inflation was high until 2009) cut policy interest rates, and reserve requirements were also reduced. Chapter 6 discusses in more detail the role of monetary policy in the GCC countries and shows that despite the peg to the US dollar, the GCC monetary authorities' decisions do have an impact on local interest rates and inflation.

The interaction of tight credit markets and asset price deflation weakened the financial system's balance sheets to some extent, and prompted government intervention of varying degrees in the financial sector. However, the global crisis had little adverse impact on overall bank profitability. The banking sector continued to record profitability—albeit lower, in 2008[8]—despite several banks showing a fourth-quarter 2008 loss reflecting slower loan growth, higher funding costs, higher provisioning, and negative marked-to-market valuation in investment portfolios.[9] Banks also continued to record high profits in the

[7] Possibly reflecting some uncertainties in the banking sector, the GCC currencies were trading at a depreciation in the forward market in September 2008.

[8] Only three banks, the Gulf Bank, Gulf International Bank, and Arab Banking Corporation, ended up with losses in 2008.

[9] Gulf Bank, National Commercial Bank, Kuwait Finance House, Burgan Bank, Al Ahli Bank of Kuwait, Abu Dhabi Commercial Bank, Ahli United Bank, Saudi Investment Bank, BMI Bank, Commercial Bank of Kuwait, Sharjah Islamic Bank, Gulf Finance House, Gulf Investment Corporation, Gulf International Bank, and Arab Banking Corporation.

first quarter of 2009. Weaker economic conditions, lower oil prices, weaker corporate sector performance, and lower asset prices eventually had an adverse impact on overall bank profitability in 2009. The property market correction had a further negative impact on banks asset quality.[10] NPLs—which were low at that time, possibly because of the credit expansion—rose. Fortunately, capital adequacy ratios in most countries were high going into the crisis. In addition, to shore up investor confidence, some governments provided guarantees for deposits at commercial banks (Kuwait, Saudi Arabia, and the UAE), and sovereign wealth funds were asked to support domestic asset prices (Kuwait) and provide capital injections to banks (Qatar and Kuwait). In Qatar, the government cleaned up the balance sheets of banks by purchasing equity investments in the trading book and real estate investments. All these measures helped preserve stability in the financial system. Chapter 7 discusses the sensitivity of banks' balance sheet to macroeconomic factors and individual bank's characteristics and finds that past credit expansion and low growth trigger higher rates of nonperforming loans. The chapter shows also that a systemic weakness in the GCC banking system would have affected credit and GDP growth, providing a justification for the exceptional measures taken in support of the GCC banks.

The crisis had a common effect in the banking sector, stock markets, and real estate markets of GCC countries. The global crisis and stress in international credit markets curtailed private capital inflows in the GCC countries, creating funding pressures in the banking system. The region's stock market capitalization fell by about $400 billion between end-September and end-December 2008 in a volatile market.[11] Volatility in the stock markets increased after August 2008.[12] The average correlation of the GCC markets with the global markets turned positive in the period after September 2008, as compared to a negative correlation during the period between January 2007 and September 2008, as the contagion from the global crisis dominated. The correction in local real estate prices, which had begun in the summer of 2008, intensified after the global crisis. Heightened risk aversion was particularly apparent in Dubai where the CDS spreads widened significantly, by over 1000 basis points during the crisis.

[10] This has been particularly important in Dubai given that banks' direct exposure to the construction sector and real estate mortgages as of the third quarter of 2008 was over 30 percent of total private-sector credit. In Qatar, the government purchased the real estate and equity exposures in the trading books of banks, thereby improving banks' capitalization and asset quality.

[11] Empirical work has shown that wealth effect from financial wealth is significant. There has been relatively little research on emerging economies. Peltonen et al. (2009) estimated financial wealth effects in sixteen emerging economies using dynamic panels and found that an increase of 10 percent in stock prices is associated with a 0.3 percent increase in consumption.

[12] The standard deviation of daily average returns doubled between August 2008 and February 2009 as compared to the period January 2007 to August 2008.

Spillovers within the GCC may have worsened the impact of the crisis through intra-GCC country linkages in addition to the direct effects coming from world shocks. Tight liquidity and credit conditions and some overleverage[13] led to some defaults by financial institutions within the GCC. Two Bahrain-based offshore banks—The International Banking Corporation (TIBC) and Awal Bank—owned by Saudi conglomerates defaulted on their debts. TIBC, which belongs to the Saudi Algosaibi Group, defaulted on its $2.2 billion debt, pending a group-wide debt-restructuring exercise. Awal Bank, owned by another prominent Saudi conglomerate (Al-Saad Group) sought a renegotiation of its debt. In Kuwait, Global Investment House, an investment company, was deemed to have defaulted on most of its $3 billion debt, as a result of actual default on a $200 million loan in December 2008. Investment Dar, another of Kuwait's largest investment companies, had defaulted on a $100 million loan even as it was trying to reach an agreement with creditors over a debt restructuring. The UAE Federal Government merged two Dubai-based mortgage companies (Amlak Finance and Tamweel, which together accounted for an estimated two-thirds of Dubai's housing lending market) that faced financing difficulties, with an amalgamation of the Abu Dhabi's Real Estate Bank and Emirates Industrial Bank.

Although these defaults were isolated and did not have any systemic consequences, partly due to swift actions taken by countries to reinforce stability,[14] the correlation of stock market returns within the GCC increased after the crisis. Chapter 8 discusses in more detail the impact of the global crisis and intra-GCC contagion on banks' performance post-Lehman.

Despite the global crisis, growth was overall resilient in the GCC, and the region was a stabilizing factor for the broader Middle East and North Africa region (MENA). The GCC has long been a significant source of financial flows to the neighboring Arab countries as well as to South Asian countries through

[13] Leverage was not a major issue in GCC countries except in Dubai and some investment companies in Kuwait. Hence in the banking system, the worries were related to liquidity rather than to solvency.

[14] These defaults however had an adverse impact in the stock markets. An event analysis in Kuwait shows that as compared to an average daily stock index return of –0.24 percent between September 2008 and June 2009, the average return plummeted to –2.2 percent in the seven-day period before and after the announcement of losses by Gulf Bank. The effect was felt across the GCC. In the seven-day period before and after the Global Investment House default, the average return was –1.3 percent and there was again negative returns across the GCC. In Saudi Arabia, following the default by the Algosaibi family, SAMBA's (a Saudi bank managed by this group) share prices declined by 15 percent between May 18 and June 2, 2009, compared to a decline of 5 percent for all banks. The Saudi index fell by 2.8 percent on May 16, the day after the announcement of default, but recovered immediately thereafter. The other GCC markets recorded declines by around 1 percent.

remittances, foreign aid, FDI, and trade. Throughout the last three decades, GCC countries have provided large amounts of foreign aid, with Saudi Arabia being the top Arab aid donor, followed by Kuwait, the UAE, and more recently Qatar. Remittances from the GCC are also an important source of income for many Arab and South Asian countries, and constituted a large share of total remittances receipts in these countries. The concluding chapter (Chapter 9) discusses the channels of outward spillovers from the GCC countries and estimates the magnitude of growth spillovers. The results point to the importance of understanding the GCC economy not only for itself but also for its significance for the wider region.

References

Agénor, P. R. (2003). "Benefits and costs of international financial integration: Theory and facts," *The World Economy*, 26: 1089–118.

Al-Jasser, M. and Al-Hamidy, A. (2003). "A common currency area for the Gulf region," in Bank for International Settlements (ed.), *Regional Currency Areas and the Use of Foreign Currencies*, BIS Papers No. 17 (May), 115–19.

Araujo, J., Li, B., Poplawski-Ribeiro, M., and Zanna, L.-F. (2012). "Current account norms in natural resource rich and capital scarce economies." Forthcoming IMF Working Paper. Washington DC: International Monetary Fund.

Cobham, D. and Dibeh, G. (eds) (2009). *Monetary Policy and Central Banking in the Middle East and North Africa*. London: Routledge.

Cherif, R. and Hasanov, F. (2012). "Oil exporters' dilemma: How much to save and how much to invest." IMF Working Paper, WP/12/4.

Frankel, J. and Rose, A. (2002). "An estimate of the effect of common currencies on trade and income," *Quarterly Journal of Economics*, 117: 437–66.

International Monetary Fund (IMF) (2008). "The GCC monetary union: Choice of exchange rate regime." Washington DC: International Monetary Fund. Available online at <http://www.imf.org/external/np/pp/eng/2008/082808a.pdf>, accessed May 28, 2013.

McCallum, J. (1995). "National borders matter: Canada-U.S. regional trade patterns," *American Economic Review*, 85: 615–23.

Mundell, R. A. (1961). "A theory of optimum currency areas," *American Economic Review*, 51: 657–65.

Peltonen, Tuomas A., Sousa, Ricardo M., and Vansteenkiste, Isabel S. (2009). "Wealth effects in emerging market economies." ECB Working Paper No. 1000. Frankfurt: European Central Bank

Ploeg, F. van der (2012). "Bottlenecks in ramping up public investment," *International Tax and Public Finance*, 19: 509–38.

Ploeg, F. van der and Venables, A. J. (2011). *"Harnessing windfall revenues: Optimal policies for resource-rich developing economies," Economic Journal*, 121: 1–30.

Rutledge, J. E. (2009). *Monetary Union in the Gulf: Prospects for a Single Currency in the Arabian Peninsula*. London: Routledge.

Sachs, J. D. and Warner, A. M. (1999). "The big push, natural resource booms and growth," *Journal of Development Economics*, 59: 43–76.

—— (2001). "The curse of natural resources," *European Economic Review*, 45: 827–38.

Setser, B. and Ziemba, R. (2009). "GCC sovereign funds, reversal of fortune." Center for Geoeconomic Studies, Working Paper. New York: Council on Foreign Relations.

2

The Determinants of Long-Term Growth in the GCC Countries

2.1 Introduction

The member countries of the GCC have changed considerably over the last thirty years. The fast development of the region has spurred the creation of new cities, the development of infrastructure, and the expansion of new industries that have attracted capital and a new labor force from around the world. The growth of these economies has been considerably higher than that of advanced economies or other oil exporters as the size of the GCC economies has more than doubled since 1986 (see Table 2.1). However, economic development has been accompanied by very large inflows of foreign workers and the population has increased by more than 80 percent in the GCC (with the exception of Kuwait). As a result, real Gross Domestic Product (GDP) per worker, a measure used to assess the improvements in worker productivity, has declined in Bahrain, Kuwait, and the UAE and improved at very low rates in Saudi Arabia, Oman, and Qatar (last column of Table 2.1).

The disappointing growth in GDP per worker has been a worry mostly in Bahrain, Oman, and Saudi Arabia where a large portion of the national population has relatively low incomes and where job prospects, especially for the growing young population, are scarce. Poor economic performance and youth unemployment have been one of the triggers of the political transitions taking place in the broader region. In the GCC countries, economic problems have not been as acute but the region is lagging in several development areas. The Human Development Index (HDI) compiled by the United

Table 2.1. Nominal GDP and annual growth rate of real GDP and real GDP per worker (1990 to 2009)

Country	Source	Nominal GDP, in billion US dollars, 2005	Annual growth rate, real GDP 1990–2009	Annual growth rate, GDP per worker
Bahrain (BHR)	IMF	13.5	5.3	–1.3
	PWT	20.5	5.7	–0.9
	IMF (non-oil GDP)	10.1	5.9	–0.7
	PWT/IMF (non-oil GDP)	17.1	6.2	–0.4
Kuwait (KWT)	IMF	80.8	4.4	–3.0
	PWT	111.0	4.4	–3.0
	IMF (non-oil GDP)	35.6	7.1	–0.3
	PWT/IMF (non-oil GDP)	65.8	4.6	–2.8
Oman (OMN)	IMF	30.9	4.5	0.5
	PWT	49.6	4.9	0.8
	IMF (non-oil GDP)	14.0	6.3	2.3
	PWT/IMF (non-oil GDP)	32.7	7.0	3.0
Qatar (QAT)	IMF	44.5	9.6	1.0
	PWT	68.7	9.6	1.1
	IMF (non-oil GDP)	18.6	9.7	1.2
	PWT/IMF (non-oil GDP)	42.7	9.5	1.0
Saudi Arabia (SAU)	IMF	315.8	2.9	–0.1
	PWT	465.0	3.6	0.6
	IMF (non-oil GDP)	150.7	3.5	0.5
	PWT/IMF (non-oil GDP)	299.9	4.3	1.3
United Arab Emirates (UAE)	IMF	180.6	5.4	–3.4
	PWT	195.0	6.6	–2.2
	IMF (non-oil GDP)	118.7	8.5	–0.2
	PWT/IMF (non-oil GDP)	133.1	10.2	1.4
Oil exporters (median)	PWT		3.7	3.7
Other developing c. (median)	PWT		3.8	3.8
OECD (median)	PWT		2.8	2.8

Note: The oil exporters (excluding the GCC) used in the chapter are Algeria, Angola, Azerbaijan, Brunei, Chad, Ecuador, Equatorial Guinea, Gabon, Iran, Iraq, Kazakhstan, Libya, Nigeria, Rep. of Congo, Russia, Sudan, Timor-Leste, Trinidad and Tobago, Turkmenistan, Venezuela, and Yemen.

Source: Penn World Tables 7, IMF, and authors' calculations

Nations (UN), which takes into account quality of education and life expectancy, consistently ranks GCC countries at levels below what would be predicted by their GDP per capita.

Governments in the GCC have had an explicit objective of diversification away from oil, with policies of high investment financed by oil revenues and undertaken with the help of migrant workers. Understanding the factors of growth, the role of investment, and the role of skills and the labor force, and refining our measure of success on this enterprise therefore has a value even for the smaller and richer countries of the Gulf.

The modern analysis of long-term growth and productivity started with Solow (1957). His growth-accounting model assumes that production (output), usually measured by real GDP, is obtained by combining two inputs: capital and some measure of labor (e.g. the hours of work in a year or the number of workers). Solow (1957) showed however that for the United States, the two factors of production did not explain output well, and he interpreted the remaining unexplained part as technical change or Total Factor Productivity (TFP), a measure of efficiency in the use of factors of production. The literature on TFP flourished as economists debated on the sources of growth in East Asia (factor accumulation versus a growth miracle), but surveys showed that results on TFP were fairly sensitive to assumptions (Felipe 1997). Nonetheless, a growth-accounting exercise remains a useful start to interpret data of factor accumulation and to discuss the sources of growth.

The aim of this chapter is to go beyond the raw numbers presented in Table 2.1 to explain the drivers of GDP growth and of productivity growth. We find that the GCC countries have swiftly accumulated large stocks of physical capital but the population increase and the shift away from oil mean that capital intensity has actually decreased or remained roughly constant. On the other hand, the efforts that have been made to improve human capital have had positive effects on growth, though educational attainment remains below what is achieved by countries with similar levels of income.

Finally, the growth-accounting exercise suggests that the development of Bahrain and Saudi Arabia is hampered by declining TFP. In addition, although Qatar and the UAE have grown fast in the last twenty years, their TFP growth has been low. One potential explanation is that the kind of capital that has been accumulated in the region (aircraft, computer equipment, electrical equipment) is not fully productive because the labor force is not educated enough. We also find that the poor quality of institutions and the large size of government consumption, both of which are possible symptoms of a resource curse, could explain the disappointing TFP growth.

The chapter first describes the economic data in the region. Section 2.3 discusses the process of diversification and shows how factors of production were accumulated. In section 2.4, we apply the growth-accounting framework to the GCC. Section 2.5 concludes by considering the vast cross-country literature that has attempted to explain growth by a variety of institutions. We apply the econometric estimates typically found in the literature to throw light on the determinants of TFP.

2.2 Economic Data

The dataset most commonly used in the literature to assess long-term growth is the Penn Word Tables (PWT, Heston, Summers, and Aten 2011) because this dataset corrects for the differences in purchasing power that the dollar has in different countries. However, other data sources exist that provide statistics for GDP, population, investment, etc. In particular, the World Bank, the United Nations, and the IMF provide statistics that are comparable across counties, while national statistical agencies supply some detailed data. We describe in this section the basic series needed for assessing the determinants of long-term growth and we explain which source was chosen based on our assessment of data quality.

The region hosted 40 million people in 2009, a number that tripled in thirty years, with a similar growth pattern across country (see Table 2.2). Revisions on population data are frequent in countries that attract a large population of migrant workers, and the data from the Penn World Tables (PWT) and the United Nations report lower population estimates. An increasingly large fraction of this population is of foreign origin (Chapter 3 covers the data on migrant workers in more detail). Population growth was matched by a strong increase in total employment, from around 7 million workers in the GCC in 1990 to 16 million workers in 2009.

To assess the evolution of real income and of productivity, we use the series of real GDP from the IMF and from the PWT. Data quality for this

Table 2.2. Employment and population in the GCC, in millions

Country	Bahrain	Kuwait	Oman	Qatar	Saudi Arabia	UAE	GCC
Employment							
IMF (1990)	0.12	0.53	0.52	0.25[a]	4.65	0.72	6.8
IMF (2009)	0.41	2.06	1.11	1.18[b]	8.15	3.54	16.4
Population							
IMF (1980)	0.35	1.37	1.20	0.22	9.32	1.01	13.5
IMF (1990)	0.48	2.13	1.63	0.42	15.19	1.84	21.7
IMF (2000)	0.67	2.22	2.40	0.62	20.47	3.00	29.4
IMF (2009)	1.04	3.54	2.88	1.64	25.52	4.91	39.5
Other sources							
World Bank (2009)	0.79	2.79	2.85	1.41	25.39	4.60	37.8
United Nations (2009)	0.72	1.58	1.58	1.20	14.90	4.82	24.8
PWT (2009)	1.14	2.49	2.91	0.83	25.33	4.80	37.5

[a] Source is World Bank, extrapolated from 1991 data

[b] Source is World Bank

series is variable. For instance, for many years, real GDP was not compiled in the region, except in Saudi Arabia. To obtain a measure of real GDP, statisticians must remove the effect of inflation on the nominal value of economic activity ("nominal GDP"),[1] using information on prices that are specific for each industry. As these statistics were not available in the Gulf countries, economists in international organizations estimated these prices using other prices—for instance, consumer price indices or price indices for imported products. The Purchasing Power Parity (PPP) index of the Penn World Tables also corrects for the purchasing power of dollars in different countries. Table 2.1 shows different measures of GDP that take into account inflation (all converted in 2005 US dollars). The first measure is real GDP from the IMF, which in most cases yields the smallest estimate of growth (column 4). The second measure is GDP growth in US$ PPP from the PWT, which tends to be high because inflation in the costs of production in the GCC is lower than in the US.

Although real GDP is a commonly used measure of economic activity, its meaning in the region, as well as for other major oil producers, is questionable. In countries without a significant natural resources sector, real GDP is a useful measure of the amount of production in the economy, which affects crucially many markets and sectors of the economy. Higher volumes of output create jobs, yield taxes to the government, attract investors, etc.

But in countries where oil production is very large, real GDP (which includes the volume of production in the oil sector) is not a good measure of economic activity, especially when the focus is on the private sector. On one hand, the effect of oil prices is taken away and therefore increases in oil prices—which improve profitability in the energy sector, yield revenues to the government, and boost asset prices—have no effect on the measure of real GDP. On the other hand, increases in the number of barrels of oil extracted (even if sold at half the price) do improve real GDP, although they do not translate into more jobs or higher private-sector profits.

This line of reasoning suggests two measures of economic activity for the region, and the validity of each of them will depend on the intended use of the indicator. One measure is GDP in constant US dollars (i.e., after taking into account the loss of purchasing power of the US dollar). This measure will be of interest when assessing the development of wealth and income

[1] Nominal GDP can itself be compiled in different ways. From the production side, nominal GDP is the sum of the value of output of all sectors (typically calculated by surveying companies' sales and inventories), subtracting the cost of intermediate inputs (GDP is a measure of value added). From the expenditure side, nominal GDP is the sum of consumption, private-sector investment, public expenditure, and exports minus imports. However, the production method is more reliable in the region as surveys on spending are incomplete.

in the region, or when reporting indicators of assets (or liabilities) in proportion of GDP. A second measure is a measure of real economic activity excluding production of oil and gas—what is loosely called non-oil real GDP (and more specifically, real value added in the *non-hydrocarbon* sector). This measure will be used when discussing growth, either in the context of short-term fluctuations or in the study of long-term development and diversification.

Series for non-oil real GDP are provided by the IMF since 1980[2] and the UN since 1970,[3] but the noise in the data is heightened by the focus on a smaller subset of the economy and the need to estimate a price index for the non-oil economy. As a result, the series coming from the two data sources are not consistent, especially for Saudi Arabia and the UAE, signaling an issue with the estimation procedures for prices and therefore for data quality. The collection of statistics in the UAE is also complicated by the federal structure of the country and the lack of homogeneity between statistics provided by the different statistical agencies. We also constructed a new series for non-oil GDP using the Penn World Tables value of total GDP, and subtracting from it the IMF series for oil GDP, after deflating it using oil prices. This latter series may provide a better source for cross-country comparison because it is based on the PWT prices.

Employment dynamics has been a source of economic growth but the standards of living in the GCC have also increased, with annual income per capita exceeding 20,000 US dollars in all GCC countries in 2009. Qatar, the UAE, and Kuwait are among the ten richest nations in the world. Bahrain, Saudi Arabia, and Oman are not as rich, but living standards there are equivalent to those of Portugal and the Slovak Republic, and the region stands out among its poor Middle-Eastern neighbors (see Figure 2.1). Income is however not evenly distributed. Data on income inequality is sparse in the region, but income inequality should be higher than that of Algeria, Egypt, Israel, or other developing economies (where Gini coefficients are around 40 percent; see Ali 2003).

The fortune of the region depends on its energy exports. Indeed, average income has followed closely the evolution of hydrocarbon revenues (Figure 2.2). As oil prices fell to record lows after the first Gulf War, income declined to a bottom in 1995. Since then, oil revenues have soared thanks to the tripling in oil prices and the growth of hydrocarbon production.

[2] Non-oil GDP series from the IMF World Economic Outlook and Regional Economic Outlook for the Middle East and Central Asia start in 1990. Data pre-1990 was collected manually using older individual IMF country reports.

[3] The UN reports data on value added at constant prices, excluding the mining and the utilities sectors. The utilities and non-oil mining sectors in the GCC are quite small though, so this measure is a good proxy of non-oil growth.

Figure 2.1. World rankings of income per capita (2009)

Note: Income per capita is US$ PPP 81,000 in Qatar (using IMF statistics for population), US$ PPP 52,932 in the UAE, US$ 32,826 in Kuwait (using IMF statistics for population), US$ PPP 23,539 in Bahrain, US$ PPP 21,579 in Saudi Arabia, and US$ PPP 20,505 in Oman.

Source: Heston, Summers, and Aten (2011). Map source is ThematicMapping.org

Production increased by more than 50 percent in Kuwait and the UAE and by more than 100 percent in Oman and Qatar. Production was stable in Saudi Arabia and started declining in Bahrain (the country's reserves were drained), but this did not prevent income per capita from more than doubling in the last fifteen years.

The hydrocarbon exports have supported the countries' ambitious development agendas. Governments financed infrastructure, developed cities, improved educational attainment, and managed to build a more diversified and modern economy. The strategy has been relatively successful and although the GCC countries' rankings in the UN HDI are still lagging behind their rankings in income per capita, Qatar, Bahrain, Saudi Arabia, and the UAE are now among the 20 to 30 percent most advanced countries according to the Human Development Index, a significant improvement since 1980.

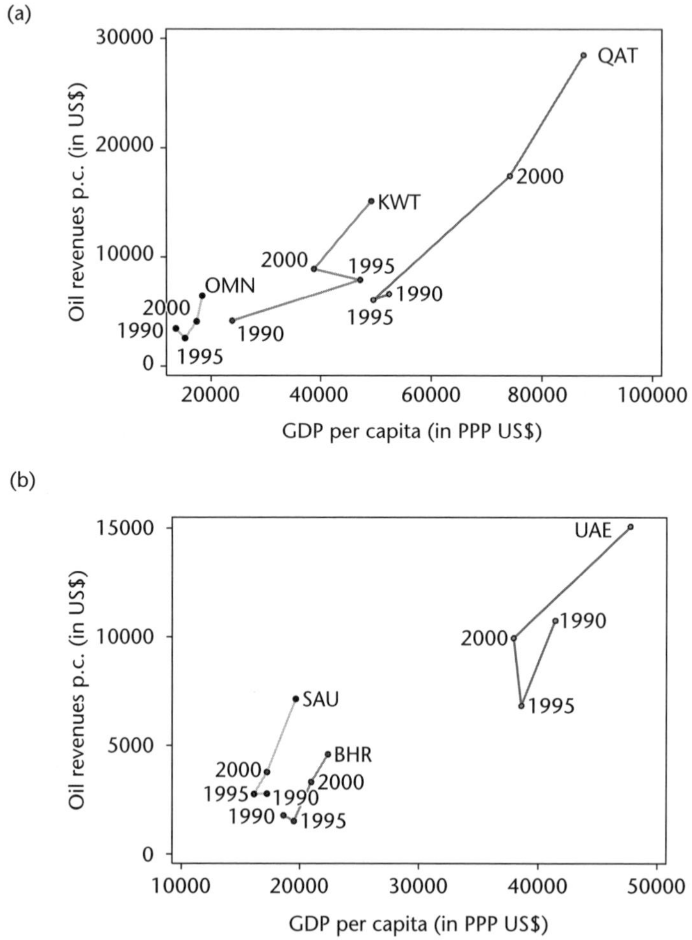

Figure 2.2. Oil production and per capita income in the region (1990–2005)
Source: US Energy Information Agency, IMF, and authors' calculations

2.3 Diversification and the Drivers of Long-Term Growth

2.3.1 Diversification

With the exception of Saudi Arabia, the GCC region's non-hydrocarbon growth performance has been above that of other oil producers or of advanced economies for the period 1980–2009. Growth in Kuwait, Qatar, and the UAE was in fact at par with that of India and China. The sectors that contributed most to non-hydrocarbon growth (and that therefore increased their share in real GDP) were the manufacturing sector in Bahrain, Oman, and Saudi Arabia (driven by petrochemicals), the construction sector in Oman and Qatar, and the transportation sector in Kuwait, Oman, Qatar, and the UAE. The financial sector also grew strongly in Qatar and the UAE (see Table 2.3).

The push for diversification was successful in the UAE where the share of oil to GDP decreased by more than 20 percent in real terms, although in nominal terms oil GDP grew faster than non-oil GDP. The share of hydrocarbon production in real GDP also decreased in Bahrain and Oman but this is explained as much by the limitations of oil resources as by growth in the non-hydrocarbon sector. In Qatar, gas production increased dramatically, driving the reduction in the share of the non-hydrocarbon sector in the economy. On average, the diversification efforts have paid off as non-oil growth reached high levels and was relatively symmetric across sectors, but oil production still accounts for more than 50 percent of GDP in Kuwait, Oman, Qatar, and Saudi Arabia.

Diversification can also be assessed by looking at the structure of exports. For the GCC, as for other resource-rich countries, non-hydrocarbon export competitiveness may be undermined through the Dutch disease effect. Despite the push for diversification across the GCC and their advantageous ability to alleviate bottlenecks through access to a perfectly elastic supply of foreign workers, hydrocarbon exports still overwhelm non-hydrocarbon exports, the bulk of which are exports of energy-intensive and subsidized manufactures. (See Chapters 3 and 4 for more discussion of the structure of non-hydrocarbon exports, subsidies, and how the GCC countries have dealt with the risk of Dutch disease).

2.3.2 The Stock of Capital

What are the main drivers of growth? The economics literature has emphasized the role of investment and of the stock of capital because capital is used in the production process.

Over the period 1980–2009, investment has not been significantly higher in oil exporters or in the GCC than in other countries. Countries invest typically around 22 percent of their production and the GCC is no exception. However, the ratio that matters to assess the extent of capital formation in the economy is investment in proportion to non-oil GDP, and this has been very high for oil-exporting countries.[4] Investment to non-oil GDP was around 33 percent over the period 1980–2000 in the GCC, and the ratio increased to 40–50 percent after 2000.

[4] One would normally want to remove the component of investment that is used in the oil sector, but this data is not available for a cross-section of countries. We therefore abstract from the difference between non-oil investment and total investment. For Saudi Arabia, oil investment represents around 10 percent of total investment only.

Table 2.3. Nominal value added by sectors, in percent of nominal non-oil GDP

	Bahrain		Kuwait		Oman		Qatar		Saudi Arabia		UAE	
	1990	2011	1990	2011	1990	2011	1990	2011	1990	2011	1990	2011
Agriculture	1	1	2	1	5	3	1	0	8	4	2	1
Manufacturing	13	19	5	6	6	25	18	23	13	22	13	13
Construction	7	6	4	5	4	11	7	9	10	9	19	17
Trade, hotels, and restaurants	14	11	15	10	21	19	11	13	9	10	29	22
Transport and communication	9	11	7	16	9	13	4	8	7	7	9	13
Finance, insurance, and real estate	35	38	26	28	18	18	17	27	19	14	19	26
Government services	24	17	19	18	25	16	38	38	27	30	8	7
Community and social services	6	8	25	22	13	15	4	4	6	4	4	4
Memorandum: oil GDP/total GDP	19	30	48	65	48	58	44	58	32	53	40	39

Note: Remaining component of non-oil GDP includes imputed bank service charges, which is usually negative.

Source: Country authorities and authors' calculations

Given a series for investment, it is possible to compute the capital stock K, using the perpetual inventory method:

$$K_t = (1 - \delta)K_{t-1} + I_t$$

where δ is the physical rate of depreciation of capital, assumed to be 6 percent.[5]

Data for investment and in particular for investment in real terms (i.e., deflating for the change in the price of investment) is of poor quality. Because national sources do not publish a deflator for investment, except in Saudi Arabia, two methods are possible. The first one is to use the deflator used in Saudi Arabia and apply it to the IMF series for investment in current prices (see Table 2.4, columns (a), (b), and (c)). This method corrects for inflation in the GCC and therefore corrects for differences in the price of investment across time. The second method uses the series provided by the Penn World Tables that also take into account the differences in costs of production across countries. As a result, investment in PWT is constantly higher than in the IMF database because production costs are low in the GCC. However, the PWT series only start in 1986 in the GCC and this is too late to compute a stock of capital in 1990. We therefore need to extrapolate the PWT investment series back to 1965 using the IMF series. The results for the capital stock are presented in columns (d) and (e) in Table 2.4.

The second method probably provides a better picture of the cross-sectional differences in investment, in particular when one wants to compare capital intensity with other developing or advanced economies. Column (e) in Table 2.4 shows that capital intensity remains high in the GCC, at par or slightly superior to capital intensity in advanced countries. However, the first method provides a better proxy of the evolution across time of capital, because the capital stock in 1990 was constructed using actual IMF series starting from 1965 (as opposed to extrapolated PWT series). This is why we will use the statistics in columns (a), (b), and (c) of Table 2.4 for the growth-accounting exercise (i.e., to decompose growth through time), although we will also use the statistics from column (d) and (e) in our attempt to compare productivity across countries.

Between 1990 and 2009, the capital stock would have increased by around 200 percent in Bahrain, Kuwait, Saudi Arabia, and the UAE. Growth in the

[5] An initial level of capital for 1960 and an assumption for δ are needed to compute the series. We use the steady-state relationship between capital and investment $K_0 = I_0/(g+\delta)$, where g is the average growth rate in the data and I_0 is investment in year 1960 (we use year 1965 for the GCC). For the non-GCC countries, if investment data in 1960 is not available, it is extrapolated from investment to GDP ratios using a linear time trend. Caselli (2005) argued the initial level of capital stock and that the specific value for δ did not affect dramatically the performance of the model in explaining the dispersion of income per capita. However, this does not imply that the assumptions are innocuous for the diagnostics of growth for individual countries.

Table 2.4. Investment and growth in the stock of capital

	Capital stock, cumulative growth rate, in percent	Capital stock per worker	Capital stock per worker	Capital stock per worker	Capital stock per worker
	1990–2009	in 2005 US$, 1990	in 2005 US$, 2009	in 2005 PPP US$, 1990 (PWT)	in 2005 PPP US$, 2009 (PWT)
	(a)	(b)	(c)	(d)	(e)
Bahrain	188	161,891	90,226	354,729	231,668
Kuwait	182	147,102	69,136	309,260	160,663
Oman	324	51,927	79,058	104,010	177,864
Qatar	621	96,131	126,516	132,199	207,856
Saudi Arabia	182	80,409	83,340	151,694	220,616
UAE	220	270,614	121,156	314,910	187,937
Other oil producers (median)				57,457	45,024
Other developing c. (median)				19,786	22,990
OECD (median)				120,110	172,024

Source: IMF, PWT, and authors' calculations. See text for details.

stock of capital would have reached 30 percent in Oman and 600 percent in Qatar. Although the GCC countries have invested massively in the last twenty years, the stock of capital per worker has been declining in Bahrain, Kuwait, and the UAE because the population increase has outpaced the rate of investment. These countries also had sizeable stocks of capital in 1990 because the oil sector was already developed, and since 1990, diversification strategies have led to the development of less capital-intensive sectors attracting a large migrant population, in particular in real estate and services. In Qatar, gas production was not yet developed in 1990 and this sector has required massive investments, yielding higher stocks of capital per capita. In Saudi Arabia and in Oman, where population growth was slower and where the energy sectors have been mature for many years, the dynamics of capital intensity have been more moderate.

2.3.3 Human Capital

A second factor that can explain growth is the level of qualification of the labor force ("human capital"). Based on the empirical literature on the returns to education, in particular Psacharopoulos (1994), Hall and Jones (1999) have suggested modeling human capital as $h=e^{\varphi(s)}$, where s is the average years of schooling of population aged 15 and over, and φ is a piecewise linear function capturing the findings that returns to education are decreasing. In

Sub-Saharan Africa this return is about 13 percent, but returns to education decrease with higher levels of education, to about 10 percent on average in the world, and to about 7 percent in OECD countries. This functional form has become standard in the growth-accounting literature and the value s is obtained from the dataset of Barro and Lee (2010).

Between 1990 and 2010, all GCC countries pushed forward plans to increase schooling. The increase in the average number of years of schooling of the population was impressive in Bahrain (from 6.5 to 9.5 years), in Saudi Arabia (from 5.9 to 8.5 years), and in the UAE (from 6.1 to 9.2 years). In Kuwait (from 5.9 to 6.3 years) and in Qatar (from 5.6 to 7.5 years), the increase was more moderate.[6] The estimated growth in the stock of human capital may however be overstated because the quality of education in the region has been disappointing, as noted for instance in the OECD's assessment of educational systems (the "PISA" study).

2.4 A Growth-Accounting Exercise

A formal growth-accounting exercise, as applied by Artadi and Sala-i-Martina (2002), is the step usually taken to investigate in more depth the role of the different factors of production. We follow Caselli's (2005) description of the model as

$$Y = AK^{\alpha}(Lh)^{1-\alpha} \tag{1}$$

where Y is output (real GDP or non-oil real GDP), K is the stock of capital in the economy, L is the number of workers, and h is the measure of human capital. A, which is a residual in equation (1) capturing the unexplained component of GDP, is called Total Factor Productivity (TFP) and is considered to be a measure of efficiency in the use of factors of production. Because there are no available series on investment in the oil sector versus investment in the non-oil sector, we are not able to subtract the capital stock in the oil sector when trying to explain GDP in the non-oil sector using capital in the non-oil sector. Similarly, we do not distinguish between employment in the whole economy and employment in the non-oil sector because employment in the oil sector is small.

The parameter α is an important parameter capturing the elasticity of growth to the stock of capital. Under the additional assumption that factors

[6] The data for Oman was not available. The World Development Indicators database of the World Bank provides numbers for the literacy rate in all the countries in the GCC, and a regression showed that the sensitivity of educational attainment to the literacy rate is 0.12 in the GCC. This coefficient was used to estimate educational attainment in Oman of 5.4 years in 1995, 6 years in 2000, 6.5 years in 2005, and 7.2 years in 2010.

are paid their marginal product, the wage rate is $w = \partial Y/\partial L = (1 - \alpha)Y/L$ and therefore α can be estimated from the share of factor payments in GDP, i.e. $\alpha=1-(wL)/Y$. Barro and Sala-i-Martin (2004: chapter 10) report α estimated from the national accounts data on factor payments for several OECD and developing countries. Their α ranges from 0.26 (Taiwan) to 0.69 (Mexico), but its value is thought to be around 0.3 to 0.5 for most countries. α can also be estimated by regressing GDP on the factors of production (i.e., estimating equation 1), but such estimations are fraught with difficulties. Simple regressions are incorrect and overestimate α because of the common issue of reverse causality: higher GDP (which results in higher profits) finances investment and therefore a higher capital stock. Disentangling the effect of capital stock on GDP from the reverse effect is difficult. Senhadji (2000) attempted such an estimation using long-term cointegration relationships and a correction for endogenenity. His results do not point to a specific range for oil exporters. Senhadji (2000) found that α was as high as 0.7 in Algeria, 0.89 in Norway, and 0.64 in Venezuela, but estimates for Ecuador, Iran, and Nigeria were all below 0.4. When no specific estimate for α is available, the literature has tended to use $\alpha = 1/3$, which is what we apply for our growth-accounting exercise.

Dividing equation (1) by the number of workers L, we define $y=Y/L$ and $k=K/L$, which leads to

$$y = A\,k^{\alpha}h^{1-\alpha}, \text{ or } y = A\,y_{KH} \quad \text{where } y_{KH} = k^{\alpha}h^{1-\alpha}$$

What does the model say about TFP? Our results are presented in Figure 2.3, where TFP in 2008 in oil-exporting countries is shown as a ratio to TFP in the US. Chart (a) shows TFP computed using GDP (vertical axis) and non-oil GDP (horizontal axis) and the stock of capital deduced from the IMF series, whereas Chart (b) shows TFP computed using the PWT series. The model suggests that TFP is higher in the GCC than in most other oil exporters. In addition, TFP is higher in the smaller countries of the region. In fact, Qatar and the UAE have productivities roughly at par with that of the US, even when TFP is calculated on non-oil GDP (horizontal axis) and when the relatively large estimate of the stock of capital from PWT is used (Chart (b)). TFP for Saudi Arabia, Oman, and Bahrain is found to be lower, around 50–60 percent of that of the US when computed on non-oil GDP.

The model also allows us to decompose the contributions to growth coming from capital, human capital, and TFP (the unknown factor). The contribution from the stock of capital can be computed using the two different series described earlier, but the choice of the series is innocuous because both series show similar changes in the stock of capital per worker between 1990 and 2009 (although the levels are different). We choose the series computed using IMF data and the Saudi Arabia price deflator for investment.

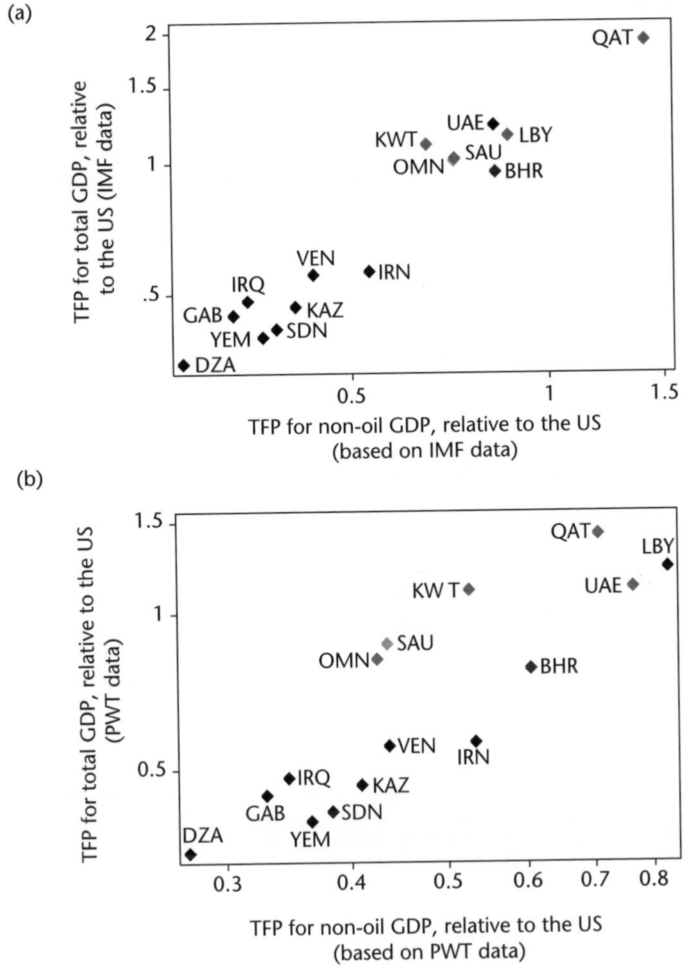

Figure 2.3. Total factor productivity relative to the US (total GDP and non-oil GDP) (logarithmic scale, 2008)

Source: IMF, PWT, and authors' calculations

Table 2.5 and Figure 2.4 show that the efforts made to improve skills were important drivers of GDP per worker in all countries but in Kuwait. However, in Bahrain, Kuwait, and to some extent the UAE, the decrease in capital intensity has been strong enough to drive a decline in worker productivity. Overall, capital and skills cannot explain the long-term performance of the GCC. In particular, the model suggests a decline in TFP in Bahrain and in Saudi Arabia even when looking at non-oil GDP.

Positive TFP growth is important because it indicates that factors of production are used efficiently. Indeed, most growth successes in the past twenty years can be attributed to positive developments in TFP (see the factors of growth for Albania, China, and the other non-oil-exporting emerging countries shown in Figure 2.6 that are offered as examples of growth success stories). Even slowly growing advanced economies such as the UK have benefitted from positive TFP. In line with the findings of a resource curse in earlier periods (Sachs and Warner 1995, 2001), many other oil producers (Algeria, Gabon, Libya, Sudan, Venezuela) also suffered from negative TFP in the period 1990–2008, despite high oil prices in the years 2002–8. The

Table 2.5. Growth accounting of GDP per capita, (contributions, in percentage points, 1990–2009)

	Model with Total GDP				Model with non-oil GDP	
	Δy (total GDP, IMF)	αΔk	(1–α)Δh	ΔTFP (total GDP)	Δy (non-oil GDP, IMF)	ΔTFP (non-oil GDP)
Bahrain	–1.3	–1.0	0.9	–1.2	–0.7	–0.6
Kuwait	–3.0	–1.3	0.1	–1.9	–0.3	0.9
Oman	0.5	0.7	0.8	–1.0	2.3	0.8
Qatar	1.0	0.5	0.7	–0.1	1.2	0.1
Saudi Arabia	–0.1	0.1	0.8	–1.0	0.5	–0.4
UAE	–3.4	–1.4	1.0	–3.0	–0.2	0.2

Source: IMF, PWT, and authors' calculations

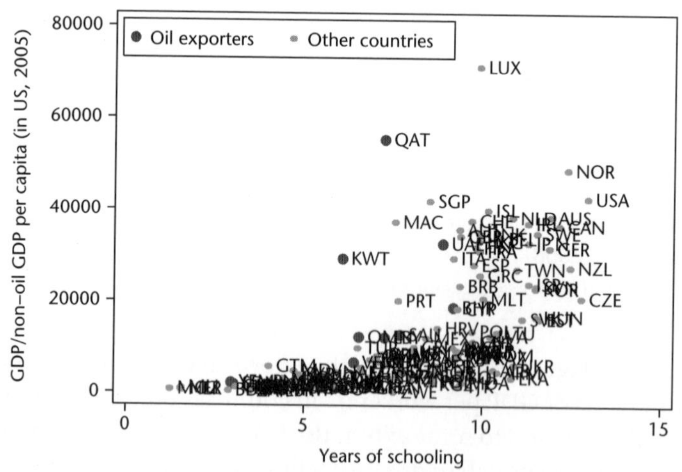

Figure 2.4. Contributions to the annual percentage change in GDP per worker (1990–2009)

Note: DZA stands for Algeria; GAB for Gabon; IRN for Iran; LBY for Libya; SDN for Sudan; VEN for Venezuela; ALB for Albania; CHN for China; POL for Poland; ROM for Romania; LKA for Sri Lanka; and GBR for Great Britain.

Source: Authors' calculations; model using total GDP for the GCC objective of the remainder of the chapter is to investigate what could have driven TFP down in the GCC region.

2.5 Total Factor Productivity and Country Characteristics

In the absence of a "standard model" of economic growth, the unexplained component of production, Total Factor Productivity, has been linked to various factors in the economic literature, either explicitly in analyses of TFP or indirectly in broader analyses of growth. There are a number of country characteristics that could matter, and formal arguments have been made to explain why the type of capital, geography, history, but also macroeconomic policy, trade openness, political and legal institutions, etc., might be important for the growth process.

2.5.1 Type of Capital

Caselli and Wilson (2004) have argued that not all investments are alike and that heterogeneity in the technology content of different capital goods can explain part of the unexplained factor of growth. In other words, countries that use more productive capital (for instance, computers if the labor force is skilled) will produce more for a given value of the stock of capital. To investigate the type of capital used in the GCC countries, we use Feenstra (2000) data on capital goods imports, which proxy for capital stocks. The use of this proxy is justified because for most countries (including for the GCC), capital goods cannot be produced domestically and are imported. The distribution of capital imports by type of capital is shown in Figure 2.5. The data shows that the GCC countries have invested large amounts in high-tech equipments, especially aircraft (Bahrain, Saudi Arabia, Qatar, and the UAE), communication equipment (Kuwait, the UAE, Saudi Arabia). In contrast, Oman has invested in relatively low-tech capital (motor vehicles).

In Figure 2.5, countries were sorted by their TFP growth between 1991 and 2008 and capital goods were sorted by their R&D content, as estimated by Caselli and Wilson (2004). This ordering shows that there is no clear pattern between the share of high-tech capital and the TFP growth. As a result, it is problematic to interpret, for instance, the disappointing growth performance of Oman in light of the lower technological content of its capital. Indeed, it is not so much the R&D content of capital that matters as it is its complementarity with country characteristics, such as human capital or geographical remoteness. In particular, Caselli and Wilson (2004) documented that for the *average country*, aircraft, computing, communication and electrical equipment are relatively inefficient given the average country's low level of human capital. As capital imports in the GCC are relatively high-tech whereas skill

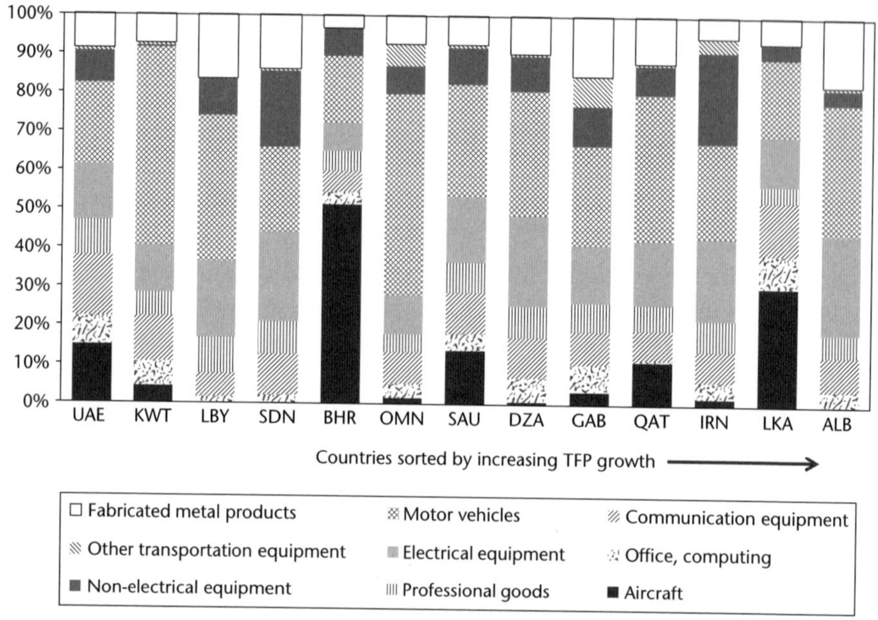

Figure 2.5. Imports of capital, by type (darker color for increasingly R&D-intensive capital)

Source: Feenstra (2000) and authors' calculations following classification in Caselli and Wilson (2004)

levels are average, one argument could therefore be that the capital stock accumulated by the GCC is not well exploited by the labor force, yielding the decreasing TFP estimates.

Caselli and Wilson (2004) however showed that computers, motor vehicles, and communication equipment are relatively efficient for countries remote from the world's largest economies. Several countries in the GCC have successfully developed their trade and transportation sector, basing this success on the geographical location between Asia and Europe. Therefore, the high-tech nature of capital in the GCC can be justified given its location.

2.5.2 Institutions and the Empirical Growth Literature

Barro (1991) estimated a reduced-form econometric model where income per capita is regressed on a vector of candidate variables that could explain growth. The results, however, were found by subsequent research to be sensitive to the inclusion of different variables. Although specifying the correct model remains elusive, the body of empirical work is now large enough that a survey of the literature should be able to identify the factors that have been found to be statistically and economically significant. This section discusses different surveys (or meta-analyses) that have been written in the recent years and uses coefficient estimates that reflect our view of the literature to assess the drivers of TFP growth in the GCC. The exercise is similar to that of Hakura (2004) who explains the low performance of the GCC (and of the rest of MENA) by using an econometric model of long-term growth, but instead of relying on a small set of regressions, we prefer to base our results on the existing literature with the objective of relying on robust relationships between growth and its determinants.

We start from the results of Sala-i-Martin et al. (2004) as a benchmark measurement of the relevance of each of the six factors. Sala-i-Martin et al. use the sixty-seven candidate regressors chosen by Sala-i-Martin (1997) to estimate all possible combinations of a growth regression with seven explanatory variables and they use Bayesian updating methods to compute the posterior probability that the coefficient of a particular variable is non-zero. Based on this methodology, they rank regressors by their potential significance, and we focus on those factors with high significance that have been most studied by economists and political scientists: initial income per capita, size of the government, macroeconomic stability, terms of trade, participation in international trade, democracy, and institutional quality.[7] Although the interpretation of some of these variables remains open to debate,[8] there is a growing consensus that the above categories, in one form or another, are all important determinants of economic growth.

INITIAL INCOME PER CAPITA AND CONVERGENCE

The negative relation between initial income per capita and economic growth is among the most robust in the empirical literature. The relation—known as beta-convergence after the customary Greek letter used as a regression coefficient—is grounded in the neoclassical growth theory of Solow (1956) and Swan (1956). The model yields predictions for the path of output but it is important to note that convergence depends on the rates of population growth, capital depreciation, and technological progress, as well as the elasticities of output to the various factors of production. The Solow–Swan model is said indeed to predict *conditional* convergence. Mankiw, Romer, and Weil (1992) estimated a regression on OECD countries

[7] Since we focus on TFP, we do not discuss the role of physical capital or of education. These have been covered in section 2.4 using estimates in line with the growth-accounting literature. Among the 25 most significant variables in Sala-i-Martin et al. (2004), we do not discuss the variables that are geographic, religious, or ethnic dummies (East Asian dummy, African dummy, Latin American dummy, fraction of tropical area, Spanish colony, fraction Confucian, fraction Muslim, fraction Buddhist) as they are not fundamentally informative about the growth process (they merely capture omitted variables). Neither do we discuss initial life expectancy because it is highly correlated with initial income per capita.

[8] For example, institutional quality might be measured as the strength of property rights, the presence of democratic institutions, or the level of bureaucracy.

that yielded a speed of convergence of 2 percent. Abreu, de Groot, and Florax (2005) conducted a meta-analysis of beta-convergence and examined the results of 619 different growth regressions from forty-eight different published papers. They found that taking stock of country differences matters for the estimated rate of convergence, which is exactly what the Solow growth model predicts. Therefore, it is difficult to attribute a large fraction of growth to convergence for very heterogeneous economies. We thus apply the commonly estimated 2 percent convergence rate only within the GCC. We apply a similar rate of convergence within non-GCC oil exporters, within non-OECD countries and within OECD countries. Figure 2.6 shows our decomposition of TFP by factors. Qatar and the UAE were the richest countries in the GCC and therefore conditional convergence would have slowed down their growth. On the contrary, countries like starting from lower levels of income, such as Sudan or China, would have benefitted from conditional convergence.

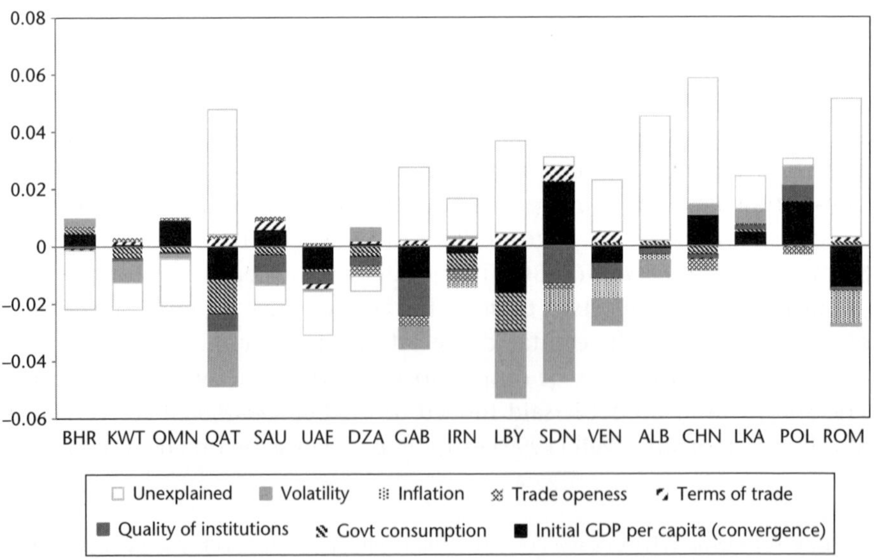

Figure 2.6. Contributions to TFP (1991–2009), in difference from median non-oil-exporting country

Note: the median non-OECD country in the sample has a TFP over the period 1990–2008 very close to 0.

Source: Sala-i-Martin et al. (2004) database, IMF, and authors' calculations. Data for inflation and terms of trade was not available for Iraq. Data for trade openness was not available for Albania, Kazakhstan, and Libya.

SIZE OF THE GOVERNMENT

The size of the public sector is potentially an important factor in growth performance, and Barro (1991) had already noted that the coefficient on government consumption was negative in growth regressions. Sachs and Warner (1995) also argued that one of the possible reasons why resource-endowed countries have tended to grow slower than resource-poor countries has to do with outsized governments. Artadi and Sala-i-Martin (2002) applied this argument to MENA and claimed that the large income that these governments receive—and subsequently spend—from oil revenues creates rent-seeking behavior. Rather than concentrate their efforts in productive activities, the incentives are for agents to concentrate on securing as big a share as possible from the oil revenues. For the GCC, the government is clearly a driving force in the economy, in particular for factor accumulation: investment, immigration, and educational improvements are to a large extent financed by the government. The argument is however that from the supply side, TFP (in the long run) is hurt by rent-seeking activities, and *unproductive* government consumption is a good proxy for this effect.

Standard regression estimates did not fully support the findings of Barro (1991) (Levine and Renelt 1992; Nijkamp and Poot 2004) but the formal Bayesian approach of Sala-i-Martin et al. (2004) found nonetheless that the effect of government share of consumption is significant and economically important: a ten percentage points increase in the share of government consumption over GDP would reduce annual growth by 0.4 percent. We apply this coefficient in our estimates, using the ratio of government consumption to non-oil GDP for oil producers, and find that for Qatar, Libya, and to some extent Kuwait, government consumption was large enough that it may have been a drag on TFP (Figure 2.6). The impact is relatively small for the other GCC countries.

INFLATION AND MACROECONOMIC STABILITY

High inflation, volatile export revenues, or variable economic growth add to the risks faced by agents and thereby worsen the prospects of economic activities that pay off in the future. These uncertain environments are therefore detrimental to investment, to skills learning, and in general to the development of businesses. Empirical studies have indeed found a significant statistical relationship between inflation and growth, even after controlling for fiscal performance, wars, droughts, population growth, openness, human and physical capital, and after allowing for simultaneity bias. Based on a cross-country regression of 101 countries over 1960–89, Fischer (1993) found that high inflation reduces output growth by reducing investment and productivity growth. Using annual data for eighty-seven countries over 1970–90, Sarel (1996) found evidence of a structural break at an 8 percent inflation rate. Inflation and growth are positively correlated below 8 percent but negatively correlated above that, suggesting that ignoring this nonlinearity would significantly underestimate the impact of inflation on growth. Ghosh and Phillips (1998) confirmed the presence of nonlinearities and found that increasing inflation from the optimal level (2–3 percent) to 5 percent reduces annual growth by 0.3 percent. Khan and Senhadji (2001) and Espinoza, Leon, and Prasad (2012) reexamined this result and found that for developing countries and for oil producers, inflation becomes costly only when it exceeds 10 percent. We choose the nonlinear specification adopted by both these papers in our application. For the GCC, inflation was lower than 10 percent during the period under study, and therefore it is unlikely that poor macroeconomic management should be a cause of low TFP in the region, contrary to the experience of Sudan and Venezuela (Figure 2.6).

VOLATILITY AND GROWTH

Output variability and exports or terms-of-trade volatility are the other commonly used measures of macroeconomic stability, and since Ramey and Ramey (1995) the literature has confirmed the negative relationship between growth and volatility. Hnatkovska and Loayza (2005) estimated that a one point increase in the volatility of GDP per capita decreases annual growth by around 0.3. Hnatkovska and Loayza (2005) also found that the negative link is stronger for poor countries, for countries with underdeveloped institutions, for countries with intermediate levels of financial development, and for countries that do not implement countercyclical fiscal policies. Similarly, Kose et al. (2006) suggested that the relationship between growth and output volatility is positive at high levels of income but negative at low levels of income, and depends on trade and financial liberalization. Loayza et al. (2007) provide a survey of some recent findings. Van der Ploeg and Poelhekke (2009) also found that a one point increase in volatility reduces growth by around 0.3 percentage points. They reinterpreted these findings for resource-rich countries and argued that volatility is indeed the key channel for the resource curse, dwarfing the Dutch disease effect that had been at the center of the literature. We apply a coefficient of 0.3 in our analysis and find that macroeconomic volatility could be a significant drag on growth for all oil producers. The standard deviation of growth per capita in Kuwait,[9] Qatar, and Saudi Arabia exceeded 5 percent since 1992.

[9] We compute the volatility after the First Gulf War for this exercise.

OPENNESS TO TRADE

Barro (1991) argued that price distortions significantly affected growth, and a growing literature has confirmed that trade openness is positive for growth (Sachs and Warner 1995; Edwards 1998), despite some critics (Rodriguez and Rodrik 2001). The recent literature has suggested that the effect of trade openness on growth is positive albeit small (for instance, Lee, Ricci, and Rigobon 2004; Billmeier and Nannicini 2009). Mookerjee's (2006) meta-analysis harvested the results of ninety-five regressions from seventy-six different papers on trade and growth and confirmed the near unanimous consensus among economists that exports orientation is positive for growth.[10] However, Makdisi et al. (2006) suggest that the link between trade and growth is weaker in MENA than it is on average. They use the same measure of openness as Sala-i-Martin et al. (2004) but find that the marginal effect of openness in MENA is only one fourth of what it is in other countries. However, it is not clear this result holds for the GCC, which had a very different tariff regime than the rest of MENA in most of the period covered. We therefore follow Sala-i-Martin et al. (2004) who find that for every four more years a country remained open in the period 1950–94, GDP growth was higher by 0.12 percent per year. The average growth of terms of trade has also been clearly associated with growth. Mendoza (1997) found that an increase of one percentage point in the terms of trade increases consumption growth by 0.05 percent, a result we take into account in our calculations. Terms of trade have been moving favorably for oil producers in the last twenty years, but the results shown in Figure 2.6 suggest that the effect was not strong enough to improve TFP in any GCC country.

INSTITUTIONS

As standard growth models failed at explaining the differences in growth across countries, the literature investigated whether non-economic factors, in particular institutions, could explain growth performance. Institutional quality is notoriously difficult to measure. Different freedom indices—political freedom, economic freedom, democracy—tend to be highly correlated to each other and insignificantly correlated to growth. Sala-i-Martin et al.

[10] There are typically two ways to measure an economy's "openness" or its disposition to trade: one is a measure of net exports (or exports plus imports) as a share of GDP, the other one is the number of years an economy is open, using Sachs and Warner's (1995) binary index of openness. For this index an economy is considered closed—and the index is set to zero—if it satisfies at least one of the following five criteria: nontariff barriers covering 40 percent or more of trade, average tariff rates of 40 percent or more, a black market exchange rate that is depreciated by over 20 percent relative to the official rate, a socialist economic system, or a state monopoly over major exports. If an economy does not exhibit any of the above traits it is considered open and receives a score of one. Sala-i-Martin et al. (2004) noted that the numbers of years the economy is open is statistically more robust than the ratio of trade to GDP in growth regressions.

(2004), for example, find that an index of political rights is not significantly correlated to growth. In a meta-analysis of the growth–democracy nexus, Doucouliagos and Ulubasoglu (2008) find that three quarters of the 470 regressions they examine do not have a positive, robust correlation between democracy and economic growth. In fact, their meta-analysis does not find any direct effects from democracy to growth.

Even though political regime variables were not found to correlate with growth, narrower measures of institutional quality were found to consistently correlate with growth. Economists and political scientists have accumulated theoretical arguments and empirical results showing that bureaucracy, corruption, or the strength of property rights matter for the growth process. However, it is important to use institutional measures parsimoniously in order to avoid multicollinearity problems. Acemoglu and Johnson (2005), for example, found that a variable capturing "contracting institutions" is significant only when the variable for "property rights institutions" is not included. Once both institutional measures are included as regressors, "contracting institutions" loses explanatory power. If the initial institutional measure is chosen appropriately, the marginal information provided by additional institutional regressors is unlikely to be significant. This is why we focused on a single variable measuring the quality of institutions, and opted for the measure of corruption of the International Country Risk Guide (ICRG), which is available for a wide range of countries. The claim is not that corruption is the only relevant feature for growth, but rather that high levels of corruption are surely symptomatic of institutional breakdown. Indeed, in the ICRG database, the correlation between the corruption and bureaucracy indices is 80 percent, and the correlation between corruption and the ICRG's composite rating is 75 percent.[11]

Ugur and Nandini (2011) conducted a meta-analysis from seventy-two different studies on corruption and economic growth. They found that corruption retards growth both directly as well as through a decline in human capital and a worsening of public finance. More importantly, they also found that corruption has a stronger negative effect in middle- and high-income countries than it does in low-income ones. Using the full sample of countries, they find that a one-point drop in the corruption index corresponds to an increase in the annual growth rate of 0.86 percent.[12] We keep this coefficient for our estimates. In several countries in the GCC (Qatar, Saudi Arabia,

[11] We prefer the corruption index to the composite rating because the former is the one surveyed by the meta-analysis of Ugur and Nandini (2011). We use this meta-analysis to calibrate the impact of corruption on growth.

[12] This coefficient is practically unchanged when removing the effect via human capital and physical capital accumulation, which are arguably already taken into account in the growth-accounting exercise.

and the UAE), the ICRG graded corruption to be worse than in the median country in our sample. As a result, the analysis suggests that poor institutions in these countries could have accounted for around –0.1 to –0.6 percentage points, per year, to the disappointing TFP of the period 1990–2008.

We conclude by summarizing our findings presented in Figure 2.4 and in Figure 2.6. Total factor productivity growth has been disappointing in the GCC in the last twenty years, as it has in many other oil exporters—although with positive growth numbers in GDP it is difficult to point at a resource curse. The emerging consensus in the growth literature is that high initial income per capita, oversized governments, instable macroeconomic environments, restrictions on trade, declining terms of trade, and poor institutions can explain declining TFP.

The GCC has had stable inflation and benefitted from terms-of-trade and trade policies in the region that were favorable to exports. However, relatively poor institutions (especially in Saudi Arabia and the UAE), oversized governments (in Kuwait and the UAE), and volatile growth in the region would have contributed negatively to TFP. Although we attempted to take into account the major lessons learnt from the growth literature, a significant part of declining TFP remains unexplained, especially in Bahrain, Oman, and the UAE. In Qatar, on the contrary, TFP was stable despite several factors that could have harmed growth (in particular the share of public consumption in GDP and the relatively poor quality of institutions).

References

Abreu, M., de Groot, H. L. F., and Florax, R. J. G. M. (2005). "A Meta-Analysis of β-Convergence: The Legendary 2%," *Journal of Economic Surveys*, 19 (3): 389–420.

Acemoglu, D. and Johnson, S. (2005). "Unbundling institutions," *Journal of Political Economy*, 113 (5): 949–95.

Ali, A. A. G. (2003). "Globalization and inequality in the Arab region." Kuwait: Arab Planning Institute.

Barro, R. (1991). "Economic growth in a cross section of countries," *Quarterly Journal of Economics*, 106 (2): 407–43.

Barro, R. and Lee, J. W. (2001). "International data on educational attainment: Updates and implications," *Oxford Economic Papers*, 53 (3): 541–63.

—— (2010). "A new data set of educational attainment in the world, 1950–2010." NBER Working Paper No. 15902.

Barro, R. and Sala-i-Martin, X. (2004). *Economic Growth*, 2nd edn. Cambridge, Mass.: MIT Press.

Billmeier, A. and Nannicini, T. (2009). "Trade openness and growth: Pursuing empirical glasnost," *IMF Staff Papers*, 56: 447–75.

Caselli, F. (2005). "Accounting for income differences across countries," in P. *Aghion* and S. *Durlauf* (eds), *Handbook of Economic Growth*, Volume 1A. New York: North-Holland, 679–741.

Caselli, F. and Wilson, D. J. (2004). *"Importing technology," Journal of Monetary Economics*, 51: 1–32.

Doucouliagos, H. and Ulubasoglu, M. H. (2008). "Democracy and economic growth: A meta-analysis," *American Journal of Political Science*, 52: 61–83.

Edwards, S. (1998). "Openness, productivity, and growth: What do we really know?" *Economic Journal*, 108 (2): 383–98.

Espinoza, R., Leon, H., and Prasad, A. (2012). "When should we worry about inflation?" *World Bank Economic Review*, 26 (1): 100–27.

Feenstra, R. (2000). "World trade flows, 1980–1997." Mimeo. Center for International Data, University of California Davis.

Felipe, J. (1997). "Total factor productivity growth in East Asia: A critical survey." ADB EDRC Report Series No. 65.

Fischer, S. (1993). "The role of macroeconomic factors in economic growth," *Journal of Monetary Economics*, 32: 485–512.

Ghosh, A. and Phillips, S. (1998). "Warning: Inflation may be harmful to your growth," *IMF Staff Papers*, 45: 672–710.

Hakura, D. (2004). "Growth in the Middle East and North Africa." IMF Working Paper, 04/56.

Hall, R. E. and Jones, C. I. (1999). "Why do some countries produce so much more output per worker than others?" *Quarterly Journal of Economics*, 114: 83–116.

Heston, A., Summers, H. A. R., and Aten, B. (2011). "Penn World Table Version 7.0." Center for International Comparisons of Production, Income and Prices, University of Pennsylvania.

Hnatkovska, V. and Loayza, N. (2005). "Volatility and growth," in L. Aizenman and B. Pinto (eds), *Managing Economic Volatility and Crises: A Practitioner's Guide*. Cambridge: Cambridge University Press, 65–100.

Khan, M. S. and Senhadji, A. (2001). "Threshold effects in the relationship between inflation and growth," *IMF Staff Papers*, 48: 1–21.

Kose, M. A., Prasad, E. S., Terrones, M. E. (2006). "How do trade and financial integration affect the relationship between growth and volatility?" *Journal of International Economics*, 69: 176–202.

Lee, H. Y, Ricci, L. A., and Rigobon, R. (2004). "Once again, is openness good for growth?" *Journal of Development Economics*, 75: 451–72.

Levine, R. and Renelt, D. (1992). "A sensitivity analysis of cross-country growth regressions," *American Economic Review*, 82: 942–63.

Loayza, N., Rancière, R., Servén, L., and Ventura, J. (2007). "Macroeconomic volatility and welfare in developing countries: An introduction," *World Bank Economic Review*, 21 (3): 343–57.

Makdisi, S., Fattah, Z., and Limam, I. (2006). "The determinants of economic growth in the MENA region," in J. Nugent and M. H. Pesaran (eds), *Explaining Growth in the Middle East*, Contributions to Economic Analysis, 278. Amsterdam: Elsevier, 31–60.

Mankiw, N. G., Romer, D., and Weil, D. N. (1992). "A contribution to the empirics of economic growth," *Quarterly Journal of Economics*, 107: 407–37.

Mendoza, E. G. (1997). "Terms-of-trade uncertainty and economic growth," *Journal of Development Economics*, 54: 323–56.

Mookerjee, R. (2006). "A meta-analysis of the export growth hypothesis," *Economics Letters*, 91: 395–401.

Nijkamp, P. and Poot, J. (2004). "Meta-analysis of the effect of fiscal policies on long-run growth," *European Journal of Political Economy*, 20: 91–124.

Ploeg, F. van der and Poelhekke, S. (2009). "Volatility and the natural resource curse," *Oxford Economic Papers*, 61: 727–60.

Psacharopoulos, G. (1994). "Returns to investment in education: A global update," *World Development*, 22 (9): 1325–43.

Ramey, V. and Ramey, G. (1995). "Cross country evidence on the link between volatility and growth," *American Economic Review*, 85 (5): 1138–59.

Rodriguez, F. and Rodrik, D. (2001). "Trade policy and economic growth: A skeptic's guide to the cross-national evidence," in B. Bernanke and K. Rogoff (eds), *NBER Macroeconomics Annual 2000*. Cambridge, Mass.: MIT Press, 261–338.

Sachs, J. D. and Warner, A. (1995). "Economic reform and the process of global integration," *Brookings Papers in Economic Activity*, 1: 1–118.

—— (2001). "The curse of natural resources," *European Economic Review*, 45 (4–6): 827–38.

Sala-i-Martin, X. (1997). "I just ran two million regressions," *American Economic Review*, 87 (2), Papers and Proceedings of the 104th Annual Meeting of the American Economic Association: 178–83.

Sala-i-Martin, X. and Artadi, E. (2002). "Economic growth and investment in the Arab world," in P. K. Cornelius (ed.), *The Arab World Competitiveness Report 2002–2003, World Economic Forum*. New York: Oxford University Press, 22–33.

Sala-i-Martin, X., Doppelhofer, G., and Miller, R. I. (2004). "Determinants of long-term growth: A Bayesian averaging of classical estimates (BACE) approach," *American Economic Review*, 94 (4): 813–35.

Sarel, M. (1996). "Nonlinear effects of inflation on economic growth," *IMF Staff Papers*, 43: 199–215.

Senhadji, A. (2000). "Sources of economic growth: An extensive growth-accounting exercise," *IMF Staff Papers*, 47: 129–57.

Solow, R. M. (1956). "A contribution to the theory of economic growth," *Quarterly Journal of Economics*, 70 (1): 65–94.

—— (1957). "Technical change and the aggregate production function," *Review of Economics and Statistics*, 39 (3): 312–20.

Swan, T. W. (1956). "Economic growth and capital accumulation," *Economic Record*, 32 (2): 334–61.

ThematicMapping.org. Country world map available online at <http://thematicmapping.org/downloads/world_borders.php>, accessed May 31, 2013.

Ugur, M. and Nandini, D. (2011). "Corruption and economic growth: A meta-analysis of the evidence on low-income countries and beyond." MPRA Working Paper, 31226.

3

The Macroeconomic Impact of Migration

3.1 Introduction

The dominance of foreigners in the labor force of the GCC countries is a very peculiar characteristic of these economies and one that has many macroeconomic consequences. Migration in the region has been steadily increasing, reaching extreme levels recently with non-nationals constituting over 90 percent of the labor force in Qatar and the UAE in 2011, 50 percent of the labor force in Saudi Arabia in 2009, and 77 percent of total employment in Bahrain in 2010. Recent efforts to "nationalize" the labor force aimed at limiting the supply of foreign workers and increasing the demand for national labor in the private sector. Nevertheless, by 2010 the GCC was the third region of immigration in the world after North America and the EU, this remaining true despite a shortage of statistics about, and hence likely underestimation of, migrants in this region.[1]

This chapter, which will focus on the macroeconomic consequences of migration, argues that the massive influxes of foreign labor have helped the region avoid one the main elements of the resource curse: the Dutch disease effect of large oil windfalls, which involves an overappreciated real exchange rate and thereby a loss of competitiveness of the export sector. The GCC countries have indeed avoided strong appreciations of their exchange rates, although this moderation has not translated into a particularly positive performance in non-oil exports. In addition, measured as the evolution of the share of non-oil exports in total exports, diversification experiences have been far from homogeneous, with relatively more success in the UAE, Oman,

[1] World Bank bilateral matrix of immigrant stocks 2010: see World Bank (2011).

and Bahrain. This chapter investigates the fundamental determinants of real exchange rates in the region, using estimation techniques that do not assume homogenous relationships.

Immigration has substantially relaxed supply shortages in the non-traded goods markets while demand has been contained via extremely restrictive immigration policies (such as various restrictions on property ownership, the absence of any naturalization process, and restricted family reunion). Theoretically, the adjustment process following an oil boom in a labor-importing country will depend on the potential effect of remittance outflows in alleviating the resulting upward pressure on the real exchange rate. Since imported workers employed in the non-tradable sector spend only part of their expenditures on non-traded goods (van Wijnbergen 1984) and remit a major part of it (especially in the GCC), further upward pressures on the real exchange rate are alleviated.

The reaction of remittances to commodity booms may therefore be of economic significance, though this link is largely unexplored in the empirical Dutch disease literature. In this chapter, we present novel evidence on the mitigating effect of international migration and remittances on the Dutch disease in the context of oil-rich and labor-poor countries.

We estimate an econometric model for the fundamental determinants of real exchange rates using a number of panel estimation techniques. We find, across our estimation methods, that the vast pool of foreign labor in the MENA net labor importers and the resulting large remittance outflows they generate act as a stabilizing factor by easing down the otherwise upward pressure on the real exchange rates caused by large oil windfalls. More specifically, we find no evidence of Dutch disease generated by large oil windfalls: the coefficient on oil export revenues is mostly negative and statistically insignificant. At the same time, the coefficient on remittance outflows is consistently negative and statistically significant across all estimation methods.

The rest of this chapter is structured as follows. Section 3.2 highlights some important facts about the GCC labor markets, including the extent of immigration and issues concerning migrants' rights, labor market segmentation, labor force growth, and unemployment. Section 3.3 discusses diversification in the GCC. Section 3.4 presents a simple theoretical model of Dutch disease in an oil-rich labor-importing economy. Section 3.5 discusses the estimator of choice and econometric model for our panel, including a treatment of cross-sectional error dependence. Section 3.6 presents our estimation results on the real exchange rate effect of remittance outflows and oil export revenues in the GCC countries. Section 3.7 concludes.

3.2 Background on GCC Labor Markets

There are two dominant features about GCC labor markets that distinguish them from the rest of MENA: (i) their high reliance on foreign (skilled and unskilled) workers, and the pervasive segmentation of labor markets between foreign workers in private jobs and nationals in public-sector jobs,[2] and (ii) the existence of large wage disparities between foreigners and nationals in the private sector, as well as between private- and public-sector wages for nationals. While these features have been a common characteristic in all GCC countries, the specific labor market issues they entailed have differed across GCC countries: in countries with relatively large indigenous populations such as Oman and Saudi Arabia, the limited scope for continued expansion in public-sector employment coupled with growing labor forces have put youth unemployment as a main concern. In these countries, governments initiated ambitious private-sector nationalization plans. However, in countries with small populations like Qatar, unemployment levels in general have been at record lows. Another common feature is very low female labor force participation rates.

3.2.1 Immigration and Remittances

In the GCC, "the employment of large numbers of foreigners has been a structural imperative [...], as the oil-related development depends upon the importation of foreign technologies and requires knowledge and skills alien to the local Arab population" (Kapiszewski 2006: 2). Migrant workers have indeed become a structural feature of GCC economies, given the long-term infrastructure development plans.

IMMIGRANTS' RIGHTS

Although most migrants benefit from the work opportunities given in the GCC, international organizations have noted some issues with the treatment of migrants and made recommendations to improve their treatment. The International Labor Organization (ILO) has called for a reform of the sponsorship system, where workers' visas depend on the employer—giving employers control over expatriate workers. This system ties migrant workers to employers and fosters abuses (IOM 2012). Many workers also arrive in the GCC with large debts due to "recruitment commissions" charged by intermediaries. In addition, working conditions and salaries are often unspecified (Plant 2008).

[2] Indeed, the prevalence of nationals, and not foreigners, in the public sector is not only a feature common to the GCC but also worldwide; however, the striking feature is that the employment of nationals in the public sector constitutes the largest share of their total employment.

The combination of employer control, large debts, and unspecified income, can lead to situations tantamount to forced labor.

Migrants, the destination countries, and the countries of origin in general benefit from these jobs and from the savings and remittances generated by the work opportunities. Survey data shows that the majority of migrant workers benefit from significantly improved economic conditions compared to what they earn in their country of origin (Plant 2008). Thus, a comprehensive approach towards ensuring migrants' rights and their fair treatment in legal systems and policies would benefit all stakeholders. Progress on this front has however been slow, despite improvements made in some of the GCC countries recently (IOM 2012). In addition, to facilitate transparency in the setting of wage conditions, the ILO has recommended that the GCC countries introduce a fair minimum wage, in line with international labor principles.

COMPOSITION OF FOREIGN WORKFORCE

The composition of the foreign labor force in the GCC countries (mostly Arab and South and Southeast Asian workers) has evolved throughout the years. While Arabs from neighboring countries dominated the Gulf foreign workforce at the beginning of the oil era owing to cultural, religious, and linguistic factors, the balance is now leaning in favor of Asian workers, in what is referred to in the literature as "de-arabization" of the Gulf labor market. The reasons for this new stream of migration relate both to favorable characteristics of the Asian workforce and increased detachment towards non-GCC Arabs.[3] Kapiszewski (2006) estimates that while Arabs constituted 72 percent of the immigrant populations across all GCC countries in 1975, this share declined to only 32 percent by 2004. Between 1975 and 2004, the share of Arabs in the foreign population declined from 22 to 15 percent in Bahrain, from 80 to 30 percent in Kuwait, from 16 to 6 percent in Oman, from 33 to 19 percent in Qatar, from 91 to 33 percent in Saudi Arabia, and from 26 to 13 percent in the UAE.

The skills composition of the foreign workforce has been diverse. The GCC countries, known for hosting a large number of low-skilled construction workers, have also successfully attracted a large number of highly skilled foreign laborers (Table 3.1). A recent UN survey indicated that all GCC countries are aiming at maintaining high-skilled immigration, despite plans to lower immigration levels in general and immigration of temporary workers in particular (Table 3.2). However, controlling unskilled immigration in countries with

[3] Lucas (2008: 61) also mentions the higher cost of labor from neighboring Arab countries, as well as the "greater ease of denying family accompaniment to the contract workers from Asia," as reasons for the shift of balance from Arab to Asian workers.

Table 3.1. Share of high-skilled migrants by region in 2000

USA	MENA	EU	CIS	GCC	LAC	SSA
42.7	22.5	21.9	19.0	18.8	15.7	2.7

Source: Docquier et al. (2010)

Table 3.2. Government views and policies on immigration, 2009

	Bahrain	Kuwait	Oman	Qatar	Saudi Arabia	UAE
View	Satisfactory	Too high	Satisfactory	Too high	Too high	Too high
Policy	Maintain	Lower	Maintain	Lower	Lower	Lower
Permanent settlement	–	Lower	No Intervention	No Intervention	No Intervention	Lower
Temporary workers	Lower	Lower	Lower	Lower	Lower	Maintain
Highly skilled workers	–	Maintain	Maintain	Maintain	Maintain	Maintain
Family reunification	Maintain	Maintain	Raise	Maintain	Maintain	Lower
Integration of non-citizens	–	Yes	No	Yes	Yes	–

Source: UN World Population Policies (2009)

large, labor-intensive, infrastructure projects is challenging when the local population is small, well-paid, and unwilling to accept unskilled jobs.

REMITTANCES

Reflecting the pattern of migrants and their high propensity to remit, remittances from the GCC in 2009 amounted to about 61 billion US dollars, 20 percent of world remittance outflows, and have constituted an important source of income for many countries in the region (see Chapter 9). Over the last decade, the GCC countries ranked among top source countries in the world, in gross terms as well as in percent of GDP (Figure 3.1). In the GCC, immigrants' incentives to remit are intensified by the countries' strict immigration rules: migrants are considered as temporary workers (even if they are essentially permanent migrants) with no potential for any naturalization process, and are thus not allowed to fully integrate in the local economy because of various restrictions on family reunion, property ownership, and rights.[4] The marginal propensity to remit in the Gulf is high for both skilled and unskilled

[4] It remains unclear whether strict immigration rules are driven by concerns in the GCC countries about maintaining their national identity and security, especially with citizens constituting a small minority of the population, or are solely based on a clear economic plan of mobilizing a cheap workforce to the provision of goods and services without adding to demand pressures (Ruhs 2009).

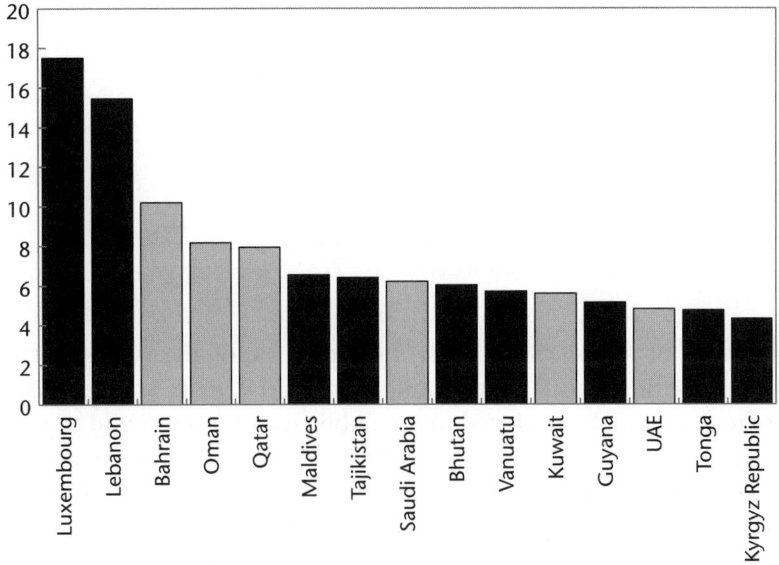

Figure 3.1. Remittance outflows in percent of GDP, average 2000–10
Source: World Development Indicators

migrants. Unskilled migrants are normally associated with higher propensity to remit as they are financially constrained, travel often alone, and leave their families back home. Docquier et al. (2011) analyze the relationship between migrants' education, the restrictiveness of immigration policies in migration destinations, and remittances. They find that skilled migrants remit more from the GCC compared to other advanced host countries. More specifically, they find that immigration policies conducted in the Gulf make the skills ratio more effective at increasing remittance outflows, while policies conducted in European countries act to reduce the amount of remittances sent home by skilled migrants.

3.2.2 Labor Market Segmentation and Wage Disparities

Labor markets in the GCC are characterized by a high degree of segmentation between the private and the public sectors and between nationals and expatriates. Foreign workers are overwhelmingly employed in the private sector and this has been the case for several decades. For instance in 2010, the share of foreigners in private-sector employment was 90 percent in Saudi Arabia and 80 percent in Bahrain. Nationals, by contrast, mainly work in the public sector, with different proportions across countries and over time (Table 3.3). In Kuwait and Qatar, the public sector accounts for close to 90 percent of total

Table 3.3. Public-sector employment as a share of total employment of nationals in the GCC

	1990	2000	2006	2008
Bahrain	68	80	38	29
Kuwait	42	75	87	86
Oman	76	–	50	47
Saudi Arabia	70	82	73	72
Qatar	–	–	89	88

Source: Baldwin-Edwards (2011)

employment of nationals. In those countries, nationals also represent the smallest share of the total population. In Bahrain, Oman, and Saudi Arabia, the share of nationals employed in the public sector is lower and unemployment is also more of a concern. These employment patterns reflect differences in oil wealth and varying degrees of saturation in public-sector employment: given their small national population and their surpluses in fiscal accounts, Qatar and Kuwait can easily offer all nationals public-sector jobs.

Significant wage disparities exist between foreigners and nationals in the private sector, and between public- and private-sector wages for nationals. Detailed wage data for Saudi Arabia show that nationals are paid significantly more than foreign workers in the private sector, and that these wage differentials decrease as the skill level of nationals and non-nationals increases. This pattern in wage gaps is even more pronounced when skills level is defined by occupation: among agricultural workers Saudi wages are nine times higher than those of expatriates, while among managers and directors there is essentially no wage gap (Figure 3.2). Wage disparities for nationals between public- and private-sector jobs are also a function of education. Differences in job security and work hours notwithstanding, for high-skilled employees, the public sector is not necessarily more lucrative than the private sector. A recent graduate with a bachelor's degree would typically be hired at a low-rank public-sector job and earn about 6,500 Saudi Riyals (SR) a month, less than the SR7,700 average wage for similarly educated Saudis in the private sector. For Saudis with secondary or lower education, however, the lowest-paying public-sector job pays about 30 percent more than a private-sector job.

Similar patterns exist in Bahrain where nationals are paid two to three times more than foreigners in the private sector, and increasingly so over the last decade. On average, over the last decade, public-sector jobs paid Bahrainis 1.7 times more than private-sector jobs. However, foreigners are paid about as much as Bahrainis in the public sector. The ratio of public to private-sector wages for foreigners has been consistently high over recent years, and increasingly so, reaching six in 2010 (Figure 3.3).

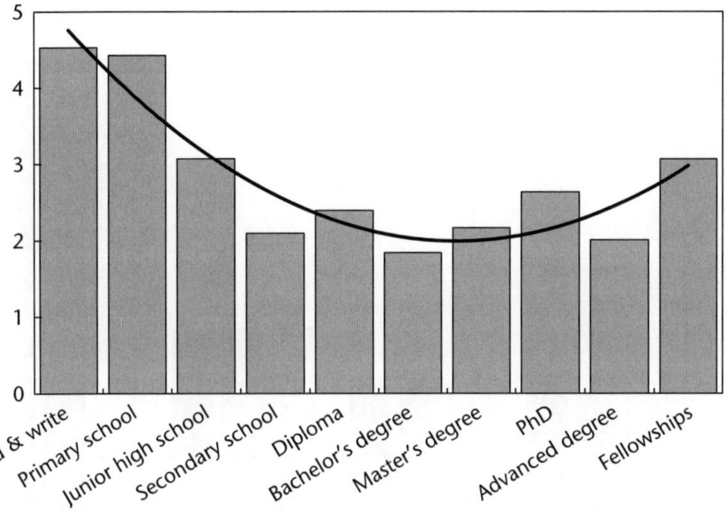

Figure 3.2. Saudi to non-Saudi monthly wages in the private sector by education, 2009 (ratio)

Source: Saudi Arabia Ministry of Labor Statistics of 2009

Wage disparities are also a function of gender, with the wage gaps between Saudis and expatriates consistently higher for males than for females. While Saudi males on average earned three times as much as expatriates in 2010, for females the average ratio was only 1.5 and in several job categories the ratio was below one.

3.2.3 Unemployment

GCC total unemployment rates (for both nationals and expatriates) have been contained, below 5 percent for most countries according to the International Labor Organization (ILO) (Figure 3.4). To a large extent, this reflects low unemployment rates for expatriates. Available data from national sources show that in 2011 the unemployment rate for Qataris, while still low at 3.9 percent, is eight times larger than the rate for both Qataris and expatriates, and in Saudi Arabia the unemployment rate of nationals is twice as large at 10.5 percent. High levels of unemployment do exist however and are concentrated among two categories of jobseekers: youth and women. Qatar is the only country in the region where youth unemployment is recorded at below 10 percent. In Saudi Arabia, for instance, high youth unemployment, which has averaged around 25 percent over the last decade, is the result of a combination of growing populations and thus labor forces (with the Saudi labor force growing 1.5 times over 1999–2009), saturation of public-sector

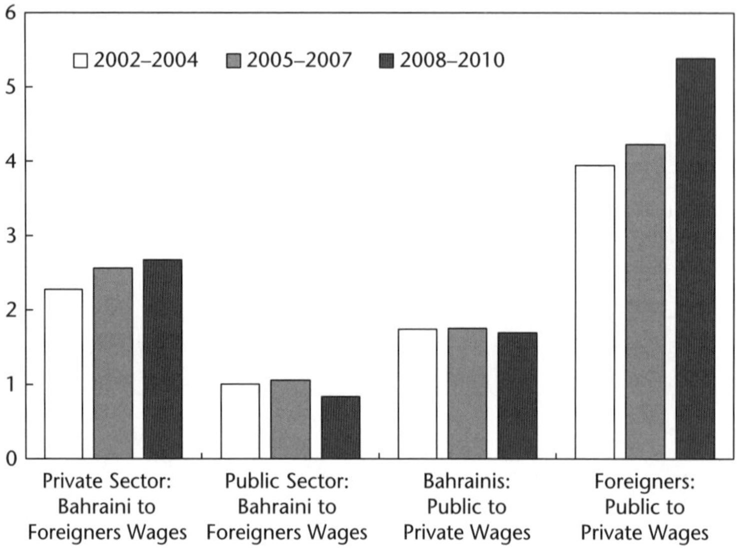

Figure 3.3. Wage ratios by sector and nationality in Bahrain, 2002–10
Source: Bahrain Labor Markets Regulatory Authority

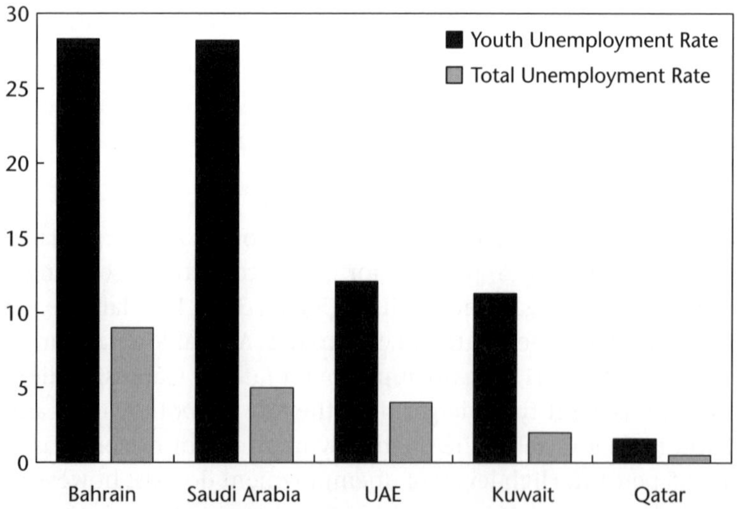

Figure 3.4. Youth and total unemployment rates (in percent, latest available date)
Source: International Labor Organization KLIM database

jobs, and private-sector job creation that has mainly benefitted foreigners. Youth unemployment is also near 30 percent in Bahrain.

Women represent the other main group of unemployed. Figures from Qatar and Saudi Arabia show nationals' unemployment rates for women about four times as high as for men in recent years, and this difference dates back at least a decade. Along with high unemployment, female labor force participation rates have been very low in some countries in the region, for instance at 12 percent for Saudi females and 34 percent for Qatari females on average over the last five years.[5] The more available country-wide rates including both national and expatriate females show significantly higher participation rates, as high as 52 percent in Qatar in 2011, 43 percent in Kuwait and 39 percent in Bahrain in 2010.

3.2.4 Nationalization

While all GCC countries' development plans target higher employment of nationals in the private sector through ambitious nationalization plans, these plans have not yet been successful in "nationalizing" the private sector.

Indeed, much of the difficulty in achieving the GCC's nationalization objectives relates to a low degree of substitutability between national and foreign workers (Fasano and Goyal 2004). Reasons for the low substitutability include a shortage of highly skilled nationals, an almost perfectly elastic supply of cheap foreign labor, a general aversion among nationals to taking menial jobs, and the role of the public sector as the dominant employer of nationals (see also Chapter 4). These factors have all contributed to generating large differences in pay between nationals and foreigners and to cementing the segmentation between the two categories of workers (Abdalla et al. 2010). They have also allowed for the coexistence of high youth unemployment alongside rapid job growth in the private sector.

Up until recently, nationalization policies in the GCC have been basically immigration policies aiming at affecting the quantity and cost of hiring foreign workers through a combination of mandatory and administrative measures. Examples are quotas on the proportion of nationals employed by private companies in specific professions or sectors and time-specific cash benefits for employing nationals. These measures however have proven difficult to monitor and implement, especially given the unlimited access of private companies to foreign labor at internationally competitive wages. Other

[5] Qatar's third National Human Development Report, as part of its efforts to support the achievement of Qatar National Vision 2030 and the program of National Development Strategy 2011–16, puts the spotlight on Qatari youth and identifies expanding education opportunities for young people and enhancing their participation in the labor force as one of the key challenges ahead.

measures have aimed at increasing the relative cost of hiring expatriates, such as regulating the supply of work permits for foreigners and imposing fees for use of expatriate labor.

More recently, immigration policies have become part of a broader effort to increase employment of nationals in some GCC countries, and it is now recognized that successful nationalization of the private workforce will also require new job creation through diversification, such as the promotion of small and medium-sized enterprises (SMEs).[6] For instance in Saudi Arabia, several labor market initiatives were co-launched in 2011, including the "Nitaqat" program, which is the updated Saudization policy. Nitaqat differs from past Saudization schemes in that (i) the percentage of Saudis required to be employed by each company is based on its area of activity and the size of its workforce, (ii) many SMEs are included in Nitaqat, as all Saudi companies with at least ten employees are required to participate, and (iii) Nitaqat involves harmonization between several government bodies to improve compliance.[7]

3.3 Diversification in the GCC

Before we provide evidence on whether the GCC economies have been harmed by a Dutch disease effect, we review the performance and composition of their non-oil sectors. As a share of total exports, non-oil exports in the GCC have remained quite low, mostly below 20 percent, though there was some improvement in the last two decades in Oman and in the UAE (Figure 3.5). The performance of non-oil exports looks more promising when expressed in percent of non-oil GDP: the share increased in Kuwait, Oman, Saudi Arabia, and the UAE (though it remains below 20 percent), and even exceeded 100 percent in Oman.

[6] While a large part of job creation takes place in small and medium-sized enterprises, SMEs are generally more financially constrained than large firms and less likely to have access to formal finance. In the GCC and the MENA region in general, SME financing through banks is very limited. Data shows that SME loans represented only 2 percent of total loans over the last few years in the GCC. However, there has been an increased focus in the GCC on SME development. For instance, Saudi Arabia has substantially scaled up programs to alleviate financing obstacles for SMEs, which are viewed as major job creation vehicles. The Saudi Industrial Development Fund supports bank lending to SMEs, and several specialized credit institutions provide additional lending. In Qatar with record low unemployment rates, SME development is solely for the purpose of diversification, infrastructure development, and privatization.

[7] Under Nitaqat, companies are classified according to a basic color scheme: red and yellow for noncompliant companies subject to sanctions, and green or premium for companies that fulfill Saudization requirements and accordingly receive benefits. Sanctions and benefits are defined in terms of companies' ability to apply for or modify work permits for expatriates. For instance, red companies are not allowed to apply for or renew work permits, and existing foreign employees will be able to take jobs with companies categorized as green or premium.

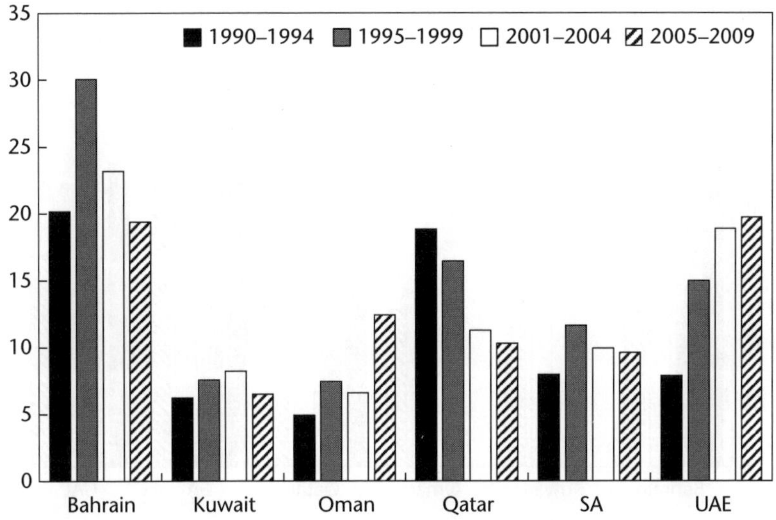

Figure 3.5. Share of non-oil exports in total exports (in percent)
Source: IMF and authors' calculations

What are GCC countries exporting other than hydrocarbons? With the exception of Oman and the UAE, around 50 to 60 percent of non-oil exports in the GCC are petrochemicals (Figure 3.6). It is important to single out petrochemical industries because this sector is heavily subsidized by the hydrocarbon sector and thus its performance is artificially boosted by the subsidy policies (see Chapter 4 for a discussion on subsidies). Other non-oil exports include agricultural (live animals, animal products, vegetables products, prepared foods, and beverages), mineral products, base metals, electrical machinery in most GCC countries, in addition to free-zone exports in Dubai. Qatar and the UAE are also examples of countries that have managed to have diversified services export sectors (transportation, including airlines, tourism related to international sports events, etc.).

3.4 Simple Theoretical Model

In this section, we develop a simple theoretical model to illustrate the mechanism through which immigration and remittances help alleviate potential real exchange rate appreciation in the oil-exporting, labor-poor, GCC states. We augment the Dixit and Norman (1980) dual trade general equilibrium model allowing for migration of labor and remittances. We consider

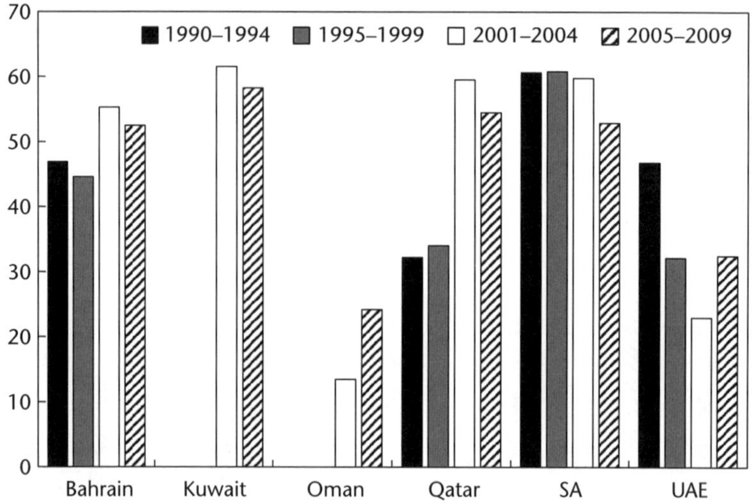

Figure 3.6. Share of petrochemical exports in total non-oil exports (in percent)
Source: IMF and authors' calculations

a resource-rich economy with the following equilibrium conditions (where subscripts denote partial derivatives):

$$e(q,u) = g(q,L) + N \text{ where } L = M(N) + I \tag{1}$$

$$e_q(q,u) = g_q(q,L) \tag{2}$$

$$w_M = g_M(q,L) < w_I = g_I(q,L) \tag{3}$$

Equation (1) is the income–expenditure equilibrium. The expenditure side is represented by the concave expenditure function $e(q,u)$ expressed in terms of the relative price of non-traded with respect to traded goods q, and the aggregate welfare level u. The implicit assumption here is that the price of tradables is normalized to one so that everything is expressed in terms of the (non-resource) tradable good. The production side consists of a convex non-resource production function represented by $g(q,L)$ and an inflow of foreign exchange resource rents represented by N. We are assuming here that oil production does not employ any resources, so the increase in oil revenue simply shows up as an increase in transfers received from abroad. The labor force L consists of the indigenous population I and the immigrant workers M. Changes in the labor force are driven only by changes in the inflow of foreign labor so that $dL = dM$ (since $dI = 0$), which is in turn driven by resource rents, i.e. $dM = M_N dN$ where $M_N > 0$. The latter effect reflects the long-standing GCC policy response to oil price shocks of increased demand for and import of foreign workers, as well as a supply-side "Alberta effect" where a booming oil sector attracts immigrants seeking to share the rents (Corden 1984).

Equation (2) reflects equilibrium in the non-traded goods market. As the first derivative of the expenditure function with respect to q represents demand for non-traded goods, and similarly the first derivative of the production function with respect to q represents the supply of non-traded goods,[8] equation (2) simply says that the non-traded goods market clears. With the economy's excess demand for the tradable good always met by the rest of the world, excess demand for all goods becomes the excess demand for non-tradables. The real exchange rate (the relative price of the non-tradable good) adjusts to clear the non-tradable goods market. The final equation represents equilibrium real product wage determination under perfect competition and assumes that the marginal product wage of migrants is lower than that of the locals. This seems to be a stylized fact in GCC countries with (almost perfectly) segmented labor markets where nationals are mainly employed in the highly paid public sector, and migrants are distributed across construction and other sectors based on their skill levels. However, we assume away any heterogeneity in the migrants' wages. The non-traded sector in our setup is labor-intensive, hence $g_{qM} > 0$ by Rybczynski's theorem (in a two-sector model, an increase in the endowment M leads to a (more than proportional) increase in the supply of the good that was M-intensive). Finally, we assume for now that there are no remittance transfers by the GCC immigrants to their families in their home countries, and allow for this possibility in the next section.

Total differentiation of equations (1) and (2) and simple manipulations produce the following expression for the change in real exchange rate dq in terms of the change in the resource windfall (dN):[9]

$$dq = \frac{1}{\Omega}\left[\eta\lambda(1 + g_M M_N) - qM_N \varepsilon_{qM}\frac{g_q}{M}\right]dN \tag{4}$$

$$\Omega = g_q\left(\varphi_{qq} - \varepsilon_{qq}\right) > 0 \tag{4a}$$

[8] The production function can also be expressed as the inner product of the price q and the optimal supply function $x(q,L)$ $g(q,L) = q * x(q,L)$. With production decisions assumed to maximize total profit, the optimally chosen supply function is thus obtained by differentiating the production function with respect to their prices. Similarly, minimizing expenditure to attain a target utility u at given prices q gives us the Hicksian compensated demand function, which is the first derivative of the expenditure function with respect to q.

[9] For details of the derivation, please see the technical appendix at the end of the chapter.

where $(\phi_{qq} = qg_{qq} / g_q > 0)$ is the elasticity of supply of non-traded goods with respect to the real exchange rate; $(\varepsilon_{qq} = qe_{qq} / e_q < 0)$ is the corresponding non-traded goods' demand elasticity with respect to the real exchange rate; $(\eta = ee_{qu} / e_q e_u > 0)$ is the income elasticity of demand for non-traded goods; $(\lambda = qe_q / e > 0)$ is the share of non-tradables in total expenditure; and $(\varepsilon_{qM} = Mg_{qM} / g_q > 0)$ is the elasticity of supply of non-traded goods with respect to inflows of immigrant workers.

Equation (4) suggests that a resource windfall *dN* generates two opposite effects on the real exchange rate. First, there is a positive demand-side effect (first term in brackets) which is increasing in the income elasticity of demand for non-tradables η and in the share of non-tradables in total expenditure λ. This is the standard spending effect of a resource windfall where additional (public and private) spending partly falls on non-traded goods. In our model, such demand effect is exacerbated by the inflow of foreign workers who also consume non-traded goods, and is increasing in migrants' wages g_M and in the immigration response to increased windfalls M_N. Second, a negative supply-side effect is at play since the oil boom is accompanied by an influx of foreign labor (second term in brackets). This depreciative supply-side effect is higher the more elastic is non-tradable supply with respect to increases in immigrant workers ε_{qM} and the greater their productivity g_q/M. In the GCC context, this is equivalent to relaxing supply shortages or bottlenecks by importing almost everything: physical capital (or rather, unskilled construction workers) and human capital in the form of skilled workers (we do not now distinguish between both types of inputs). Finally, equation (4a) which defines the denominator of equation (4) gives the standard result in such models that the higher the real exchange rate elasticities of supply and demand for non-tradables, the lower the real appreciation caused by any factor included in the right-hand side of equation (4).[10]

The upshot is that a real depreciation is possible if the supply-side effect of immigrants is large enough and their contribution to domestic demand small enough. This seems to be unlikely in this setup where migrants are assumed to spend all their incomes in the GCC host countries. We now relax this restrictive assumption and allow immigrants to save and remit a proportion of their incomes back to their home countries. In fact,

[10] It can also be shown that a resource windfall followed by the import of foreign workers is strictly welfare-enhancing by solving for *du*, and that the resulting change in domestic wages is ambiguous by solving for *dw*. The change in domestic wages includes the negative effect of the import of foreign labor and the resulting increase in labor force, as well as the positive effect reflecting the adjustment process through which Dutch disease happens: real exchange rate appreciation driven by an excess demand for non-traded good post-resource windfall raises demand for labor and domestic wages for locals and immigrants proportional to their shares in the total labor force, and hence increases overall wages. This is by definition the process through which labor is drawn out of the tradable sector to the booming non-tradable sector and Dutch disease occurs.

restrictive immigration policies in the GCC (such as various restrictions on property ownership, the absence of any naturalization process and hence a sense of "permanent temporary residence", and restricted family reunion) encourage migrants to remit even larger proportions of their incomes back home.

More specifically, we model immigrants' remittances as an exogenous fraction $\theta<1$ of their wages. Equation (1) becomes:

$$e(q,u) = g(q,L) + N - \theta w_M M \tag{5}$$

And the rest of the model equations remain the same. Total differentiation of equations (5), (2), and (3) generates the following:

$$dq = \frac{1}{\Gamma}\left\{\eta\lambda\left[1 + w_M M_N\left(1 - \theta - \theta\varepsilon_{MM}\right)\right] - qM_N\varepsilon_{qM}\frac{g_q}{M}\right\}dN \tag{6}$$

$$\Gamma = g_q\left(\varphi_{qq} - \varepsilon_{qq} + \theta\eta\lambda\varepsilon_{qM}\right) > 0 \tag{6a}$$

where $\varepsilon_{MM} = Mg_{MM} / g_M < 0$ is the elasticity of migrants' wages to the inflow of foreign workers, and all other terms are as defined above.[11]

Equation (6) for the model with remittance outflows differs from its counterpart (equation (4)) for the model without remittance transfers in that now a real depreciation is more likely. This can be seen from the first term illustrating the demand-side effect which is smaller the higher the fraction of migrants' wages repatriated back home. The term $-\theta\varepsilon_{MM}$, which is overall positive, suggests that the faster migrants' wages adjust downwards to additional inflows of foreign workers, the lower are overall remittance outflows and hence the lower is their depreciative effect. The supply-side effect is unchanged as expected. It is thus more likely here that the supply side is big enough to offset any positive demand-side effects so that a real depreciation is observed following resource windfalls. This suggests that not only will the usual Dutch disease trade-off between non-traded and non-resource traded be absent (labor only moves internationally and not intersectorally), but the non-resource tradable sector can actually expand, and pro-industrialization (as opposed to de-industrialization) occurs. This may well have been the case for the GCC countries, as they have witnessed an expansion of their non-oil sectors over the last three decades.

[11] Derivation of equation (6) is very similar to derivation of equation (4) shown in the technical appendix, and is left to the interested reader.

3.5 Estimation

Our theoretical model shows that the GCC countries can avoid the structural adjustment of a resource windfall to a new long-run structure, namely a larger non-traded goods sector, by jumping instantaneously to this new structure. This has been made possible since "all sorts of capital—skills, capital equipment, and infrastructure—can be redeployed or bought and sold on world markets, so that bottlenecks are not encountered and relative prices need not change" (van der Ploeg and Venables 2010). With remittance outflows and oil export revenues as our main right-hand-side determinants of real exchange rates in equation (6), we may not find any significant real exchange rate appreciation driven by oil export revenues. We do however expect a significant depreciative effect of remittance outflows. With no available time series on the stock of immigrants in GCC countries and given evidence of high correlation between the size of remittance transfers and the stock of immigrants, we posit that the coefficient on remittances captures both the supply-side and demand-side effects.

The macroeconomic (supply- and demand-side) shocks that fundamentally determine the equilibrium long-run real exchange rate, and hence constitute our set of control variables, have been well identified in the literature. In addition to the leading variables of interest—international transfers in the form of public windfalls (oil export revenues) and private flows (workers' remittances)—the equilibrium long-run real exchange rate is generally determined by international financial conditions, government spending, terms of trade, commercial policy, and productivity growth (Montiel 1999).

For our sample, however, we restrict regressors to remittance outflows (*rem*), oil export revenues (*oil*), government spending (*gov*), and net foreign assets (*nfa*). We do not include trade openness, the proxy for Montiel's commercial policy, as a control variable. The most common measure of trade openness, sum of exports and imports to GDP, is highly collinear with oil export revenues in the GCC. We choose to drop the terms-of-trade variable from our estimation for the same reason, as oil prices drive terms of trade for major oil exporters.

Given the dynamic nature of real exchange rates, we investigate the alleviating effect of immigration and the resulting remittance outflows by estimating a dynamic Error Correction Model (ECM) of the long-run relationship between the real effective exchange rate (*reer*)—our proxy for the relative price of non-traded goods—and its above-mentioned determinants, all measured in percent of non-oil GDP.

The prior expectation would be that oil export revenues have an appreciating effect on the real exchange rate, but that remittances have a depreciating effect. The effect of government consumption and net foreign assets is more ambiguous. For the former, the effect depends on whether government spending falls more heavily on tradable or non-tradable goods and for the latter, on whether the country is a net creditor or debtor.

Remittance outflows are potentially endogenous due to reverse causality: endogeneity of the demand for foreign labor may result in endogeneity of the resulting remittance outflows. More specifically, real exchange rate fluctuations following a boom or contraction in the oil sector (due to a change in world oil prices) generate different labor demand structures than the existing ones across sectors, namely the oil sector, the tradable non-oil sector, and the non-tradable sector. Corden (1984: 366–7) makes an indirect case for remittances' endogeneity in oil-exporting countries when discussing the "Alberta effect", where booming oil sector revenues accrue to the government, which redistributes them to the public through lower taxes and better public facilities. This policy attracts immigrants seeking to share the rents. In the Gulf countries, this adjustment is accompanied by import of foreign labor, to deal with labor supply shortages, not only in the expanding non-tradable sector but in other sectors as well (van Wijnbergen 1984). It should be noted, however, that reverse causality running from real exchange rate misalignments (following oil booms) to immigration and remittances is expected to be positive, i.e., working against our hypothesis of a negative effect of remittances on the real exchange rate. This suggests that correcting for such reverse causality can only strengthen our results.

Our basic model is estimated with the following auto-regressive distributed lag model, which we present, for illustrative purposes, with one lag on both the dependent and explanatory variables:

$$reer_{it} = \lambda_1 reer_{i,t-1} + \delta_0 oil_{i,t} + \delta_1 oil_{i,t-1} + \alpha_0 rem_{i,t} + \alpha_1 rem_{i,t-1} + \gamma_0 gov_{i,t} + \gamma_1 gov_{i,t-1} + \theta_0 nfa_{i,t} + \theta_1 nfa_{i,t-1} + \mu_i + \sigma_t + \varepsilon_{it} \quad (7)$$

where μ_i and σ_t are country and year dummies that control, respectively, for country-specific time-invariant unobserved heterogeneity and global shocks or common factors affecting all countries in the sample (such as oil price shocks). ε_{it} are error terms that are assumed to be identically and independently distributed across i and t. Our time dimension is annual data from 1980–2009 and the countries we include in the sample are labor-importing oil exporters, namely: GCC countries, Australia, Libya, Netherlands, Norway, Russia, and the United Kingdom. All variables (except net foreign assets) are expressed in logarithmic values.

Equation (7) can then be expressed in error correction form. Manipulating and rearranging terms, we separate the short-run adjustments from the long-run equilibrium relationship and capture the speed of adjustment:

$$\Delta reer_{it} = \varphi(reer_{i,t-1} - \eta_i - \tau_t - \delta oil_{i,t} - \alpha rem_{i,t} - \gamma gov_{i,t} - \theta nfa_{i,t}) + \delta_0 \Delta oil_{i,t} + \alpha_0 \Delta rem_{i,t} + \gamma_0 \Delta gov_{i,t} + \theta_0 \Delta nfa_{i,t} + \varepsilon_{it} \quad (8)$$

Where $\varphi = -(1-\lambda_1)$; $\delta = \frac{\delta_0 + \delta_1}{1-\lambda_1}$; $\alpha = \frac{\alpha_0 + \alpha_1}{1-\lambda_1}$ etc.; $\eta_i = \frac{\mu_i}{1-\lambda_1}$; $\tau_t = \frac{\sigma_t}{1-\lambda_1}$

- $(reer_{i,t-1} - \eta_i - \delta oil_{i,t} - \alpha rem_{i,t} - \gamma gov_{i,t} - \theta nfa_{i,t})$ is the long-run relationship between the REER and its fundamental determinants. More specifically, it is the deviation of $reer_{i,t-1}$ from its predicted value given by $(\eta_i + \delta oil_{i,t} + \alpha rem_{i,t} + \gamma gov_{i,t} + \theta nfa_{i,t})$. These are the long-run coefficients that we report below.
- $\delta_0 \Delta oil_{i,t} + \alpha_0 \Delta rem_{i,t} + \gamma_0 \Delta gov_{i,t} + \theta_0 \Delta nfa_{i,t}$ are the short-run adjustments which are assumed to be homogeneous for the pooled ECM and allowed to vary across countries in the PMG model (see below).
- φ is the error correction term or speed of adjustment. It must be negative and less than one (in absolute value), for a stable equilibrium to exist. The larger is φ, the faster is the speed of adjustment back to the long run.

We estimate two variants of the model. We first use a pooled ECM model to estimate a homogeneous cross-country response of the real exchange rate to its determinants. Unit root and cointegration tests indicate that all model variables, except for oil revenues, are nonstationary and cointegrated.[12] We therefore estimate the pooled ECM without oil revenues, keeping in mind that government consumption is strongly correlated with oil revenues. More specifically, since in oil-exporting countries oil revenues are the main source of budget financing, including government spending, which is the main mechanism through which oil revenues are injected to the economy, would be a good proxy for spending booms out of oil windfalls (see also Chapter 5).

For robustness, and since we are including countries at different stages of development, we also estimate a separate version of the ECM that accommodates potential heterogeneity in individual countries' responses. For this, we use the pooled mean group (PMG) estimator (Pesaran, Shin, and Smith 1999), which allows the short-run coefficients to vary across countries, while imposing homogeneous long-run responses. This is particularly relevant when dealing with real exchange rates: while it is expected that short-run real exchange rate movements are affected by country-specific factors, long-run real exchange rate changes are driven by the same fundamentals.

[12] Based on a number of unit root tests such as Im, Pesaran, and Shin (2003) and Pesaran (2007). Panel cointegration tests included Kao's (1999) homogeneous residual test and the Fisher test.

The PMG estimator does not require pre-testing for the presence of unit roots in the panel variables.[13] Since the PMG estimates the model for each country separately, it does not allow us to include year fixed effects. As a result, an important issue which arises in this heterogeneous setting is potential error cross-sectional dependence, i.e., the potential for errors to be contemporaneously correlated across panel members due to unobserved (global) common factors. These major oil producers are indeed all exposed, potentially in different ways, to common global factors of changing world oil prices. In order to ensure that regressions residuals are cross-sectionally independent across countries, we use a recently developed augmented version of the PMG estimator suggested by Binder and Offermanns (2007) in our panel. The ECM is augmented by cross-sectional averages of all the variables of the model, which are taken as proxies of the common factors. Just like all the variables in the model, the countries' responses to these global factors are thus allowed to be heterogeneous in the short run. The literature also suggests assuming a common country response to global factors and hence correcting for cross-section dependence by simple cross-sectional demeaning of model's variables prior to estimation. We report results from both approaches below.[14]

3.6 Results

Our findings in Table 3.4 show the important stabilizing effect of immigration and remittance outflows on the real exchange rates of GCC countries.

[13] Pesaran et al. (1999) show the consistency of the PMG estimator in the case of I(0) and I(1) regressors. In the PMG model, the parameters of interest (long-run coefficients and speed of adjustment) are obtained by maximizing a concentrated log-likelihood function of the panel data model (defined as the product of likelihoods of each group). Starting with an initial estimate of the long-run homogenous parameters (such as static fixed effects), estimates of error-correction coefficients and the other short-run coefficients (including country-specific intercepts and error variances) can be computed (also using maximum likelihood) as the averages of the estimated coefficients for each cross-section. These average estimates can then be used to obtain an updated estimate of the long-run parameters. The same process is repeated until convergence is achieved. The long-run parameters are consequently nonlinear functions of the short-run parameters.

[14] Several practical points on the PMG estimation are worth noting. First, the time dimension of the data has to be long enough to allow estimation of the model for each of the cross-sections separately. Second, the lag order has to be long enough to ensure that the residuals of the error correction model are serially uncorrelated but not too long to cause a serious loss of degrees of freedom. In this respect, there is a trade-off between the loss of degrees of freedom when including too many lags (relative to the time series dimension) and the loss of consistency when including too few lags. Augmenting the model with lags addresses the potential endogeneity of remittances. In this respect, Pesaran (1997) and Pesaran and Shin (1999) show that for inference on the long-run parameters, sufficient augmentation of the order of the autoregressive distributive lag model can simultaneously correct for the problem of residual serial correlation and endogenous regressors. The optimal number of lags is best chosen according to an information criterion such as Akaike Information Criterion (AIC) or the Schwarz Bayesian Criterion (SBC).

Table 3.4. Effect of remittance outflows on the REER, 1980–2009

Dependent variable: REER	Pooled ECM	Pooled Mean Group	
Long-run coefficients	(1)	(2)	(3)
Oil export revenues		−0.049	−0.017
Remittance outflows	−0.254*	−0.274***	−0.133***
Error correction coefficient	−0.110***	−0.133*	−0.311**
Countries	11	8	8
Country fixed effects	Yes	Yes	Yes
Year fixed effects	Yes	CSD	CSA

Note: ***, **, and * indicate significance respectively at the 1, 5, and 10 percent levels. In regressions (1) and (3), we use two lags. In regression (2), we use the Akaike Bayesian optimal lag selection criterion. CSA means that the model was augmented with cross-sectional averages of variables. CSD means that all model variables were cross-sectionally demeaned prior to estimation. Controls, not reported here, include government spending and net foreign assets (which are positive and significant for regressions (2) and (3)).

Source: Authors' calculations

Across all models, we find that remittance outflows significantly depreciate the *reer* in this group of countries. The correlation of remittance outflows with the stock of immigrants suggests that importing foreign workers does indeed mitigate Dutch disease, as expected. Oil export revenues, in contrast, do not seem to exert the expected appreciative effect on the *reer* (Table 3.4). For the major labor importers in the sample, namely the GCC and Libya, if oil booms are always accompanied by imports of foreign labor, it may be that the usual Dutch disease-type bottlenecks are simply not present. In addition, saving a large share of oil revenues in foreign currencies may also mitigate Dutch disease. Norway is often seen as an example of a country that has successfully avoided Dutch disease through sound management of resource windfalls.[15] Consequently, in this set of countries, there is little to suggest that Dutch disease is a serious problem.

The coefficient that captures the speed of adjustment is significant at the 1 percent level, suggesting a strong long-run relationship and feedback effects between the real exchange rate and its fundamental determinants.

Our results can be interpreted in light of the diversification efforts of the GCC countries. First, our analysis suggests that while the Gulf countries' open immigration policies and consequent access to a perfectly elastic supply of foreign labor have played a significant role in alleviating the bottlenecks and relative price pressures that often tend to crowd out non-oil exports in oil-exporting economies, the current level of diversification in most GCC countries has not yet reflected such considerable advantage.

[15] See Gylfason (2006).

Second, GCC countries adopting active policies to boost the employment of nationals in the private sector, which has been historically dominated by foreigners, might face a trade-off between creating new jobs in the private sector and shifting existing jobs from foreigners to nationals. Job creation initiatives that promote economic diversification, such as the development of SMEs, are intended to add to labor demand in the non-oil economy, and therefore require improvements in competitiveness. Nationalization policies aimed at increasing the share of nationals in the private sector may on the other hand reduce the number of foreign workers and reduce competitiveness. In their pursuit of jobs for nationals, GCC countries will therefore need to maintain competitiveness, as raising the share of nationals in private-sector employment is not a simple matter of substituting foreign for national workers.

The experience of other labor-importing countries shows that it is possible to combine a high reliance on foreign workers with strong jobs growth for nationals. Singapore, for example, has seen consistent increases in employment of nationals over the past decade, with employment of both nationals and expatriates going up in boom years (whilst the brunt of job losses during downturns was borne by foreign workers). Underpinning this, Singapore's immigration policies have simultaneously attracted highly skilled foreign workers and restricted the inflow of low-skilled workers (Ruppert 1999).

3.7 Conclusion

This chapter has attempted to show the stabilizing effect of immigration and the resulting remittance outflows on the real exchange rates of the GCC countries. This is particularly important for these major oil exporters who face the risk of Dutch disease and the ensuing undermining of competitiveness in non-oil export sectors. Using a number of estimation techniques, our findings not only suggest a significant negative depreciative effect of remittance outflows but also show the absence of any Dutch disease threat of oil windfalls in a panel of resource-rich, labor-poor economies. This result suggests that the GCC countries have managed to avoid the structural adjustment of a resource windfall (creating a spending boom and a relative increase the price of non-traded goods) that typically dictates an expansion of the non-traded sector at the expense of the non-oil traded sector. As the GCC countries continue in their plans to diversify from oil and increase the employment of nationals in the private sector, it will be important to keep in mind what lies behind this success.

Technical Appendix

Derivation of equation (4):

Keeping in mind (as explained above) that $dL = dM = M_N dN$ (since $dI = 0$), total differentiation of equation (1) gives:

$$e_q(q,u)dq + e_u du = g_q(q,L)dq + g_M(q,L)M_N dN + dN \qquad \text{(A1)}$$

Total differentiation of equation (2) gives:

$$e_{qq}(q,u)dq + e_{qu}(q,u)du = g_{qq}(q,L)dq + g_{qM}(q,L)M_N dN \qquad \text{(A2)}$$

Combining equation (A1) with equations (2):

$$e_u du = (g_M M_N + 1)dN \qquad \text{(A3)}$$

Replacing the value of *du* in (A3) in (A2), we get:

$$(g_{qq} - e_{qq})dq = \left[\frac{e_{qu}}{e_u}(g_M M_N + 1) - g_{qM} M_N\right] dN \qquad \text{(A4)}$$

Multiplying and dividing the left side of equation (A4) by $qe_q = qg_q$ allows us to express the left side of (A4) as:

$$\Omega \frac{dq}{q} = g_q\left(\frac{qg_{qq}}{g_q} - \frac{qe_{qq}}{e_q}\right)\frac{dq}{q} \qquad \text{(A5)}$$

And similarly multiplying and dividing the left side of equation (A4) by $qe_q = qg_q$, and additionally multiplying and dividing the first term by *e* and the second term by *M*, we get:

$$\left[\frac{1}{q}\frac{ee_{qu}}{e_q e_u} * \frac{qe_q}{e}(g_M M_N + 1) - \frac{g_{qM}M}{gq}\frac{g_q M_N}{M}\right] dN \qquad \text{(A6)}$$

Equating (A5) and (A6) and replacing the defined elasticities in both gives equation (4).

References

Abdalla, I. M., Al-Waqfi, M. A., Harb, N., Hijazi, R. H., and Zoubeidi, T. (2010). "Labour policy and determinants of employment and wages in a developing economy with labour shortage," *Labour*, 24: 163–77.

Baldwin-Edwards, M. (2011). "Labour immigration and labour markets in the GCC countries: National patterns and trends." Research paper, Kuwait Programme on Development, Governance and Globalisation in the Gulf States.

Binder, M. and Offermanns, C. J. (2007). "International investment positions and exchange rate dynamics: A dynamic panel analysis." CFS Working Chapter No. 2007/23.

Corden, W. M. (1984). "Booming sector and Dutch disease economics: Survey and consolidation," *Oxford Economic Papers*, 36: 359–80.

Dixit, A. and Norman, V. (1980). *Theory of International Trade*. Cambridge: Cambridge University Press.

Docquier, F., Marfouk, A., Özden, C., and Parsons, C. (2010). "Geographic, gender and skill structure of international migration." Report written for the Economic Research Forum.

Docquier, F., Rapoport, H., Özden, C., and Salomone, S. (2011). "Remittances, migrants' education and immigration policy: Theory and evidence from bilateral data." CReAM Discussion Paper No. 19/11. London: Centre for Research and Analysis of Migration.

Fasano, U. and Goyal, R. (2004). "Emerging strains in GCC labor markets." IMF Working Paper No. 04/71. Washington DC: International Monetary Fund.

Gylfason, T. (2006). "The Dutch disease: Lessons from Norway." Paper prepared for Trinidad and Tobago Chamber of Commerce and Industry.

ILO (2013). "Domestic workers across the world: Global and regional statistics and the extent of legal protection." Geneva: International Labor Organization.

Im, K., Pesaran, M. H., and Shin, Y. (2003). "Testing for unit roots in heterogeneous panels," *Journal of Econometrics*, 115: 53–74.

IOM (2012). "The Middle East and North Africa: Annual report 2011." Geneva: International Organization for Migration.

Kao, C. (1999). "Spurious regression and residual-based tests for cointegration in panel data," *Journal of Econometrics*, 90: 1–44.

Kapiszewski, A. (2006). "Arab vs. Asian migrant workers in the GCC countries." Paper presented at the United Nations Expert Group Meeting on International Migration and Development in the Arab Region, Beirut, May 15–17, 2006.

Lucas, R. E. B. (2008). "International migration and economic development: Lessons from low-income countries." Stockholm: Expert Group on Development Issues, Swedish Ministry for Foreign Affairs.

Montiel, P. J. (1999). "Determinants of the long-run equilibrium exchange rate: An analytical model," in L. E. Hinkle and P. J. Montiel (eds), *Exchange Rate Misalignment: Concepts and Measurement for Developing Countries*. New York: Oxford University Press, 264–90.

Pesaran, M. H. (1997). "The role of economic theory in modelling the long run," *The Economic Journal*, 107: 178–91.

—— (2007). "A simple panel unit root test in the presence of cross-section dependence," *Journal of Applied Econometrics*, 22: 265–312.

Pesaran, M. H. and Shin, Y. (1999). "An autoregressive distributed lag modelling approach to cointegration analysis," in S. Strom (ed.), *Econometrics and Economic Theory in the 20th Century: The Ragnar-Frisch Centennial Symposium*. Cambridge: Cambridge University Press, 371–413.

Pesaran, M. H., Shin, Y., and Smith, R. (1999). "Pooled mean group estimation of dynamic heterogeneous panels," *Journal of the American Statistical Association*, 94: 621–34.

Plant, R. (2008). "Temporary contract labour in the Gulf states: Perspectives from two countries of origin." Paper for the Gulf Forum on Temporary Contractual Labor, International Labor Organization, Geneva.

Ploeg, F. van der and Venables, A. J. (2010). "Absorbing a windfall of foreign exchange: Dutch disease dynamics." OxCarre Working Papers No. 052.

Ruhs, M. (2009). "Migrant rights, immigration policy and human development." UNDP Human Development Reports Research Paper No. 2009/23.

Ruppert, E. (1999). "Managing foreign labor in Singapore and Malaysia: Are there lessons for GCC countries?" World Bank Policy Research Paper No. 2053. Washington: World Bank.

United Nations (2009). "World Population Policies 2009." New York: United Nations Department of Economic and Social Affairs, Population Division.

Wijnbergen, S. van (1984). "Inflation, employment, and the Dutch disease in oil-exporting countries: A short-run disequilibrium analysis," *Quarterly Journal of Economics*, 99: 233–50.

World Bank (2011). "World Bank prospects: Migration and remittances dataset." Available online at <http://econ.worldbank.org>, accessed May 28, 2013.

4

Government Spending, Subsidies, and Economic Efficiency

4.1 Introduction

The activities of the government have a heightened importance in the Gulf countries because oil revenues accrue to the government and the way they are spent or saved affects the whole economy. Parts of the receipts from oil exports are saved in sovereign wealth funds or central bank reserves, and the remainder is spent and therefore channeled to the economy via a large public-sector wage bill, via public infrastructure, subsidies for industries, and subsidies and provision of services for nationals. The diversification process has also required large amounts of government money as structural and development policies remained based on government intervention. Thus, the overall bill for the public sector is high, between 36 percent and 74 of the economy (excluding the oil sector; see Table 5.2 in Chapter 5) and above what is common for either emerging or advanced economies.

The nature of expenditure is also quite different. In the United Kingdom, social protection (pensions, welfare benefits) contributes to one third of total spending, and health care and education spending account each for around 15 percent of spending. In contrast, Saudi Arabia and the UAE are investing massively in education (more than 25 percent of government spending; see Figure 4.1). Spending on economic affairs (mostly support to the business sector, but *excluding implicit subsidies*, which are not measured in fiscal accounts) is also large, especially in Bahrain, Kuwait, and Qatar where it takes more than 20 percent of the budget. Such numbers witness the considerable interest that the Gulf governments have in pushing for private-sector

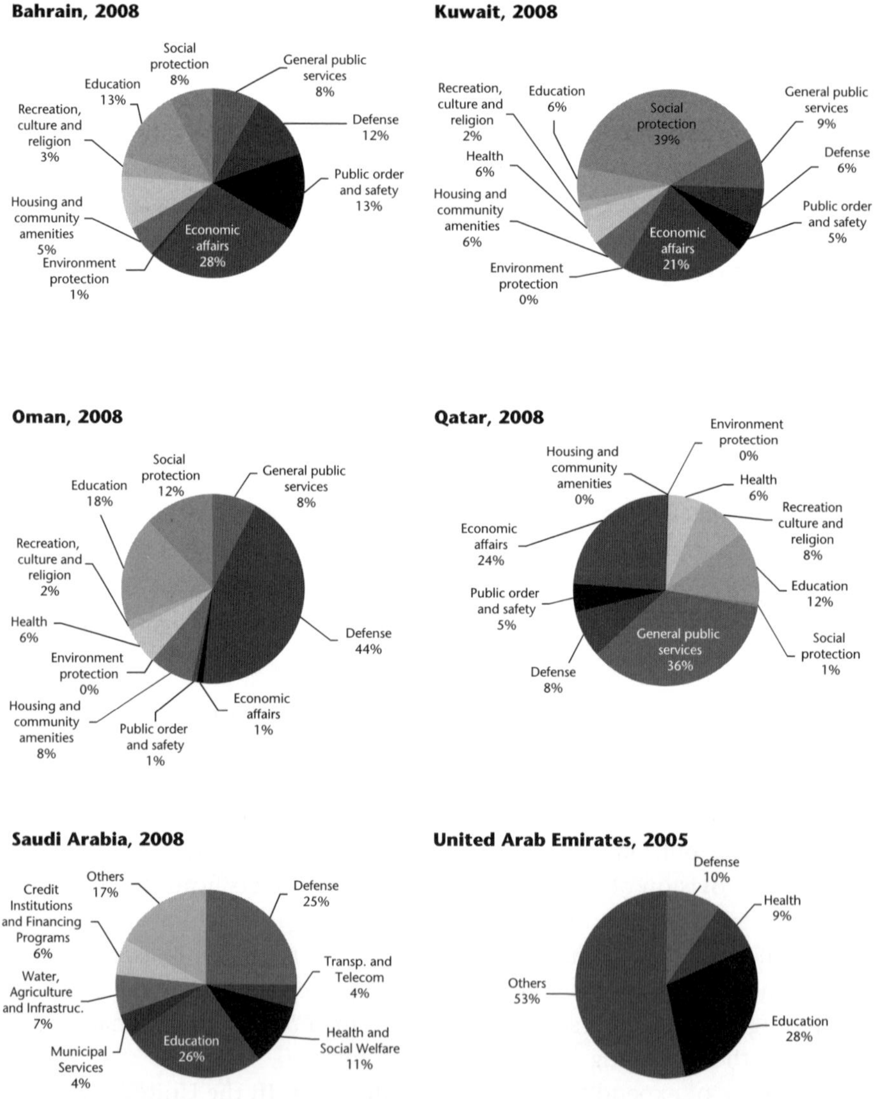

Figure 4.1. Budgetary spending, by outlay

Source: IMF, World Bank, Al Rajhi Bank (for Saudi Arabia)

development and diversification. On the other hand, spending on health and pensions in the Gulf remains under check as the national population—which is the one that benefits from welfare spending—is young. Social safety nets are also underdeveloped in countries where unemployment has historically been low though unemployment benefits have recently been introduced in Oman and Saudi Arabia. In a region where neighbors are affected by wars and political instability, military spending is also higher as a proportion of the budget than in most advanced countries. Oman and Saudi Arabia spend more than 25 percent of their budget on the army.

Government spending serves several objectives in the GCC. The first one is to develop the private sector, diversify the economy away from oil, and create jobs. A large share of spending supports energy-intensive industries, real estate developments, infrastructure, and tourism (the economic affairs outlay in Figure 4.1). A natural question to ask is whether the strategy is efficient in economic terms. We have shown in Chapter 2 that the increase in income per capita was below what could have been expected given the massive accumulation of capital. This result points at possible inefficiencies in the strategy, and the literature has indeed argued that large governments and price distortions created by subsidies reduce growth. We review these arguments in section 4.2 and discuss how they apply to the GCC.

The second purpose of government expenditure is to distribute a large part of oil revenues to the population, in a way that is compatible with the diversification objective. Government spending directly benefits nationals, through high public-service wages, public investment that feeds contractors and subcontractors, and the improved provision of public goods (infrastructure in particular). Section 4.3 describes the problem of a government that wants to distribute oil money as an "inverse" Ramsey (1927) problem of optimal taxation/subsidies. The second-best policy (when lump-sum transfers are not available) is to use subsidies across a wide range of goods (as opposed to the focus on energy chosen by the GCC). Section 4.4 discusses the additional distortions coming from agents' incentives to queue for subsidies as opposed to participating in private markets. A model of the labor market is given as an example where high wages and employment in the public sector reduce private and total employment. Finally, government spending can also be used as a tool to stabilize the economy, as is done in many advanced and emerging countries. This macroeconomic stabilization role will be investigated in Chapter 5.

4.2 Government Spending and the GCC Development Strategy

We discuss in this section the role of public investment and support to businesses in the development strategy of the GCC.

4.2.1 Public Investment

Capital-intensive economies are more productive and achieve higher levels of income, a result that justifies the use of public investment for the aim of diversification. Nevertheless, sound investment decisions should be taken depending on the rates of return for those investments. From a microeconomic perspective, if rates of return for domestic investment are lower than the rates of return that can be achieved by investing in foreign assets, investing domestically is inefficient.

Macroeconomists take a wider approach by looking at the long-term effects of investment on growth, and the growth-accounting exercise performed in Chapter 2 would suggest that investment has indeed contributed to worker productivity growth in Oman, Qatar, and Saudi Arabia. However, the second message coming from the growth-accounting exercise is that efficiency has been lower in the GCC than in other fast-growing emerging markets. Interpreting Pritchett (2000), it could be that the decline in TFP reflects in fact the low quality of investment undertaken in the GCC. Massive investment spending would not have been translated into useful capital because with oil revenues flowing, investment decisions might not have been made carefully. Pritchett (2000) argues that the accumulation of capital we used in Chapter 2 should in fact be modeled as:

$$K_t(\gamma) = (1-\delta)K_{t-1}(\gamma) + \gamma I_t$$

where $\gamma < 1$ is the efficacy of investment, i.e., the rate at which investment spending (which is what is measured in I_t from the national accounts) is transformed into a productive unit of capital (what K_t is supposed to capture). A situation where $\gamma < 1$ would indicate that the investment did not contribute to productive capital because the process of investment (investment decision, implementation, etc.) was inefficient.

A simple investigation of the data tends to confirm Pritchett's hypothesis that public investment can be inefficient. First, oil-rich countries invest more the bigger the size of their oil sector (Figure 4.2).[1] This suggests that the availability of resources, as opposed to the expected rates of return, is the major factor behind investment decisions. Governments spend a lot on public investment because they can, and not necessarily because those investments are needed. In the GCC, 30 to 50 percent of investment can be attributed directly to the government and this share is probably higher when taking into account subcontracting and the indirect role of the government. Second, countries that have developed sound institutions for the selection, implementation, and evaluation of public-sector projects (as measured by the PIMI index of Dabla-Norris et al. 2012) have benefitted from higher incomes given the factors of production available (higher TFP; see Figure 4.3). Although the

[1] The share of investment going to the energy sector is around 10 percent in Saudi Arabia. Although the numbers are higher in the rest of the GCC, especially in Qatar, the correlation shown in Figure 4.2 is not due to reverse causality.

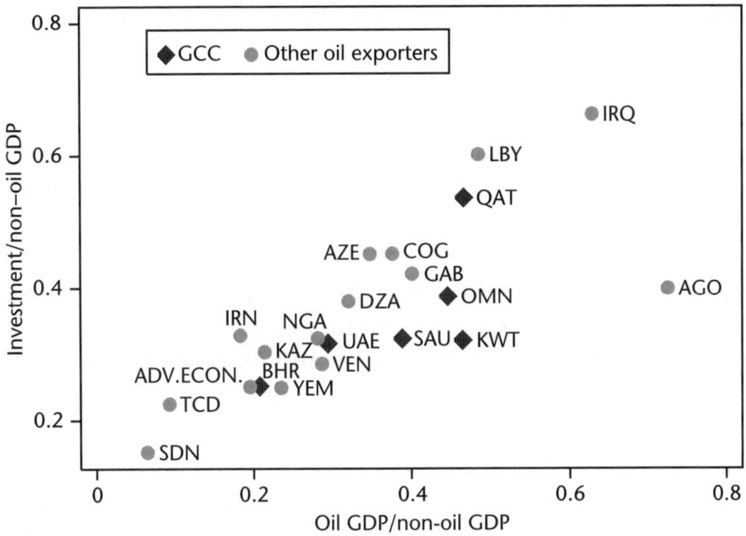

Figure 4.2. Investment/non-oil GDP and oil GDP/non-oil GDP (1980–2009)

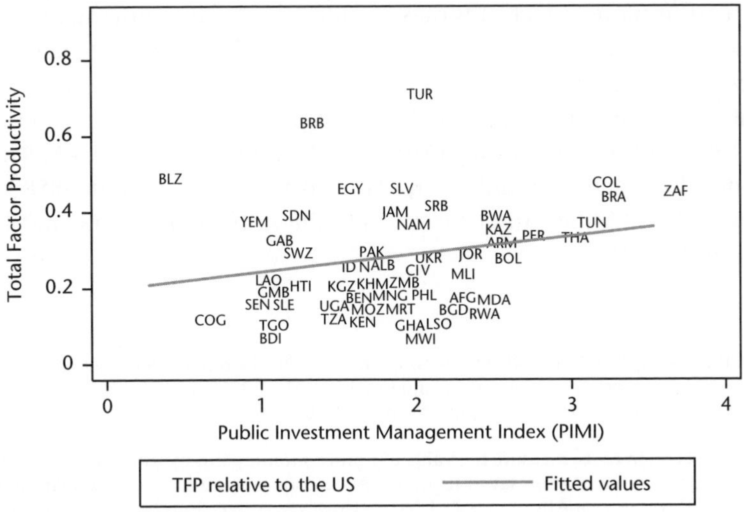

Figure 4.3. Total Factor Productivity and the Public Investment Management Index

Source: Dabla-Norris et al. (2012) and authors' calculations

PIMI index is not available for the GCC, the evidence is that oil exporters[2] have institutions of a lower quality than other emerging markets. Of course, a similar story can be built with other data on institutions, e.g., the World Bank's Country Policy and Institutional Assessment (CPIA). Therefore, the particular link between public investment, PIMI, and growth may be difficult to differentiate from what was found with other indexes of institutions (see also Chapter 2).

In addition, even the medium-term macroeconomic returns from investment can be poor proxies for the benefits of public investment. In many situations, the benefits of public investment are non-monetary and cannot be converted into dollar equivalents.[3] The benefits of some investments are also highly uncertain and far remote in the future, which raises the additional question of the correct coefficient of risk aversion and the appropriate discount rate. For instance, to take an extreme case, how would one price the value of organizing a World Cup for a small country in search of international prestige? In short, it seems difficult to judge, in simple economic terms, of the efficiency of investment strategies that have been as transformative as those in the GCC.

4.2.2 Support to the Corporate Sector and Subsidies

In addition to the development of infrastructure, the diversification strategy in the GCC has been built on a multiform support to the private sector. This is witnessed by the outlay "Economic Affairs" in Figure 4.1 that represents more than 20 percent of government spending in Bahrain, Kuwait, and Qatar. Furthermore, direct subsidies or indirect subsidies (pricing under market rates) are large and amount 10 to 30 percent of government expenditure, with energy and utility subsidies the largest items (see Table 4.1). According to the International Energy Agency (IEA), the subsidization rate for fuel would exceed 65 percent for Kuwait, Qatar, Saudi Arabia, and the UAE. The IEA estimates that energy subsidies implicitly cost the government US$8 billion in Kuwait, US$4 billion in Qatar, US$44 billion in Saudi Arabia, and US$18 billion in the UAE.

[2] The PIMI average is 1.16 for oil exporters, against 1.76 for the other emerging markets, and the difference is significant at the 1 percent confidence level. The PIMI is available for the following oil exporters: Azerbaijan, Chad, the Republic of Congo, Gabon, Kazakhstan, Nigeria, Sudan, Trinidad and Tobago, and Yemen.

[3] Economists often try to measure the value of non-economic gains by using conversion factors. For instance, the value of time saved in transports can be converted into its dollar equivalent using hourly wages (e.g. one hour saved = US$10). However, conversions become increasingly difficult—and unconvincing—when what is being converted is not priced in markets. For instance, the value of a life saved thanks to secure transportation is sometimes converted into a dollar equivalent using the value of life insurance or the outcome of court decisions, but these conversions are uncertain and often perceived as unacceptable.

Table 4.1. Subsidies and opportunity costs/implicit subsidies, 2010

Subsidies in 2010, in US$ million	Bahrain	Kuwait	Oman	Qatar	Saudi Arabia	UAE
Energy[a]	–	7,620[a]	1,334	4,150[a]	43,520[a]	18,150[a]
Electricity and water	543	8,260[e]	503[c]	495[e]	–	3,370[d,e]
Food	114	481	–	82[b]	1,100	111[d]
Memorandum items						
GDP, in US$ million	22,656	132,569	57,851	127,332	448,360	302,039
Government expenditure, in US$ million	4,789	50,474	19,583	26,958	136,030	64,549

[a] Includes implicit oil, gas, and electricity subsidies (source: IEA)
[b] Includes transfers
[c] All utilities subsidies excluding fuel for power generation
[d] Abu Dhabi only; 2011 statistics
[e] May overlap with energy subsidies
Source: IEA and individual government statistics

The bulk of these subsidies is however not accounted for in central government financial statistics because many subsidies are only "opportunity costs" of publicly owned companies that are selling domestically at prices below international prices (but above production costs). For the same reason, the statistics cannot distinguish between subsidies to corporates and subsidies to households.

Subsidies are a tool for industrial policy and contribute to a broader plan to support businesses with a view to diversifying the economy and creating jobs. Has this strategy been successful and what should the policy be, looking forward?

In the GCC, diversification means developing a non-oil sector in the economy, and as shown in Chapter 3 the largest share of non-oil exports is petrochemicals, an industry heavily reliant on energy subsidies. Therefore, if diversification is believed to be only meaningful when it creates activities that are viable in the absence of oil revenues and government support, then it can be construed that the GCC have not fared well in their long-term diversification plans. But such an extreme view would only be justified if the exhaustion of oil and gas reserves was an impending prospect, ruling out the possibility of any adjustment (Luciani 2007). This is indeed not the case for most GCC countries, especially Kuwait, Saudi Arabia, and Qatar where proven reserves are around or exceed 100 years at current extraction rates.

Two questions are therefore worth considering. First, are subsidized industries providing positive productivity and technology spillovers to the rest of the non-oil sector in the economy? Second, are subsidized industries imposing high opportunity costs; in other words, how costly and distortionary are these subsidies?

Answering the first question is a task that goes beyond the scope of this book and relates to the broader question of the success of industrial policies. Nonetheless, it seems reasonable to expect both direct and indirect positive spillovers from the petrochemical industry on the rest of the non-oil economy. For instance, in Saudi Arabia, since the petrochemical sector opened up to private companies in 1995, investments have been made, both jointly with SABIC (Saudi's largest petrochemical company, 70 percent of which is owned by the government) and independently of it. The downstream sectors also attract FDI, a potential source of transfers of technology. Finally, petrochemical manufacturing requires constant innovation, and direct spillovers from such industries to other sectors of the economy could be of importance in the diversification process.

Since at existing levels of subsidies petrochemical companies are viable in the region, a long-term policy of gradually increasing feedstock prices without eliminating their competitive advantage could help ensure their long-term viability when resources are near depletion. This strategy is currently followed in the case of Industries Qatar, for example. Nonetheless, the high-technology content and capital intensity of petrochemical industries makes them inadequate as engines of job creation in the larger countries of Oman and Saudi Arabia.

Looking at the drawbacks of the strategy, direct financial costs may not be very high. Feedstock is sold at prices below international prices to petrochemical and aluminum producers, but is often sold above the average cost of production (although not always above marginal cost). In Qatar, condensates, a by-product of gas production that exhibits near-zero production costs, are a feedstock to Industries Qatar. In Saudi Arabia part of the gas used as feedstock in petrochemical industries is associated gas, derived as a by-product of crude oil.

However, there are implicit financial costs: in particular the opportunity cost of not exporting the feedstock and selling it at international prices. When downstream producers are government-controlled, the price at which the oil company sells to the downstream company does not matter because the eventual owner (the state) cashes in the profits (in the form of exports of petrochemicals, for instance) and internalizes the opportunity cost of selling below international prices and overutilizing the feedstock. Hence, these subsidies would be innocuous in terms of the efficient use of fuel. However, when subsidies accrue to the private sector, the opportunity costs of subsidies are not internalized.

In these cases, subsidies encourage wasteful consumption, lead to excessive carbon emissions, attract smugglers, reduce incentives to increase extraction, reduce incentives to build efficient plants, and create barriers to investment in alternative energies. For instance, Fattouh and El-Katiri (2012) show that energy efficiency in power generation is below the world average (40 percent) in Qatar, Kuwait, Saudi Arabia, and the UAE, despite these countries' capacity to use advanced technologies. In particular, the UAE and Saudi Arabia are among the least energy-efficient countries in the world for power generation. In Saudi Arabia, the growing demand for gas led to the 2000 Gas Initiative to speed up exploration of its gas fields. But despite proven gas reserves estimated at 8 trillion cubic meters, over 4 percent of the global gas reserves, Saudi Arabia is not exporting its natural gas.

4.3 An Inverse Ramsey Model

Subsidies are sometimes justified because they can protect the poor. There is ample evidence, however, that generalized, untargeted subsidies are an inappropriate tool to support lower-income households. This is because larger subsidies are received by the ones who consume most, who are also the households with highest income. For instance, Arze del Granado et al. (2010) reviewed the evidence for twenty developing countries and found that on average, gasoline subsidies accrue for 61 percent to households in the highest consumption quintile, whereas households in the lowest quintile (the 20 percent poorest households) received only 3 percent of the subsidies (including free education, subsidized healthcare, etc.). The distribution of subsidies is less skewed for other products but this pattern of regressive subsidies is common for energy and utilities.

Subsidies can also be a simple way for the government to redistribute the natural wealth of the country (oil revenues) to its nationals, independent of their income level. While lump sum transfers to households would be the first-best solution from an economic efficiency point of view, and would also allow the government to target subsidies to nationals, there may be several reasons why governments prefer to give subsidies (including in the form of free health care and education). First, governments may think that markets do not always lead to efficient outcomes; for instance, they may believe that their citizens would underinvest in their education if they had to pay its full cost. Second, subsidies act as conditional transfers and allow governments to determine acceptable conditions for citizens to receive government money (one needs to work to receive wage subsidies, to study to receive education allowances, etc.).

Third, several authors have suggested that retaining direct control of how oil money is spent allows the political establishment to evade transparency and accountability (Morrison 2009; Birdsall and Subramanian 2004). In the words of Sala-i-Martin and Subramanian (2003): "oil accounts for a substantial share of total government revenues. As such, the government has little incentive to provide services efficiently because the discipline exerted by the need to tax the public is largely absent: oil revenues are manna from heaven and keep flowing regardless of what the public sector delivers." Finally, direct redistribution policies would open national debates on the fair distribution of resources and reduce the power of government. Only advanced regions (Alaska, Alberta) have been able to apply such policies (Auty and Gelb 2001).

Governments use therefore indirect methods, which include hiring for the public sector at relatively high wages (see Chapter 3), subsidizing salaries for nationals in the private sector (in particular for youth), subsidizing consumption of goods (free electricity, subsidized health care and mortgages), and providing education to nationals. Richer countries tend to provide larger subsidies. Figure 4.4 shows for instance the subsidization rate on fuel as a function of the size of the oil sector in the economy.

Subsidies, the development of public infrastructure, and the provision of public-sector jobs are different ways for the government to redistribute its oil revenues. The problem of the government is therefore similar (but in reverse) to the Ramsey (1927) problem of optimal taxation commonly studied in public economics, where a government that needs to tax the private sector searches for the optimal way to allocate the distortions due to taxes across markets (see, for instance, Cullis and Jones 1992). Three channels of spending seem most relevant: public-sector employment, the provision of public capital, and subsidies. This section presents the general (inverse) Ramsey problem of an oil-rich government.

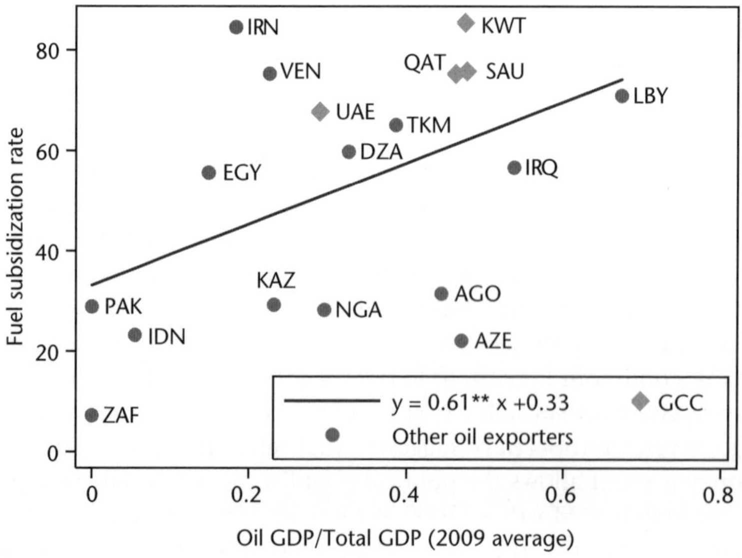

Figure 4.4. Subsidies and size of the oil sector

Source: International Energy Agency and authors' calculations

Assume that production is a linear function of labor used in the private sector L_p,

$$Y = AL_p \tag{1}$$

and that the stock of public capital G affects productivity: $A = A_0(1+G)$. Wages in the private sector w_p are set competitively by firms taking as given the level of productivity A: max $\pi = Y - w_p L_p$ implies $w_p = A = A_0(1+G) = w(1+s_w)$ where $w = A_0$ is the wage that would prevail absent of any public investment. In this very simplified model, public investment G is equivalent to a multiplicative subsidy on private-sector wages ($G = s_w$).

Households are endowed with time (divided between work and leisure), equal to D, and can consume tradables T (with a price equal to 1), non-tradables NT (with a price p_{NT}), and enjoy leisure $0 < x < D$, with a utility function: $u(c_T, c_{NT}, x)$.

The government can subsidize labor (by increasing the stock of public capital, which has the same effects as subsidizing wages in this model) and can provide subsidies on non-tradable consumption goods. We assume tradable goods cannot be subsidized because otherwise the international demand for these goods would generate large losses to the government—with little benefits for the nationals.[4]

The household problem is to maximize utility given a budget constraint[5]

$$\begin{aligned} &\max u(c_T, c_{NT}, x), \text{ subject to} \\ &c_T + p_{NT}(1 - s_{NT})c_{NT} = w(1+s_w)(D-x) \end{aligned} \tag{2}$$

An interior solution is such that the ratios of marginal utilities equal relative prices (net of subsidies):

$$(\partial u / \partial c_{NT}) / (\partial u / \partial c_T) = p_{NT}(1 - s_{NT}) \tag{3}$$

$$(\partial u / \partial x) / (\partial u / \partial c_T) = w(1 + s_w) \tag{4}$$

The problem of a benevolent government is to maximize utility of the representative household, taking into account the optimal behavior of the workers (equations 3 and 4) and using the oil resources to subsidize labor and the

[4] Note that the Ramsey problem requires that one good cannot be taxed: if all goods are taxable or can be subsidized, the problem is trivial as the optimal policy is to tax/subsidize all goods with the same rate, ensuring that relative prices are not distorted. The literature has usually assumed that leisure is not taxable, but this assumption is innocuous for the general results given by the model.

[5] The symmetry with the original Ramsey problem (see, for example, Auerbach 1985) is clear when rewriting the constraint as $c_T/(1+s_w) + p(1-s_{NT})/(1+s_w)\, c_{NT} + w\, x = w\, D$. The choice of subsidies s_w, s_{NT} is equivalent to a choice of relative prices for c_T and c_{NT}.

consumption of non-tradables. The amount of the subsidies is limited by the budget constraint of the government, which is such that the total cost of subsidies equals oil rents X (net of any extraction costs):

$$ws_w(D-x)+p_{NT}s_{NT}c_{NT}=X \tag{5}$$

The problem of the government is identical to the one solved by Ramsey (1927), except that X, s_w, and s_{NT} are positive (the original Ramsey problem is for a government taxing households to finance a given government expenditure).

The objective of the government can be shown to be equivalent to reducing the overall deadweight losses due to government intervention. As can be seen from Figure 4.5, subsidies generate welfare losses that are larger for commodities the demand for which is most sensitive to prices. The left panel of Figure 4.5 shows the demand curve (quantities of the commodity demanded are shown on the horizontal axis, for a price p on the vertical axis) for a relatively inelastic commodity. A subsidy s reducing prices from p_1 to $p_1 - s$ increases consumer welfare by the light grey trapezoid AECD, whereas the cost to the government is the rectangle ABCD. The loss for the economy is W_1, the area of the dark grey triangle EBC. This social loss is the symmetric loss to that due to taxes, first described by Dupuit (1844) and popularized by Harberger (1964). When demand is more elastic (right panel of Figure 4.5), the welfare loss is greater because the subsidy-induced distortion is larger when subsidies have a bigger impact on demand. This is why $W_2 > W_1$.

Auerbach (1985) provides a modern treatment, and the analytical solution of the Ramsey problem shows that when demand[6] for the different "commodities" (non-tradables, tradables, and leisure) is insensitive to the prices of other commodities (i.e., commodities are neither substitute nor complement), the solution for the government is to tax (in our case, subsidize) commodities that are least elastic to prices. This solution ensures that the marginal deadweight loss, per additional unit of dollars distributed to nationals, is equalized across commodities and therefore that it is not possible to reduce overall deadweight loss by increasing subsidies in one commodity and reducing subsidies in another one.

The model therefore provides predictions on the scale of public investment and the pervasiveness of subsidies and distortions in an oil-rich economy. It is indeed optimal to subsidize all commodities that can be subsidized, as opposed to focusing subsidies on a narrow range of goods. In addition, the

[6] Demand could refer either to Hicksian or to Marshallian demand (see Auerbach 1985: 93).

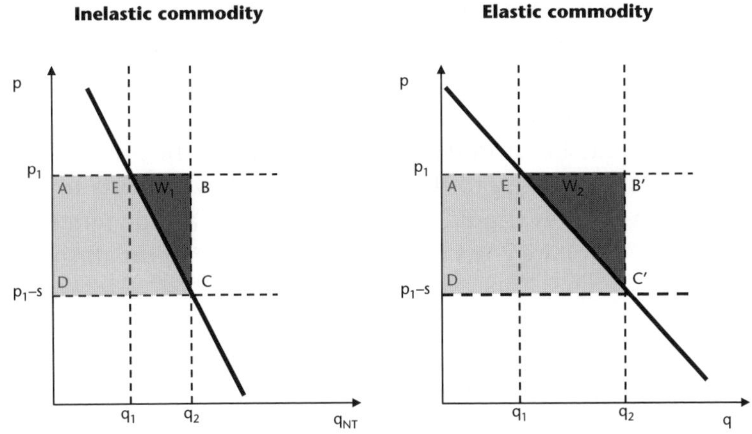

Figure 4.5. Subsidies and welfare losses

model implies that commodities for which demand is least elastic to prices should be subsidized at higher rates. This implies it would be more efficient to subsidize basic needs at higher rates, in particular food, health care, and education.[7] The Ramsey solution that reduces allocative inefficiency is therefore compatible with the equity objective of subsidizing basic needs. In addition, there are long-term growth benefits that come from increasing skills, which are not taken into account in this chapter (Chapter 2 showed that the contribution of human capital to long-term growth in the GCC has been positive in the last twenty years, although there is scope for improvements in educational attainment).

The model does not support the GCC region's heavy spending on energy subsidies. There are no justifications for concentrating subsidies on a narrow range of products and energy subsidies are also very distortive: according to the Ramsey model, they are therefore not an efficient way to distribute oil wealth. Demand for energy is typically very sensitive to prices, with elasticities around –0.7 (see for instance Iimi 2010). Al-Faris (2002) also found that the price elasticity of electricity demand is between –1.1 and –3.4 in the GCC countries.[8] On top of this allocative efficiency argument,

[7] Bread, cereals, oil and fat, fruit and vegetables have been found to have low price elasticity in the GCC, between –0.2 and –0.35; see Seale et al. (2003). Ringel et al.'s (2005) review of the literature for the US suggests a price elasticity of –0.17 for health care services. Shires (1995) found demand elasticities in college education to be relatively low, between –0.05 and –0.2; see also Heller (1997) for a survey.

[8] On the other hand, Narayan and Smyth (2007) found that demand for oil is inelastic to prices in the region. It is however difficult to estimate price elasticities of demand in the GCC because prices are often controlled and not very volatile, which makes estimates less robust.

one should also remember that energy subsidies benefit disproportionally richer households. There are also negative environmental externalities to the use of fuels, which have in fact prompted many countries to increase taxation on these products.

Finally, the model has normative implications for the optimal phasing-out of subsidies. According to the Ramsey model, when cuts to subsidies are envisaged, subsidies should be decreased across a wide range of products, because the welfare costs of inefficiencies depend on all the relative prices.

4.4 Distortions in Labor Markets

In the previous section, we described market subsidies that affect continuously the final price of goods, in the tradition of the public finance literature. Government spending can however generate other distortions, especially in dynamic settings. For years, in Egypt, college graduates were entitled to public-service jobs. Because the number of graduates exceeded the needs of the government, college graduates had to queue for public-service jobs and discontent grew (Richards and Waterbury 2007). In Saudi Arabia, since the 1970s, the Real Estate Development Fund (REDF) has been extending interest-free loans to Saudi citizens who own land plots, with a maturity of twenty-five years. By 2010, the REDF had a total of 77.6 billion Saudi Riyals of loans outstanding. In recent years, new credit was limited by the size of the REDF's balance sheet (and by the repayment of loans reaching maturity) and amounted to only SR 2 billion annually, around one fourth of the volume of new applications, resulting in an applicant waitlist that could exceed ten years (IMF 2006). The scheme has affected the demand for loans issued by private banks, and as a result of capacity constraints, the REDF's business model has recently shifted to guaranteeing loans of commercial banks and covering any interest rate payments.

In most of the GCC, highly paid public-sector positions are also used as another channel to redistribute oil revenues. These positions are preferred, especially by women, over private-sector jobs, but the government is of course unable to hire all the candidates in the more populated states.[9] Wage disparities between public- and private-sector jobs are striking in the GCC. Combining data on private-sector monthly wages from Saudi Arabia's Ministry of Labor with data on monthly public-sector wages from the

[9] For instance, in Saudi Arabia, the saturation of public-sector jobs, coupled with increasing labor forces, has made job creation for nationals in the private sector a policy priority (see Chapter 3).

Ministry of Civil Services suggests that for Saudis with secondary or lower education, the lowest-paying public-sector job pays about 30 percent more than a private-sector job (see also Chapter 3). Nevertheless, differences in job security and work hours notwithstanding, for high-skill employees, the public sector is not necessarily more lucrative than the private sector. A recent graduate with a bachelor's degree would typically earn about 6,500 Saudi Riyals a month, less than the 7,700 Saudi Riyals average wage for similarly educated Saudis in the private sector.

Other government subsidies include unemployment benefit schemes which have been recently introduced in both Oman and Saudi Arabia. In Oman, more than 60,000 private-sector employees were reported to have quit their private-sector jobs after the announcement, based on royal orders, of a monthly unemployment allowance of 150 Omani Riyals ($390) and plans to increase hiring in the public sector. Statistics also show that more than 70,000 citizens of the total number of 200,000 registered were over 25 and most of them were women. Similarly in Saudi Arabia, the Hafiz program of unemployment benefits was initiated in 2011. The program pays unemployed Saudis 2,000 Riyals ($533) a month for up to one year, which is lower than the minimum public-sector wage and also lower than any private-sector wage except that for illiterate Saudis. The number of beneficiaries has nonetheless exceeded one million, of which 82 percent were females, with the initial number of applicants exceeding 1.7 million.[10] The high percentage of female recipients in both countries reflects low labor force participation rates among females: in Saudi Arabia, the labor force participation rate for Saudi females has been about 12 percent on average over the last few years.

This section proposes a simple model of the labor market with public and private employment. The model captures the intuition that recruitment of public servants can induce a large disincentive to take private-sector positions. This intuition is in line with empirical evidence. For instance, Behar and Mok (2012) estimate, using panel data on 194 countries, that public employment fully "crowds out" private-sector employment, with the implication that the net effect of public employment on the unemployment rate is null. Using our simple model, we compute the conditions under which this empirical finding holds, i.e., the conditions under which the disincentive to take a private-sector job is so strong that overall employment is unaffected, or even decreased, as public servants are being hired. Our model has a similar take to Gelb et al. (1991). Gelb et al. (1991) simulate a two-sector Harris-Todaro model where an increase in wages in cities (for instance, due

[10] Based on the Al Riyadh newspaper citing an announcement by the executive director of the Hafiz program.

to an oil windfall) attracts workers from the rural sector. Unemployment increases in cities and the government's attempt to decrease unemployment by promoting urban jobs (financed by taxation) is self-defeating because it increases further the incentive to leave farming to find employment in cities.

Our model assumes there are three types of nationals: workers in the private sector L_p, workers in the public sector L_g, and, given an exogenous labor force L, unemployed workers are $L_u = L-L_p-L_g$ (the number of workers L_p, L_g, and therefore L_u will be determined in equilibrium).

Nationals can look for jobs in the private sector and get a salary w_p, but they can also apply or queue for government jobs, which pay higher salaries ($w_g>w_p$). We assume that if a national applies for a government job and is unsuccessful, he or she remains unemployed and earns a lower income w_u, representing the value of leisure and of social benefits provided by the government. Therefore we assume $w_u<w_p<w_g$. Without loss of generality, we normalize w_u to 0.

The probability of being unemployed after applying for a government job is (this probability will be solved in equilibrium):

$$v = \left(L - L_p - L_g\right)/\left(L - L_p\right);\ 0 < v < 1$$

The probability of succeeding in capturing a government job is:

$$1 - v = L_g / \left(L - L_p\right)$$

The equilibrium condition in the labor market for nationals is similar to a no-arbitrage condition:[11] the expected wage of queuing for a government job must equal the income guaranteed in the private sector. The income earned with a job in the private sector is equal to the income paid by the firm (w_p) plus the subsidies provided by the government ($s\ w_p$), which implies that the equilibrium condition in the labor market is

$$(1+s)w_p = v\ w_u + (1-v)w_g = (1-v)w_g \tag{6}$$

since we set earlier $w_u = 0$.

Let us assume that wages in the private sector are a decreasing function of L_p (we discuss below the case where private-sector wages are determined by

[11] We have assumed implicitly that the job seeker is risk-neutral. His or her utility is simply linear in income.

migrants' reservation wages). With a production function using labor L_p and a stock of capital K:

$$Y = L_p^{\theta} K^{1-\theta}; \quad 0 < \theta < 1$$

Wages are set competitively to: $w_p = \theta L_p^{\theta-1} K^{1-\theta}$. This yields:

$$\partial w_p / \partial L_p \;=\; (\theta - 1) w_p / L_p < 0. \tag{7}$$

Equation 6 and Figure 4.6 provide the key insights into the impact of government decisions on the labor market. Figure 4.6 shows the equilibrium in the labor market, i.e., the solution of the following equation obtained by replacing w_p using equation (6):

$$(1+s) w_{Lp} = \; (1-v) w_g => (1+s)\theta L_p^{\theta-1} K^{1-\theta} = L_g w_g / \left(L - L_p\right)$$

The comparative statics in the labor market are intuitive: if the government increases the labor subsidy from s_0 to $s_1 > s_0$, the returns to working in the private sector increase and employment in the private sector increases (see dashed line on left-hand-side panel). This will reduce unemployment *ceteris paribus*. If the government increases its payroll ($w_g L_g$), it increases the expected payoffs of queuing for a government job and reduces the incentive to accept a private-sector job. This effect implies that an increase in government employment L_g can reduce private-sector employment (see dashed line on right-hand-side panel).

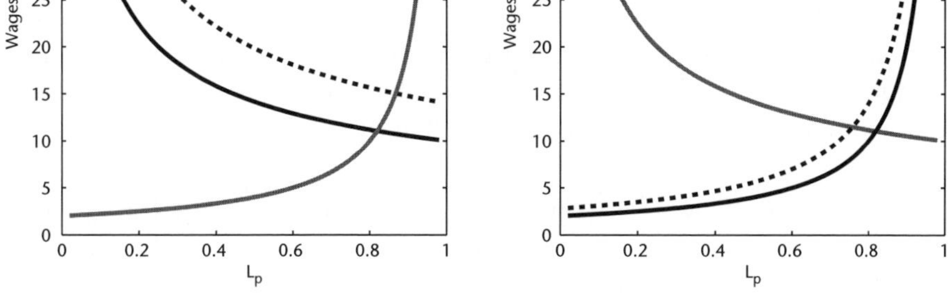

Figure 4.6. Equilibrium in the labor market

What is the effect of government employment on overall unemployment? We need to differentiate the equilibrium condition $(1+s)\, w_p\, (L-L_p) = L_g\, w_g$ and investigate whether $dL_p/dL_g < -1$ (i.e., whether one additional government job reduces private-sector employment by more than one job because of the incentive to queue).

Differentiating the equilibrium condition yields:

$$(1+s)\left(\partial w_p/\partial L_p\left(L - L_p\right) - w_p\right)dL_p = w_g dL_g$$

Therefore

$$dL_p/dL_g = w_g/\left[(1+s)(\partial w_p/\partial L_p\ (L - L_p) - w_p)\right] \tag{8}$$

Note that $dL_p / dL_g < 0$ because $\partial w_p / \partial L_p < 0$. In addition, from equation (7):

$$\partial w_p/\partial L_p\ (L - L_p) - w_p = w_p\left((\theta-1)\left(L - L_p\right)/L_p - 1\right)$$

Therefore $dL_p/dL_g < -1$ if and only if

$$w_g > (1+s)w_p\left((1-\theta)\ \left(L - L_p\right)/L_p + 1\right) \tag{9}$$

It is therefore possible that with high levels of public wages, increases in government hiring decreases overall employment. For instance, if only 50 percent of nationals are working in the private sector and if $\theta = 0.5$, then $(1+s)\, w_p\, ((1-\theta)\,(L-L_p)/L_p + 1) = 1.5\,(1+s)\, w_p$. Government hiring would increase unemployment if government salaries are 50 percent higher than private-sector salaries, net of wage subsidies. This calibration is roughly in line with evidence in the GCC, although the share of public employment is lower in Saudi Arabia (see, e.g., Behar and Mok 2012).

The model has assumed until now that wages in the private sector respond to changes in the (domestic) labor supply. To a large extent, however, private-sector wages are determined by the reservation wages of expatriate workers. The main result of the model is unchanged under the assumption that private-sector wages are exogenous (in which case the labor demand curves are horizontal in Figure 4.6). In particular, an increase in public employment reduces private-sector employment; and setting $\partial w_p/\partial L_p = 0$ in equation (8), one finds that

$$dL_p/dL_g = -w_g/\left[(1+s)w_p)\right] < -1 \text{ if and only if } w_g > (1+s)w_p \tag{10}$$

The condition in equation (10) implies that overall employment falls when public employment increases, as long as public-sector wages are higher than private-sector wages. This condition is met more easily than the condition in equation (9), because private-sector wages do not go up as workers are moved into public-service jobs, and therefore the gap between public wages and private wages is wider when private wages are determined by the reservation wages of foreign workers. Note also, from equation (9) that "crowding-out" of private employment by public hiring is stronger the higher public-service wages and the lower private-sector wage subsidies.

4.5 Conclusion

Government spending is high in the GCC and even ratios of spending to GDP underestimate the pervasive role of government in the economy. Oil revenues accrue to the government and the way the oil money is spent has decisive impacts on the non-oil sector. Capital accumulation by the public sector has been strong and contributed to the high levels of income per capita, as discussed in Chapter 1. However, it is difficult to sustain the quality of investment when volumes are so high, and the evidence suggests that the institutions that matter for public investment decisions are weaker in oil-exporting countries.

Large government subsidies also alter markets. Subsidies affect the demand for education, the labor supply in the private sector, the demand for mortgage financing, the consumption of energy, etc., and in a "first best" view of the world, these subsidies are inefficient. Some inefficiency should however be expected for rich countries that distribute oil revenues to their population, since this situation mirrors that of a government that collects distortionary taxes to finance public goods. The relevant question, which is well-studied in the public finance literature, is how to distribute oil windfalls (with "negative" taxes) in the least distortive fashion. The Ramsey theory is applicable here and the answer is that subsidies should be distributed across a wide range of goods (and services), with higher rates of subsidies for goods whose demand is least price-elastic: in practice, basic needs such as food, education, and health care. In addition, the Ramsey theory suggests that when subsidy policies are under review (because of the government has less money available or wants to save more), changes to subsidies should be across the board, so that relative prices are not affected.

Some subsidies however create perverse mechanisms in dynamic contexts. In particular, mortgage subsidies and high wages in the public sector have created "queues": the benefits of landing a public-sector job (or getting a subsidized mortgages) may be so high that some would rather wait and stay unemployed (or rent an apartment) in the hope of obtaining the coveted benefit later in time rather than going for an alternative (private-sector job;

commercial bank mortgage). These distortions are highly inefficient and may be worsened by further government intervention: for instance, a wave of hiring in the public sector may decrease labor supply to the private sector (or increase unemployment) since job seekers understand that the probability of landing a government job has increased. Therefore, the distributive policies in the GCC should be evaluated carefully, taking into account both theory and experience with specific government programs, so that these kinds of egregious distortion be removed.

References

Al-Faris, A. R. F. (2002). "The demand for electricity in the GCC countries," *Energy Policy*, 30: 117–24.

Arze del Granado, J., Coady, D., and Gillingham, R. (2010). "The unequal benefits of fuel subsidies: A review of evidence for developing countries." IMF Working Paper No. 10/202. Washington DC: International Monetary Fund.

Auerbach, A. (1985). "The theory of excess burden and optimal taxation," in A. Auerbach and M. Feldstein (eds), *Handbook of Public Economics, vol. I.* Amsterdam: Elsevier Science Publishers (North-Holland), 61–127.

Auty, R. M. and Gelb, A. H. (2001). "Political economy of resource-abundant states," in R. Auty (ed.), *Resource Abundance and Economic Development.* Oxford: Oxford University Press, 126–44.

Behar, A. and Mok, J. (2012). "Does public sector employment fully crowd out private sector employment?" Forthcoming IMF Working Paper. Washington DC: International Monetary Fund.

Birdsall, N. and Subramanian, A. (2004). "Saving Iraq from its oil," *Foreign Affairs*, 83 (July/August): 77–89.

Cullis, J. and Jones, P. (1992). *Public Finance and Public Choice: Analytical Perspectives.* London and New York: McGraw-Hill, ch. 16.

Dabla-Norris, E., Brumby, J., Kyobe, A., Mills, Z., and Papageorgiou, C. (2012). "Investing in public investment: An index of public investment efficiency," *Journal of Economic Growth*, 17 (3): 235–66.

Dupuit, J. (1844). "De la mesure de l'uti1ité des travaux publics," *Annales des Ponts et Chaussées*. Translated and reprinted in K. Arrow and T. Scitovsky (eds), *AEA Readings in Welfare Economics*, 8 (1969): 255–83.

Fattouh, B. and El-Katiri, L. (2012). "Energy subsidies in the Arab world," *Arab Human Development Report*, Research Paper Series, UNDP.

Gelb, A. H., Knight, J., and Sabot, R. (1991). "Public sector employment, rent seeking and economic growth," *The Economic Journal*, 101: 1186–99.

Harberger, A. (1964). "Taxation, resource allocation and welfare," in *The Role of Direct and Indirect Taxes in the Federal Reserve System*. Princeton: Princeton University Press for the NBER and Brookings Institution, 25–75.

Heller, D. E. (1997). "Student price response in higher education: An update to Leslie and Brinkman," *Journal of Higher Education*, 68: 624–59.

Iimi, A. (2010). "Price elasticity of nonresidential demand for energy in South Eastern Europe." Policy Research Working Paper 5167, World Bank.

International Energy Agency (2010). "World Energy Outlook." Online database available at <http://www.iea.org/subsidy/index.html>, accessed May 31, 2013.

International Monetary Fund (IMF) (2006). "Saudi Arabia financial system stability assessment." IMF Country Report No. 06/199. Washington DC: International Monetary Fund.

Luciani, G. (2007). "The GCC refining and petrochemical sectors in global perspective," in E. Woertz (ed.), *Gulf Geo-Economics*. Dubai: Gulf Research Center.

Morrison, K. (2009). "Oil, non-tax revenue, and the redistributional foundations of regime stability," *International Organization*, 63: 107–38.

Narayana, P. K. and Smyth, R. (2007). "A panel cointegration analysis of the demand for oil in the Middle East," *Energy Policy*, 35: 6258–65.

Pritchett, L. (2000). "The tyranny of concepts: CUDIE (Cumulated, Depreciated, Investment Effort) is not capital," *Journal of Economic Growth*, 5: 361–84.

Ramsey, F. P. (1927). "A contribution to the theory of taxation," *The Economic Journal*, 37: 47–61.

Richards, A. and Waterbury, J. (2007). A Political Economy of the Middle East, 3rd edn. Boulder, Col.: Westview Press.

Ringel, J., Hosek, S., Vollaard, B., and Mahnovski, S. (2005). "The elasticity of demand for health care: A review of the literature and its application to the military health system." Washington DC: RAND National Defense Research Institute.

Sala-i-Martin, X. and Subramanian, A. (2003). "Addressing the natural resource curse: An illustration from Nigeria." NBER Working Paper No. 9804. Cambridge, Mass.

Seale Jr, J., Regmi, A., and Berstein, J. (2003). "International evidence on food consumption patterns." United States Department of Agriculture, Economic Research Service. Technical Bulletin Number 1904.

Shires, M. A. (1995). "The master plan revisited (again): Prospects for providing access to public undergraduate education in California (draft)." Santa Monica: Rand Institute, DRU-965-LE.

5

Fiscal Policy for Macroeconomic Stability

5.1 Introduction

Macroeconomic stability is important for long-term growth and the literature has discussed several channels through which volatility can reduce growth.[1] Firms are likely to make important mistakes when planning is done in an uncertain environment (Ramey and Ramey 1991). As a result, when investment decisions are irreversible or when it is costly to switch production, investors may decide to wait before investing in order to gather more information about the future (McDonald and Siegel 1986; Bertola 1994). Firms also hit liquidity constraints more frequently in volatile environments. When financial institutions are underdeveloped, liquidity constraints limit investment (Aghion et al. 2010).

The empirical literature has found indeed that a one percentage point increase in volatility tends to reduce annual growth by around 0.3 percent, and the negative link is stronger for countries with poor institutions, intermediate levels of financial development, and for countries that do not implement countercyclical fiscal policies—all characteristics that apply to some extent to the GCC (Hnatkovska and Loayza 2005; Kose et al. 2006; van der Ploeg and Poelhekke 2009).

In the GCC as in many other oil-exporting countries, growth has been very volatile over the last thirty years, and this is why in Chapter 2 we attributed part of the disappointing growth in TFP to this factor. In the period 1976–90, the standard deviation of GDP growth exceeded 7 percent in all countries

[1] This chapter is an extension of a paper written with Abdelhak Senhadji (Espinoza and Senhadji 2011). The authors are grateful to A. Senhadji for allowing us to use parts of his work in the present chapter.

Table 5.1. Standard deviation of GDP growth per capita in percent, 1976–2007

	1976–1990	1991–2007	
Country	GDP per capita	GDP per capita	Non-oil GDP per capita
	PWT 7	PWT 7	IMF
Bahrain	11.8	3.1	2.6
Kuwait	16.6	12.1	36.7
Oman	8.7	3.6	4.4
Qatar	5.8	9.8	11.3
Saudi Arabia	7.7	5.5	3.3
UAE	7.1	4.3	4.4
OECD (median country)	2.1	1.8	1.4
Oil exporters (median country)	9.2	8.8	6.5
Other developing countries (median country)	5.8	4.8	3.4

Source: PWT 7, IMF, and authors' calculations

but Qatar, above what is typical for either advanced or developing countries (Table 5.1). The recent period has been more favorable. Nevertheless, the standard deviation of growth per capita has been around or above 4 percent in all the GCC countries but Bahrain, whereas before the Great Recession volatility had decreased to less than 2 percent in advanced economies.

Policymakers can use both fiscal and monetary policy to stabilize economic cycles. However, since the GCC countries have long pegged their currencies to the US dollar,[2] domestic interest rates in the region have closely tracked US rates. As a result, conventional monetary policy loses power to stabilize the economy. Chapter 6 analyzes this issue further, whereas in this chapter we show the importance of fiscal policy as a tool for macroeconomic stabilization.

The GCC economies faced the Great Recession—as the 2008–9 world recession became known—in a strong position, supported by several years of high oil prices and fiscal surpluses that alimented the build-up of government savings and foreign reserves. Despite a major drop in government revenues in 2009, fiscal space was available for countercyclical measures, and overall GCC real government spending remained high, supporting non-oil growth. Also in 2009, Saudi Arabia in conjunction with other G20 countries assigned several percent of GDP of spending to a fiscal stimulus package motivated by the need to kick-start the world economy. We assess in this chapter the effectiveness of fiscal policy and the use that the GCC countries have made of this tool in the last thirty years.

[2] Kuwait is an exception, as its currency has been pegged to a basket of currencies since 2007.

There is little recent research on the effect of fiscal policy in the GCC[3] and therefore having an estimate of the impact of spending shocks is important. Our focus is on spending as opposed to revenues because most of the revenue comes from hydrocarbon exports and little is derived from non-oil taxes. Hence, fiscal policy is tantamount to expenditure policy in the region. We show, using panel and simple Vector Auto-Regression (VAR) models, that fiscal expenditure is a major driver of growth cycles in the non-oil economy. We find that the fiscal multiplier (i.e. the volume of domestic economic activity that is generated by a dollar of government spending) is positive and statistically significant, and varies between 0.2 and 0.5 the first year spending is increased. Expenditure on public investment (capital expenditure) is found to have stronger effects than current expenditure (public wages, spending on goods and services, etc.).

The VAR models also show that 20 to 60 percent of the variance of unexpected non-oil GDP growth can be explained by fiscal shocks. To a large extent these shocks reflected oil revenues. Indeed, our results suggest that fiscal consolidations, forced by low oil prices, were an important cause of GDP contraction in 1986–7 and in 1998–2000, whereas an expansionary fiscal stance would have pushed activity after the First Gulf War and in the five years between 2003 and 2008. In addition, several GCC governments ran expansionary policies during the Great Recession with the objective of mitigating the negative impact of external factors.

We first provide some background on government spending in the GCC (section 5.2) and on the recent literature on fiscal multipliers (section 5.3). The estimates of fiscal multipliers, using both panel and VAR techniques, show that government spending has a strong effect on non-oil growth (section 5.4). In the last sections of the chapter, we discuss whether fiscal policy has been pro-cyclical or countercyclical, and assess the contribution of fiscal policy to economic cycles in the region, using variance and historical decompositions.

5.2 Background

In the GCC, governments exert a strong influence on the economy and government spending accounts for between 35 and 80 percent of non-oil GDP (see Table 5.2). Current expenditure forms the bulk of government

[3] An exception is Nakibullah and Islam (2007) who study the effect of fiscal policy in Bahrain. They find that temporary shocks have little effect whereas permanent shocks are important. They take into account the global environment of Bahrain by controlling for US fiscal shocks and find that a US expansionary shock has negative spillovers on Bahrain.

Table 5.2. Characteristics of GCC economies and government expenditure

Average 2000–9	Bahrain	Kuwait	Oman	Qatar	Saudi Arabia	UAE
Government expenditure/non-oil GDP	0.36	0.79	0.66	0.64	0.66	0.36
Current expenditure/total expenditure	0.76	0.88	0.72	0.70	0.80	0.83
Capital expenditure/total expenditure	0.24	0.12	0.28	0.30	0.20	0.17
Hydrocarbon-related revenues/total revenues	0.77	0.73	0.84	0.66	0.86	0.73
Investment income/total revenues[b]	0.01	0.22	0.04	0.24	0.02	0.12
Taxes and others/total revenues	0.22	0.05	0.12	0.11	0.12	0.14
Government expenditure and oil prices						
R-square (1991–2007)[a]	0.10	0.29	0.30	0.55	0.79	0.20
Imports of goods and services/nominal GDP	0.71	0.35	0.39	0.35	0.34	0.68
Share of non-national in total population (2005)	0.41	0.62	0.24	0.72	0.27	0.79

[a] Regressions of the growth rate of nominal spending on contemporaneous and lagged oil price inflation.

[b] Investment income for Bahrain includes other capital revenues.

Source: IMF and authors' calculations

spending, but capital expenditure represents nonetheless more than 12 percent of spending in all GCC countries, and reaches 30 percent of GDP in Oman and Qatar. Government revenues come from hydrocarbon exports and investment income and as a result, non-oil fiscal revenues and in particular income taxes, corporate taxes, and VAT are small (less than a third; see again Table 5.2). Government spending is therefore the main instrument of fiscal policy.

Because government revenues coming from the non-oil economy are small, government spending is eventually constrained by oil revenues and the historical pattern has indeed been that expenditure followed oil prices. The R-square of the regression of government expenditure on oil prices is highest in Qatar and Saudi Arabia, where it reaches 80 percent (Table 5.2). Indeed, Fasano and Wang (2002) show using a VAR model of revenues and expenditure that around 80 percent of the variance of expenditure shocks in Saudi Arabia can be explained by shocks in revenues. The proportion would be around 65 percent for Qatar. In the last crisis, as oil prices collapsed, the announcements from several countries that the government would maintain or even increase expenditure despite low oil prices was therefore a significant change from past practice.

This policy shift raises the question of the effect of government spending on activity. Theory suggests several determinants of the size of fiscal multipliers, depending on the model chosen. In a neoclassical model of a closed economy, Woodford (2011) shows that the size of the fiscal multiplier is lower the harder it is to employ new resources and the easier it is for the private sector to reduce consumption and investment to leave space for government spending (in that case government spending is "crowding out" private spending). In addition, if monetary policy does not react to fiscal expansion (if the interest rate is constant), the multiplier reaches 1 because private spending is fully determined by intertemporal optimization, and optimal private-sector decisions are unchanged if interest rates are fixed (Woodford 2011). In a Keynesian model, multipliers are lower in more open economies because a larger faction of the increase in government spending is spent on imports, which do not contribute to domestic production. In a Mundell-Fleming model, multipliers are larger under fixed exchange rate regimes because the interest rate is not affected by the fiscal expansion. Ilzetzki, Mendoza, and Végh (2010) have indeed shown using a panel of forty-four countries that multipliers are larger in closed economies and in economies with fixed exchange rates.

How does the GCC fare with respect to the determinants of the fiscal multiplier identified in the literature? Imports are large in the GCC—between 35 and 70 percent (Table 5.2)—and it is therefore possible that "leakages" from government spending to imports reduce the effect of government spending on growth. In other words, government money spent on wages or on capital expenditure could finance imports and therefore not contribute to GDP. In particular, stimulus spending would take in many cases the form of capital spending that would require importing machinery and material. On the other hand, the GCC currencies are fixed to the US dollar, and therefore movements in interest rates would not dampen the effect of fiscal policy.

Finally, it is relatively easy in the GCC to mobilize factors of production because a large portion of the new labor force comes from abroad and the governments are wealthy and do not need to tap into private funds to spend. With a large foreign workforce, even in the public sector, increases in government spending could leak out as outward remittances and not be spent in the domestic economy. The multipliers could therefore be small, as in many open emerging economies, but the issue has to be settled empirically.

5.3 The Empirical Literature on Fiscal Multipliers

The estimation of many macroeconomic relationships raises the concern of potential endogeneity of the explanatory variables. In the particular case at hand, the relationship of interest is that between an indicator of economic growth and an indicator of fiscal spending.

The problem is that the relationship might be bidirectional (i.e., fiscal spending influences economic growth and vice versa). Failing to control for the endogeneity of spending may lead to the well-known *simultaneity bias*. Economists have identified two sources of endogeneity when estimating fiscal multipliers:

(a) In good times, spending is reduced (lower employment benefits) and taxes are higher (*automatic fiscal stabilizers*) and therefore the correlation between spending and activity tends to be negative, and as a result the multipliers are underestimated by OLS. We can safely rule out this channel in the GCC since, as we have already shown, fiscal policy boils down to government spending and there is very little "*automatic*" spending in the region (unemployment benefits are insignificant).

(b) Systematic countercyclical policies may give the impression that fiscal expansions have limited effects since they will be implemented during bad times (*endogenous fiscal policy*). This source of endogeneity is likely to be of a lesser importance in the GCC than in other countries because, historically, spending has been limited by oil revenues and driven by diversification objectives.

The literature has tackled the issue of endogeneity from two angles (see also the surveys in Spilimbergo et al. 2008 and Spilimbergo et al. 2009).

(a) Case studies have looked at specific experiments. For instance, Romer and Romer (2008) analyzed the effect of tax policy changes using detailed information on policy decisions to identify the size and timing of policy changes in the US. This allows them to identify structural shocks (changes in taxes exogenous to the business cycle) and estimate the effects on GDP in an OLS quarterly model (a VAR is also analyzed for robustness).

(b) VAR identification procedures have been used in an attempt to take into account the endogenous fiscal response. Blanchard and Perotti (2002) estimated a quarterly VAR on the US with output, tax revenues, and total spending, and the key to the identification procedure was to recognize that the use of quarterly data virtually eliminates the endogeneity bias: fiscal policy cannot react fast enough to be endogenous to current quarter activity. The second element in their identification procedure was to estimate directly the behavior of the automatic fiscal stabilizers (applying the OECD method; see Giorno et al. 1995) to constrain the structural coefficient and thus deduce some reduced-form coefficients in the VAR. More sophisticated identification procedures exist and do not need to assume contemporaneous exogeneity. For instance,

> Mountford and Uhlig (2008) use sign restrictions in a standard VAR model to identify fiscal shocks as positive shocks to fiscal spending that are uncorrelated with monetary and business cycle shocks.[4]

The literature that covers a cross-section of countries has taken the VAR route to reduce the importance of the endogeneity bias, since finding detailed information on specific spending programs for many countries is cumbersome. For instance, IMF (2008) estimates impulse responses for the G7 countries using quarterly VARs with Choleski ordering of the output gap, the GDP deflator, the structural fiscal balance, and the cyclical fiscal balance. Perotti (2005, 2006) uses a different identification procedure but the methodology is also based on a quarterly structural VAR of fiscal variables, GDP, the GDP deflator, and the ten-year nominal interest rate.

Panel methods have also been common. Ilzetzki and Végh (2008) used Instrumental Variables models and system GMM on quarterly data from forty-nine countries to investigate both the size of multipliers and the importance of pro-cyclicality, and found that although IV models were inconclusive, the GMM models suggested that pro-cyclicality existed but that fiscal multipliers had also been underestimated, especially for developing economies, for which the elasticity was estimated to reach 0.73, implying a multiplier of around 1 for the GCC.

By and large, much of the fiscal multiplier literature has considered advanced economies. A recent survey is provided by Romer (2011). The literature on emerging markets is not as vast, and has not considered the GCC separately. The next section provides our estimates of fiscal multipliers using panel and VAR models for this group of countries.

5.4 Econometric Estimates of Fiscal Multipliers

We follow the literature in estimating panel models for the region and VAR models country by country. The description of the data used is presented in Table 5.3. Panel models allow us to increase statistical power by pooling data from the six GCC countries. As a result, it is easy to distinguish in these models the impact of current expenditure from that of capital expenditure, and to control for many external factors. However, panel models assume homogeneity in the estimated elasticities, and the identification of fiscal policy shocks is easier with VAR models. In addition, the variance and historical decomposition of shocks in time series models, discussed in section 5.5, is also useful to provide a narrative of the drivers of growth cycles.

[4] See, for instance, the discussion on VAR identification in Perotti (2005) for more details.

Table 5.3. Data sources

Data	Source	Note
Non-oil real GDP growth (GCC excl. Saudi Arabia)	IMF (2010b) and IMF Article IV country reports (1980–90)	
Saudi Arabia non-oil real GDP growth	Saudi Arabia Monetary Authority	National Accounts, constant prices (base 100 in 1999)
Government expenditure (GCC excl. Saudi Arabia)	IMF (2010b) and IMF Article IV country reports (1980–90)	Central government, deflated by the CPI
Saudi Arabia government expenditure	Saudi Arabia Monetary Authority	Central government, deflated by the CPI
Inflation (excl. Saudi Arabia)	IMF (2010b) and IMF Article IV country reports (1980–90)	CPI inflation
Saudi Arabia inflation	Saudi Arabia Monetary Authority	
Oil price	IMF (2010a)	WTI (West Texas Intermediate)
World interest rate	IMF (2010a)	Fed Funds Rate

5.4.1 Panel Model

The data for the six members of the GCC are presented in Figure 5.1. Some co-movement between non-oil growth and spending appears, except in the UAE. In the UAE, fiscal data have gaps because there is no consolidated budget. We eventually dropped the data for the UAE as they drastically reduced the significance of the panel results.

We first estimate a simple panel model of non-oil real GDP as a function of growth in public expenditure using Pooled OLS (Table 5.4, POLS, columns 1, 5, and 9), random effects (RE, columns 2, 6, and 10), and fixed effects (FE, columns 3, 7, and 11). We also estimated a model excluding contemporaneous spending, so as to check the robustness of the results with regard to endogeneity of government spending (lag FE model, columns 4, 8, and 12).[5]

For all regressions including the lag FE models, the coefficients for contemporaneous, lagged, and twice-lagged fiscal expenditure are positive and significant. For the models that include capital expenditure only, the third lags are also significant (all t-statistics presented are computed using standard errors robust to heteroskedasticity). Overall, our estimates suggest that the short-term fiscal multiplier[6] is around 0.3 for total government expenditure (columns 1 to 4), 0.2–0.3 for capital expenditure (columns 5 to 8), and 0.2–0.4

[5] We also used different IV models (not reported). We tried oil prices as an instrument, but because high oil prices also benefit the petrochemical industry (the production of which is included in the non-oil GDP data), improve confidence, and ease financial conditions, exogeneity of the instrument was unlikely. Lagged spending proved also to be a weak instrument. As a result, we found the lag FE model, in which endogeneity is removed by construction, to be a safer alternative.

[6] The fiscal multiplier is computed as the elasticity divided by the ratio of capital (or current or total) expenditure to GDP. The elasticity is $\alpha = (\Delta Y/Y)/(\Delta G/G)$ and therefore the multiplier is $\Delta Y/$

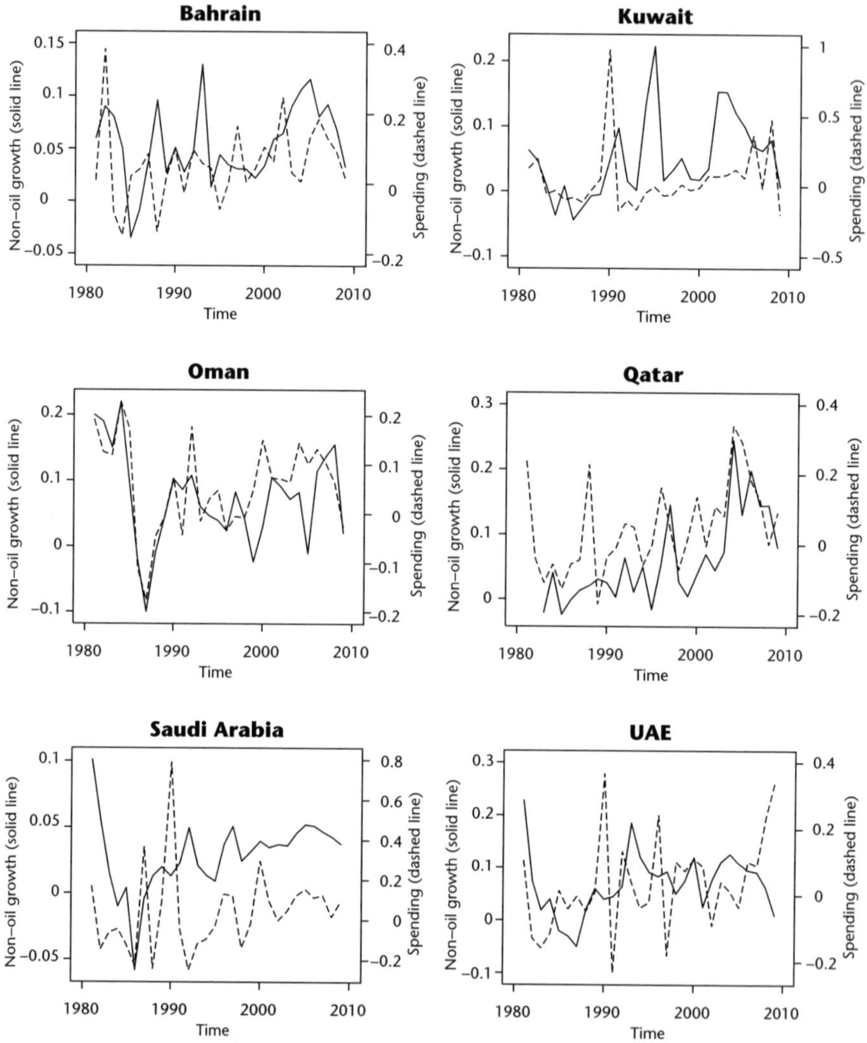

Figure 5.1. Non-oil real GDP growth and real growth in total government expenditure
Source: IMF and IMF country reports

for current expenditure (columns 9 to 12). A possible explanation for why the multiplier on capital expenditure is weaker than that for current expenditure is the relatively long gestation lags for capital formation. It can take several years of investment before productive capacity is operational.

$\Delta G = \alpha\ Y/G$. The ratio Y/G has evolved over time, which is why we use the historical average to calibrate it (see Table 5.2).

Indeed, the long-run multiplier estimates suggest that the effect of capital expenditure on non-oil GDP is significantly higher than that for current expenditure: the long-run multiplier on capital expenditure is 0.6–1.1 versus 0.3–0.7 and 0.4–0.7 for current and total spending, respectively. Endogeneity did not seem to be a major issue since removing contemporaneous spending did not change statistical significance, although the multipliers were found to be smaller.

We tested the robustness of these results to the inclusion of several control variables: inflation, oil prices, interest rates, and world growth (Table 5.5). Oil prices can affect non-oil growth either via the petrochemical industry (the demand for petrochemicals is highly correlated to oil prices), via increased liquidity and business confidence, or via fiscal expenditure—but this latter channel should ideally be attributed to government spending. Contemporaneous oil prices were not significant but lagged oil price changes were found to affect non-oil growth. The contemporaneous correlation between fiscal spending and growth is therefore entirely attributed to the effect of fiscal policy when the contemporaneous oil price is dropped (a more appropriate identification of shocks is done thanks to the VAR historical decomposition; see next section).

The Fed Funds rate and its lags, as well as world GDP growth were not significant. Finally, current inflation was strongly correlated with growth and was also included. Overall, the short-run multipliers would remain around 0.2–0.3 in most models, and the long-run multiplier would be 0.6 for capital spending and 0.3 for current spending.

5.4.2 *Fiscal Policy and Economic Cycles*

We now investigate the importance of fiscal shocks on the dynamics of GDP using Vector Auto-Regressions. We estimate VAR models for each country linking real world GDP, real government expenditure (we follow Ilzetzki and Végh 2008 in deflating all fiscal variables by the CPI), and non-oil real GDP.[7] In a VAR, it is important to keep the number of variables to its minimum. Adding endogenous variables in particular (such as inflation) is very costly in degrees of freedom. We therefore did not include as control variables the Fed Funds Rate, which was not significant in the panel, nor inflation, because it was not essential to a discussion of fiscal multipliers. We did however include world growth in order to disentangle external from domestic components

[7] We use total government expenditure, despite the criticism formulated in Ilzetzki and Végh (2008) against the inclusion of interest payments and transfers in the data, because we do not have such detailed description of expenditure before 1990. In any case, both transfers and interest payments represent a very small portion of spending in the GCC (interest payments averaged 4.8 percent of total spending and rarely exceeded 10 percent of spending).

Table 5.4. GCC panel fiscal multipliers—dependent variable: non-oil real GDP growth

Variables	(1)	(2)	(3)	(4)	(5)	(6)	(7)	(8)	(9)	(10)	(11)	(12)
	Total Expenditure				Capital Expenditure				Current Expenditure			
	POLS	RE	FE	Lag FE	POLS	RE	FE	Lag FE	POLS	RE	FE	Lag FE
Δ Expenditure	0.233***	0.233***	0.233***									
	[4.088]	[5.102]	[4.934]									
Δ Expenditure (t–1)	0.160***	0.161***	0.161***	0.201**								
	[3.475]	[6.151]	[6.083]	[3.490]								
Δ Expenditure (t–2)	0.0891***	0.0892**	0.0897*	0.0908**								
	[2.722]	[2.221]	[2.173]	[3.186]								
Δ Capital Expenditure					0.0513***	0.0513***	0.0511**					
					[2.771]	[4.077]	[4.063]					
Δ Capital Expenditure (t–1)					0.0459**	0.0459***	0.0457***	0.0336*				
					[2.430]	[6.794]	[6.692]	[2.512]				
Δ Capital Expenditure (t–2)					0.0453***	0.0453***	0.0450***	0.0286**				
					[3.510]	[8.971]	[8.764]	[4.056]				
Δ Capital Expenditure (t–3)					0.0337***	0.0337***	0.0336***	0.0316**				
					[2.687]	[4.784]	[4.758]	[4.146]				
Δ Current Expenditure									0.235***	0.235***	0.241***	
									[3.277]	[7.553]	[6.968]	
Δ Current Expenditure (t–1)									0.103**	0.103***	0.108**	0.103*
									[2.427]	[4.030]	[3.674]	[2.190]
Δ Current Expenditure (t–2)									0.0436	0.0436	0.0472	0.0437
									[1.543]	[1.041]	[1.045]	[1.300]

Constant	0.0366***	0.0367***	0.0365***	0.0454***	0.0512***	0.0512***	0.0512***	0.0556***	0.0364***	0.0364***	0.0355***	0.0501***
	[7.545]	[6.877]	[6.395]	[9.218]	[9.416]	[21.16]	[44.20]	[51.32]	[5.455]	[5.533]	[5.321]	[8.744]
N.obs	156	156	156	156	139	139	139	139	144	144	144	144
R-squared	0.408		0.408	0.223	0.201		0.199	0.096	0.282		0.286	0.07
Breusch-Pagan p-value		0.255				0.143				0.306		
*** p < 0.01, ** p < 0.05, * p < 0.1, t-statistics in brackets												
S-T multiplier	0.33	0.33	0.33	0.29	0.33	0.33	0.33	0.22	0.44	0.44	0.45	0.19
L-T multiplier	0.69	0.69	0.69	0.42	1.13	1.13	1.13	0.60	0.71	0.71	0.74	0.27

Source: IMF, country authorities, and authors' estimates

Table 5.5. GCC panel fiscal multipliers, controlling for inflation and oil prices

Variables	(1)	(2)	(3)	(4)	(5)	(6)	(7)	(8)	(9)	(10)	(11)	(12)
	Total Expenditure (FE)				Capital Expenditure (FE)				Current Expenditure (FE)			
Δ Expenditure	0.233***	0.206**	0.218***	0.192***								
	[4.934]	[4.453]	[5.680]	[5.179]								
Δ Expenditure (t–1)	0.161***	0.150***	0.121**	0.111**								
	[6.083]	[7.770]	[3.529]	[3.076]								
Δ Expenditure (t–2)	0.0897*	0.0941	0.0420	0.0451								
	[2.173]	[1.852]	[1.005]	[0.899]								
Δ Capital Expenditure					0.0511**	0.0422**	0.0346	0.0266				
					[4.063]	[3.605]	[1.901]	[1.532]				
Δ Capital Expenditure (t–1)					0.0457***	0.0418***	0.0298**	0.0269*				
					[6.692]	[7.122]	[2.892]	[2.218]				
Δ Capital Expenditure (t–2)					0.0450***	0.0377***	0.0297**	0.0230*				
					[8.764]	[7.395]	[3.403]	[2.295]				
Δ Capital Expenditure (t–3)					0.0336***	0.0327***	0.0200	0.0198				
					[4.758]	[4.760]	[1.689]	[1.619]				
Δ Current Expenditure									0.241***	0.208***	0.171*	0.131
									[6.968]	[6.464]	[2.392]	[1.681]
Δ Current Expenditure (t–1)									0.108**	0.0924**	0.0479	0.0285
									[3.674]	[3.467]	[0.771]	[0.432]
Δ Current Expenditure (t–2)									0.0472	0.0589	0.00589	0.0157
									[1.045]	[1.076]	[0.161]	[0.376]
Δ Oil Price (t–1)		0.0438**		0.0398		0.0778**		0.0683**		0.0696**		0.0686**
		[3.009]		[1.942]		[4.253]		[3.564]		[2.869]		[2.785]
Inflation			0.355**	0.358**			0.632**	0.627**			0.503	0.533
			[3.519]	[3.231]			[3.509]	[3.505]			[1.926]	[1.808]

Constant	0.0365***	0.0367***	0.0318***	0.0319***	0.0512***	0.0501***	0.0368***	0.0357***	0.0355***	0.0352***	0.0330***	0.0326***
	[6.395]	[6.093]	[9.224]	[8.443]	[44.20]	[72.92]	[12.91]	[10.86]	[5.321]	[4.853]	[7.097]	[7.562]
Observations	156	151	155	150	139	134	138	133	144	139	143	138
R-squared	0.408	0.429	0.456	0.476	0.199	0.274	0.354	0.422	0.286	0.333	0.349	0.401
*** p < 0.01, ** p < 0.05, * p < 0.1, t-statistics in brackets												
S-T multiplier	0.33	0.29	0.31	0.16	0.33	0.27	0.22	0.17	0.45	0.39	0.32	0.24
L-T multiplier	0.69	0.64	0.54	0.50	1.13	0.99	0.73	0.62	0.74	0.67	0.42	0.33

Source: Country authorities and authors' estimates

when interpreting growth cycles. In addition, we checked the robustness of our results to including oil prices as an exogenous variable.

The model was estimated on 1980–2008 data since data was unavailable for most countries before that period. Data was available for Saudi Arabia, but the coefficients were unstable when using data between 1968 and 1975. The variables were converted into logarithms[8] so that the ratio of the impulse responses can be thought of as elasticities. The short-term multiplier (one year) is then obtained by dividing the elasticity by the ratio of spending to GDP. The two-year multiplier is obtained by assuming the expenditure shock is maintained over two years.

For each country in the GCC, the following VAR is estimated by OLS for a vector y_t of world GDP, real government expenditure, and non-oil real GDP. The VAR has three lags,[9] and additional exogenous variables X_t are added as control variables:

$$y_t = \sum_{k=1}^{3} \varphi_k y_{t-k} + \beta X_t + \varepsilon_t; \quad E[\varepsilon_t \varepsilon_t{}'] = \Sigma$$

The identification procedure is based on a Choleski orthogonalization of the covariance matrix of errors Σ, with fiscal expenditure ordered before non-oil growth, i.e., it is assumed there is no immediate effect of non-oil growth on fiscal expenditure. This identification procedure assumes that because budgets are voted much ahead of their implementation, the causality runs from spending to non-oil growth and not the other way around. The assumption is common in the literature and easily justifiable when using quarterly VARs, since fiscal policy cannot be adjusted within a quarter. But we only have annual data in the GCC, and therefore the VARs are estimated on annual data. The assumption is therefore a stronger one. World growth is ordered first in the VAR, to capture the effect of the global environment.

In addition, we checked how robust the results are to including oil prices as an exogenous variable. It is not always easy to disentangle shocks to oil prices from shocks to government spending because GCC spending has been strongly correlated with oil revenues. Table 5.6 summarizes the elasticities of government spending to oil prices found in the VAR when oil prices were included. In Saudi Arabia, as also noted in Table 5.1, the link between spending and oil prices is very strong. On the other hand, oil price was not significant in the UAE regression. Our preferred specification, presented in Figures

[8] The variables are cointegrated, which is why estimation in log level remains appropriate. The VAR results were very similar when using growth rates instead of log levels.

[9] For Saudi Arabia, the AIC criteria and the LR tests suggest using three lags while the BIC (Schwartz) criteria suggested using two lags only. There were no major differences on the impulse response functions using two or three lags. The three-lag structure was kept identical for all counties.

5.2 to 5.10, is however the one without oil prices because we think the main channel via which oil revenues affect the non-oil is via government spending.

We show in Figure 5.2 the effect of a shock to government spending (normalized to a permanent one dollar increase) on non-oil GDP. The multiplier is estimated to be around 0.3–0.5 in the year of the shock in Bahrain, Kuwait, Oman, and Qatar, and to increase to around 0.7 after two years in Kuwait, Qatar, and the UAE. The multipliers are statistically different from 0 in all countries at the 90th percent confidence level. When adding oil prices as a control variable, the multipliers are similar in the first year but tend to be higher in the second year (1 for Kuwait and Qatar, and 2 for Bahrain and the UAE). These results are roughly in line with the results of the panel model: dropping the UAE (which was dropped in the panel given the poor quality of data), the average multiplier is 0.3 in the first year and 0.5 after two years (1.0 when oil prices are added as a control variable). There is some heterogeneity in the data, which could not be captured by the panel model. In particular, the multiplier is smaller in Saudi Arabia (0.1 after one year and 0.2 after two

Table 5.6. Elasticity of spending to a permanent increase in oil price in the VARs

	Bahrain	Kuwait	Oman	Qatar	Saudi Arabia	UAE
1 year	0.27	–0.02	0.12	0.10	0.51	–0.20
2 year	0.27	0.13	0.12	0.26	0.77	–0.10

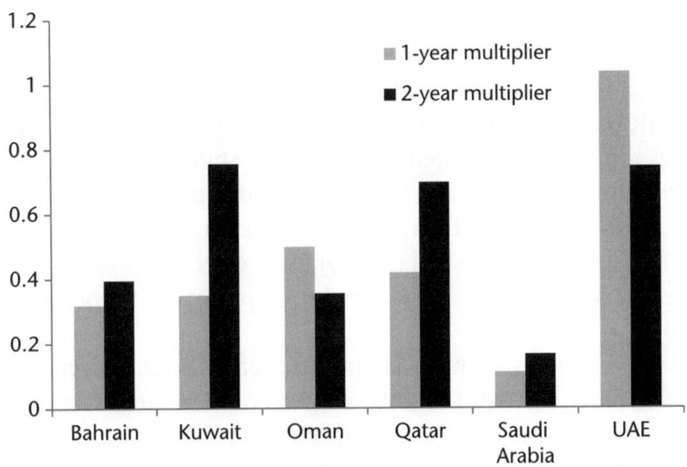

Figure 5.2. Fiscal multiplier (impact of total government spending on non-oil GDP)

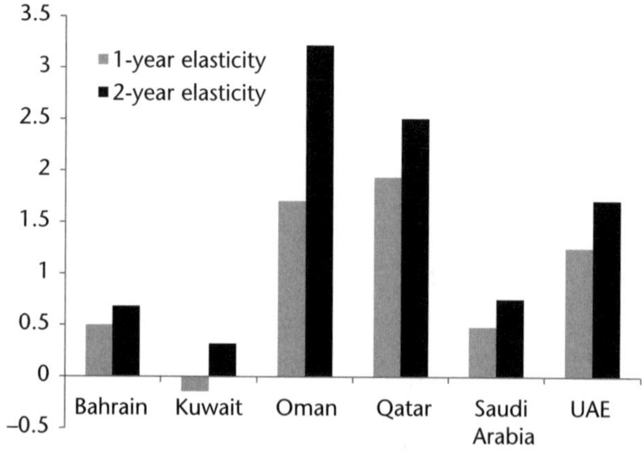

Figure 5.3. Impact of world growth on non-oil growth in the GCC

years, irrespective of whether oil prices are included) and larger in Bahrain and the UAE.

Positive shocks in the world economy spill over to the GCC (Figure 5.3). The elasticity of individual countries to GDP is higher than 1 in the small and very open economies of Qatar, UAE, and Oman. The elasticity is however lower in Saudi Arabia, Kuwait, and Bahrain. The main difference, when adding oil prices, is that the elasticity of non-oil growth to world growth is much lower for Qatar and is positive in the first year after the shock for Kuwait.

5.5 Contribution of Fiscal Policy to Economic Cycles

We use the same VARs to assess whether fiscal policy has been pro-cyclical or countercyclical in the region. Our measure of cyclicality is the orthogonalized impulse response of government spending to shocks in non-oil GDP. One should remember however that since our identification strategy assumed that fiscal policy cannot react within a year to news on non-oil GDP growth, the VARs may underestimate the reactivity of fiscal policy. Figure 5.4 presents the impulse response functions, normalized for a permanent 1 percent shock to non-oil GDP.

Fiscal policy appears to have been historically countercyclical in Saudi Arabia and in Oman. In Saudi Arabia, a 1 percent (permanent) negative shock in non-oil GDP would have triggered a strong expansion in government spending in the next year, although the increase would have been quickly

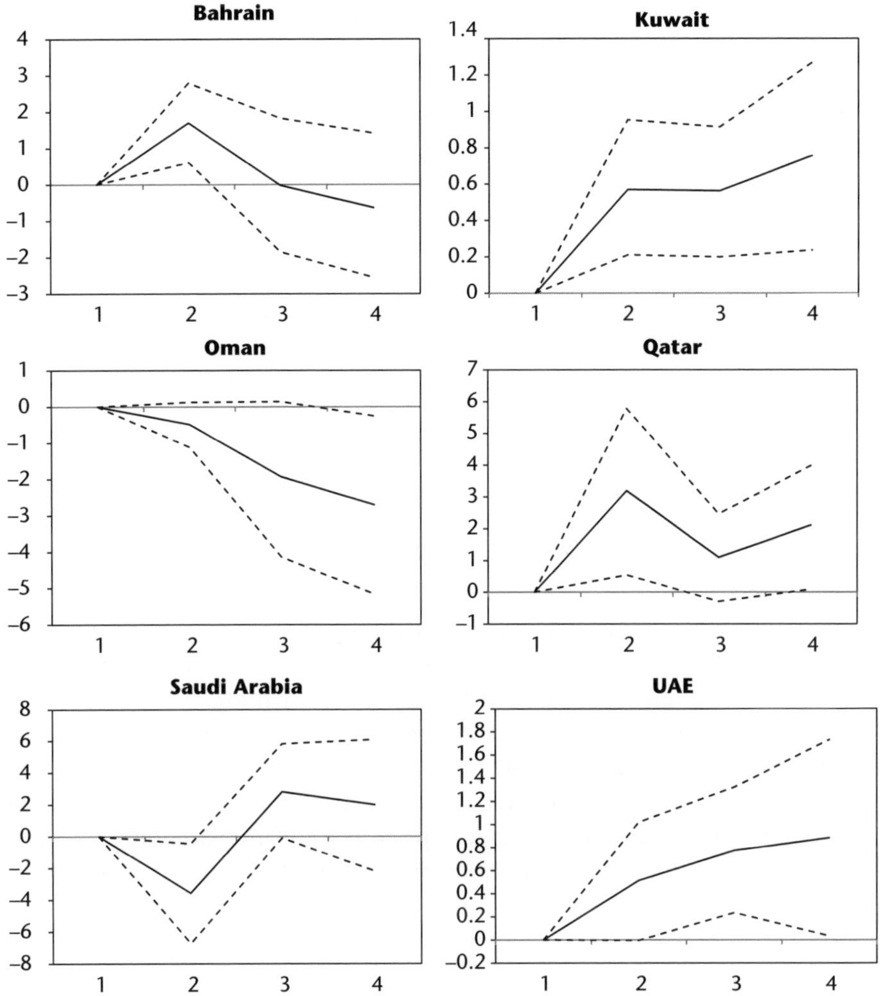

Figure 5.4. Pro-cyclicality of fiscal policy: Response of government spending to non-oil GDP shocks, in percent deviation from baseline

Note: Impulse Response Function for a permanent 1 percent shock to non-oil real GDP; 16th and 84th percentile error bands

offset the subsequent year (surprisingly, this result is robust to including oil prices as a control variable). In the other four countries of the GCC, fiscal policy would have been pro-cyclical, and the elasticity of spending to non-oil growth would have been high in Qatar and in Bahrain. When controlling for oil prices, the elasticity of spending to growth is not significantly different from 0 in Kuwait and Qatar, which suggests that our finding of pro-cyclicality in these two countries is really due to the importance of oil revenues in driving both government spending and non-oil growth.

Table 5.7. Non-oil GDP growth: Forecast Error Variance Decomposition two years ahead

	Bahrain	Kuwait	Oman	Qatar	Saudi Arabia	UAE
World growth	0.06	0.00	0.41	0.17	0.26	0.18
Govt expenditure	0.38	0.65	0.17	0.62	0.17	0.28
Non-oil GDP	0.56	0.35	0.42	0.21	0.57	0.53

Note: In Kuwait, the regression of non-oil growth on oil prices also includes two dummy variables for the years 1991 and 1992.

We use the VARs to assess to what extent government expenditure drives non-oil GDP cycles. We first look at the Forecast Error Variance Decomposition (FEVD), which summarizes the contribution of the orthogonalized shocks[10] to the variance of the stochastic component of non-oil GDP growth (Table 5.7). In Qatar and Kuwait, government spending would have contributed more than 60 percent to this variance (50 percent when controlling for oil prices). In the other GCC countries, government spending would have contributed to between 17 and 38 percent of the variance (17–28 percent when controlling for oil prices).

World growth contributed less to volatility than might be expected given the high elasticities estimated earlier, because world growth is actually much more stable than growth in the GCC. The FEVD attributes 18 to 26 percent of the unexpected variance in GDP to shocks in world growth (except for Oman where the share goes to 41 percent). The Kuwait and Bahrain economies would not have been affected by world growth shock. These results are again mostly unaffected by adding oil price as a control variable.[11]

We now compute the historical decomposition of non-oil GDP growth. A historical decomposition relies on the moving average representation of a VAR:

$$y_{t+j} = \hat{y}_{t+j} + \sum_{s=0}^{\infty} \Psi_s u_{t+j-s} = \underbrace{\hat{y}_{t+j} + \sum_{s=j}^{\infty} \Psi_s u_{t+j-s}}_{y_{t+j}^F | t} + \underbrace{\sum_{s=0}^{j-1} \Psi_s u_{t+j-s}}_{V_{t+1,t+j}}$$

[10] i.e., after identifying the shocks by Choleski ordering, with world growth order first, followed by government expenditure and non-oil GDP shocks.

[11] Note however that the variance that is being decomposed is different when oil prices are added as control variables, since the FEVD is a decomposition of the unexpected/stochastic component of a variable. Also, the FEVD cannot identify oil price shocks since the oil price was included as an exogenous variable (the historical decomposition is more interesting for this purpose—see Figures 5.5 to 5.10 and the related discussion). It is nonetheless clear from simple correlations that oil prices matter directly and indirectly via government spending. The "reduced-form" relationship between oil prices and non-oil growth can be measured by the R^2 in the univariate regression of oil prices on non-oil growth, which has been above 40 percent for all countries.

where $\hat{y}_{t+j}$ is the deterministic part of y_{t+j} $y_{t+j}^{F}|t$, is the forecast of y_{t+j} based on information available at time t, and $V_{t+1,t+j}$ is the component in y_{t+j} that is due to shocks that occurred between t and $t+j$. u_t are the innovations that have been obtained thanks to the Choleski decomposition of Σ and Ψ_s is the matrix containing the orthogonalized impulse responses of the VAR.

The historical decomposition is useful because it allows us to explain growth and cycles from past shocks of world growth, fiscal spending, and oil prices using the coefficients Ψ_s (the impulse response functions, summarized in Figures 5.2 and 5.3), the structural shocks u_t, and the deterministic part $\hat{y}_{t+j}$, which is a function of oil prices in particular.

According to the historical decomposition, restrictive fiscal policy was the cause of the GDP contractions in Saudi Arabia in 1986 and in the mid-1990s (Figure 5.5). Expansionary policies would have pushed activity in the late 1980s and in the years 2005–10, despite negative contributions from the world business cycle. These cycles in spending were strongly related to oil prices, although since 2000 the oil price boom has been large enough for the Saudi government to be able to save. As a result, spending has been more stable and the 2009 announcement that fiscal policy would explicitly aim at stabilizing growth goes one step further. The VAR does indeed show that Saudi government policy was countercyclical in 2009–10.

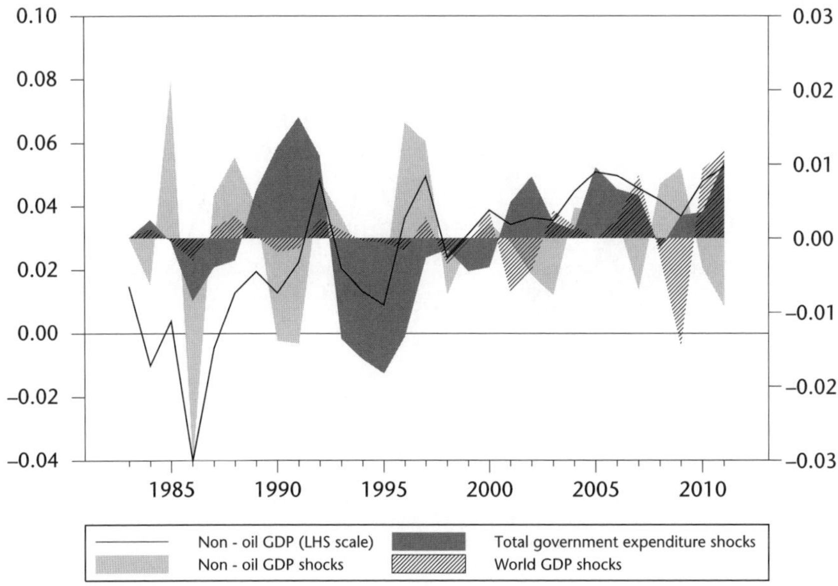

Figure 5.5. Saudi Arabia (non-oil GDP growth on LHS scale, contributions on the RHS)

In the UAE and in Kuwait, growth has been very volatile (Figure 5.6 and Figure 5.7) and fiscal policy as well as external shocks mattered. The boom in the UAE in 1993 has been attributed to a spike in government spending, but much of the growth in 2003–7 is unexplained, although some of it can be attributed to a favorable external environment. The UAE is a very open economy, and its service sector includes ports and airlines that are highly dependent on world trade. The recent fall in growth is clearly associated with the global crisis. In Kuwait, the First Gulf War affected government operations but public spending and growth rebounded in 1993. Oil prices and government spending also stimulated growth in 2003–5 but fiscal policy has been contractionary since 2010–11.

In Qatar, external and fiscal shocks have contributed to the high volatility of the economy (Figure 5.8). Non-oil growth was low in the first half of the 1990s as oil prices fell and the world economy slowed down. Government spending was restrained in the late 1990s and this drove down GDP growth from 1997 to 2003, until the persistent increase in oil prices allowed expansionary fiscal policies. The boost in public investment, aimed at scaling up gas production, contributed significantly to pushing non-oil GDP growth to 40 percent in 2006. The global downturn and the moderation in oil prices since 2008 have brought back growth to single digits.

Oman has suffered two recessions in the last thirty years (see Figure 5.9). The first one, in 1986–7, can be attributed to the fall in oil prices, which also

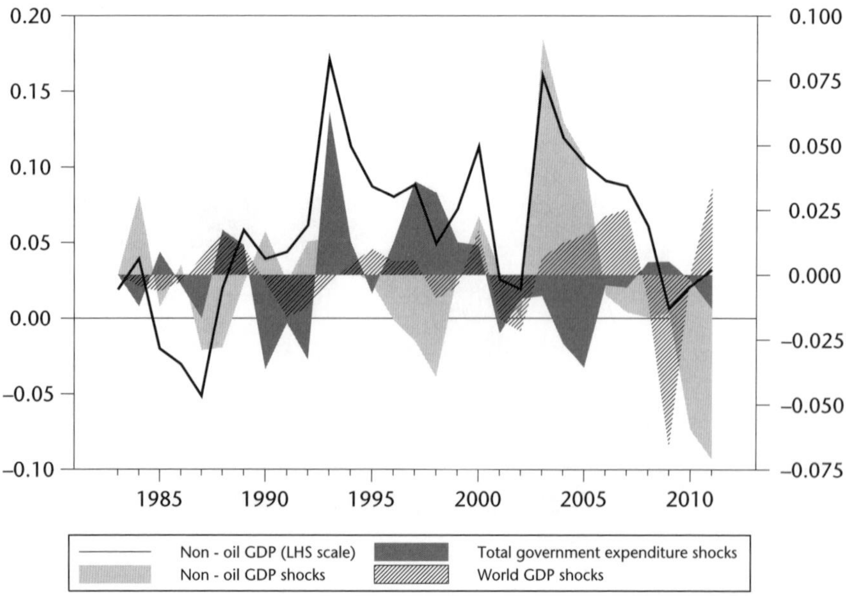

Figure 5.6. UAE (non-oil GDP growth on LHS scale, contributions on the RHS)

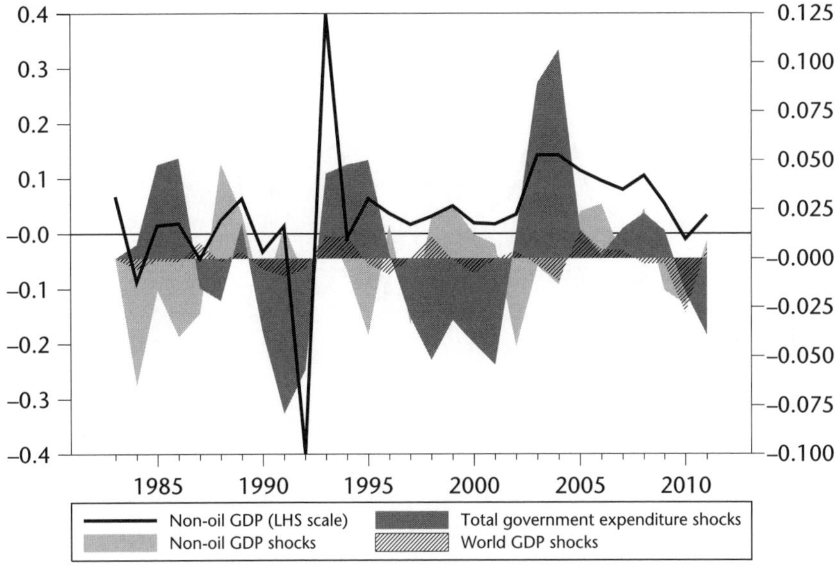

Figure 5.7. Kuwait (data post-1996 is from IMF; data pre-1996 is from UN). Dummies for estimation in 1991 and 1992

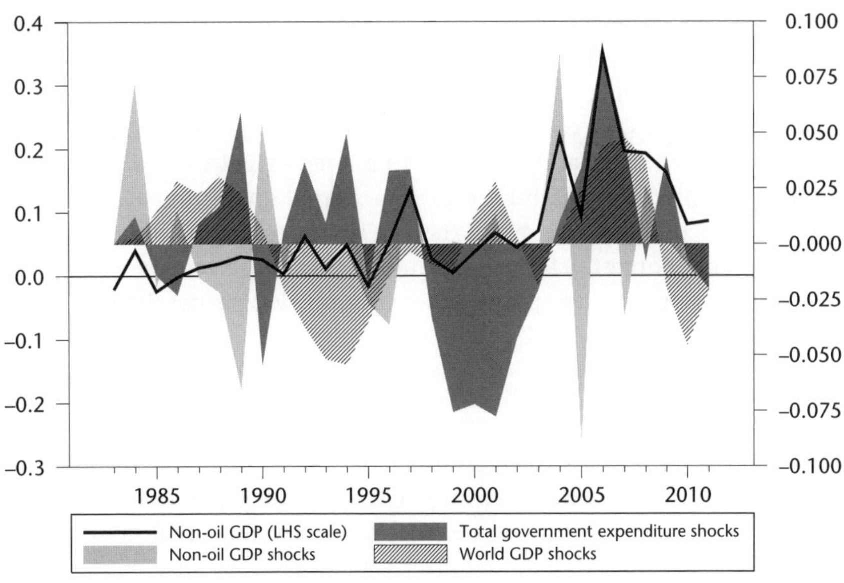

Figure 5.8. Qatar (non-oil GDP growth on LHS scale, contributions on the RHS)

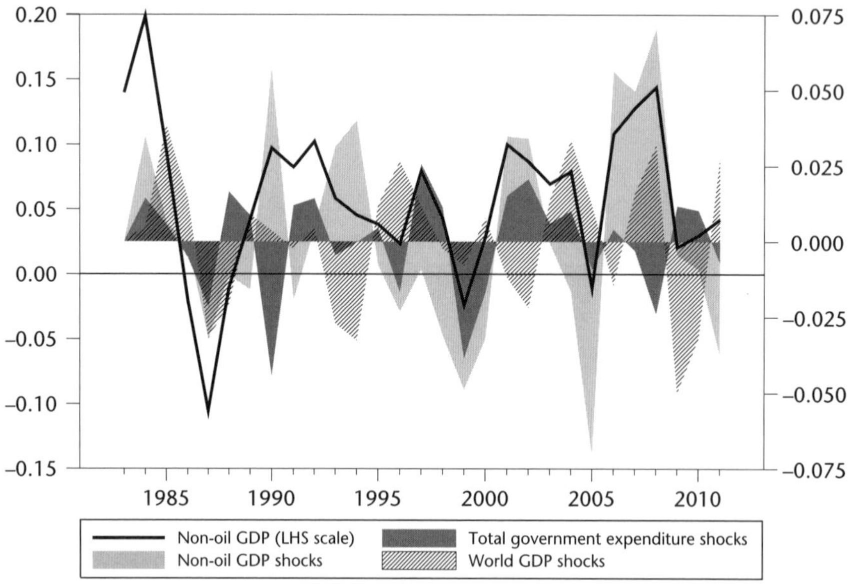

Figure 5.9. Oman (non-oil GDP growth on LHS scale, contributions on the RHS)

constrained government spending. The second recession, in 1999, was again brought about by tight fiscal policy (oil prices had been low for two years) although domestic factors (a fall in private consumption and the completion of the large LNG project and of the Salalah port) also contributed.

Finally, for Bahrain, the VAR is only useful to explain the sources of growth after 2000 (before that, the historical decomposition attributes the shocks to domestic sources, as can be seen from Figure 5.10). The strong growth recorded between 2001 and 2009 was to a large extent due to government spending, high oil prices, and a positive external environment. The global crisis stopped this positive cycle, despite the government maintaining its spending, and domestic factors, including bank deleveraging and social unrest, have contributed to pulling the economy down since 2009.

5.6 Conclusion

In the GCC, governments wield considerable control over the economy and the main instrument of macroeconomic management remains government spending, in countries with fixed exchange rates and a small tax base (and therefore negligible automatic stabilizers). It is therefore important to assess the effectiveness of fiscal policy. The existing literature does not provide

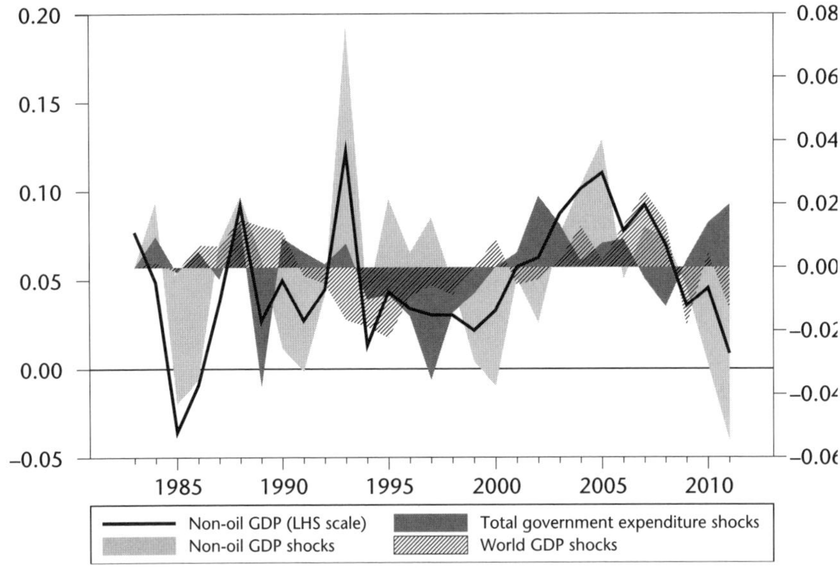

Figure 5.10. Bahrain (non-oil GDP growth on LHS scale, contributions on the RHS)

readily available estimates for the size of fiscal multipliers, i.e, the increase in GDP that can be obtained by decreasing the government balance by one dollar. Depending on country characteristics (open versus closed economy, fixed versus flexible exchange rate regimes) and on the instrument of fiscal policy (taxes versus government expenditure), and depending on the theoretical framework (Keynesian versus neoclassical) and on the econometric model used (VAR, case studies, etc.), multipliers have been found to be anywhere between 0 (e.g., IMF 2008) and 1 (e.g., GMM model in Ilzetski and Végh 2008).

We estimated several models for the GCC and found that the short-term multipliers are between 0.2 and 0.4 in most specifications. The long-term capital spending multipliers would be larger, and they were estimated between 0.6 and 1, whereas current spending multipliers in the long run would be between 0.2 and 0.4 according to the majority of our models.

The effect of government spending in the GCC is likely to depend on the distribution between capital and current spending and the import content of the programs implemented. For Saudi Arabia, where spending is scaling up, government expenditure will be distributed between capital spending in the oil infrastructure and utility sectors (with a fairly high import content) and current spending focused on second-generation reforms (education, health, the judiciary), areas that are likely to have a lower import content and therefore stronger multipliers. Econometric estimates provide merely baseline numbers and it is therefore important to apply judgment, based on the detailed distribution and timing of expenditure, when assessing the effect of different spending programs.

We also discussed the contribution of fiscal policy to economic stabilization. The VARs suggest that fiscal policy would have been countercyclical in Saudi Arabia and Oman. However, for the other countries of the region, policy would have been pro-cyclical. Enhancing fiscal management is important for all oil producers that seek to limit a volatility-driven resource curse. Fiscal frameworks can help (see IMF 2012) and there is scope for improvement in the region.

References

Aghion, P., Angeletos, G. M., Banerjee, A., and Manova, K. (2010). "Volatility and growth: Credit constraints and the composition of investment," *Journal of Monetary Economics*, 57 (3): 246–65.

Blanchard, O. and Perotti, R. (2002). "An empirical characterization of the dynamic effects of changes in government spending and taxes on output," *Quarterly Journal of Economics*, 117: 1329–68.

Bertola, G. (1994). "Flexibility, investment and growth," *Journal of Monetary Economics*, 34: 215–38.

Espinoza, R. and Senhadji, A. (2011). "How strong are fiscal multipliers in the GCC? An empirical investigation." IMF Working Paper 11/61. Washington DC: International Monetary Fund.

Fasano, U. and Wang, Q. (2002). "Testing the relationship between government spending and revenue: Evidence from the GCC countries." IMF Working Paper 02/201. Washington DC: International Monetary Fund.

Giorno, C., Richardson, P., Roseveare, D., and Noord, P. van den (1995). "Estimating potential output, output gaps and structural budget balances." OECD Economics Department Working Papers, No. 152. Paris: OECD Publishing.

Hnatkovska, V. and Loayza, N. (2005). "Volatility and growth," in J. Aizenman and B. Pinto (eds), *Managing Economic Volatility and Crises: A Practitioner's Guide*. Cambridge: Cambridge University Press, 65–100.

Ilzetzki, E., Mendoza, E., and Végh, C. (2010). "How big (small?) are fiscal multipliers?" NBER Working Paper No. 16479. Cambridge, Mass.: National Bureau of Economic Research.

Ilzetzki, E. and Végh, C. (2008). "Procyclical fiscal policy in developing countries: Truth or fiction?" Mimeo. University of Maryland.

International Monetary Fund (IMF) (2008). "Fiscal policy as a countercyclical tool," chapter 5 in *World Economic Outlook*, October. Washington DC: International Monetary Fund, 159–96.

—— (2010a). *World Economic Outlook: Rebalancing Growth, April 2010*. Washington DC: International Monetary Fund.

—— (2010b). *Regional Economic Outlook: Middle East and Central Asia, October 2010*. Washington DC: International Monetary Fund.

—— (2012). "Towards a GCC monetary union: The role of fiscal policy and institutions." Washington DC: International Monetary Fund.

Kose, M. A., Prasad, E. S., Terrones, M. E. (2006). "How do trade and financial integration affect the relationship between growth and volatility?" *Journal of International Economics*, 69: 176–202.

McDonald, R. and Siegel, D. (1986). "The value of waiting to invest," *Quarterly Journal of Economics*, 101 (4): 707–27.

Mountford, A. and Uhlig, H. (2008). "What are the effects of fiscal policy shocks?" NBER Working Paper No. 14551. Cambridge, Mass.: National Bureau of Economic Research.

Nakibullah, A. and Islam, F. (2007). "Effect of government spending on non-oil GDP of Bahrain," *Journal of Asian Economics*, 18 (5): 760–74.

Perotti, R. (2005). "Estimating the effects of fiscal policy in OECD countries." CEPR Discussion Paper No. 4842. London: Centre for Economic Policy Research.

——— (2006). "Public investment and the golden rule: Another (different) look." IGIER Working Paper No. 277. Milan: Bocconi University Innocenzo Gasparini Institute for Economic Research.

Ploeg, F. van der and Poelhekke, S. (2009). "Volatility and the natural resource curse," *Oxford Economic Papers*, 61: 727–60.

Ramey, G. and Ramey, V. (1991). "Technology commitment and the cost of economic fluctuations." NBER Working Paper No. 3755. Cambridge, Mass.: National Bureau of Economic Research.

Romer, C. (2011). "What do we know about the effects of fiscal policy? Separating evidence from ideology." Speech at Hamilton College, November 7, 2011.

Romer, C. and Romer, D. (2008). "The macroeconomic effects of tax changes: Estimates based on a new measure of fiscal shocks." Unpublished ms. University of California, Berkeley.

Spilimbergo, A., Symansky, S., Blanchard, O., and Cottarelli, C. (2008). "Fiscal policy for the crisis." IMF Staff Position Note, December 29, 2008, SPN/08/01.

Spilimbergo, A., Symansky, S., and Schindler, M. (2009). "Fiscal multipliers." IMF Staff Position Note, May 20, 2009, SPN/09/11.

Woodford, M. (2011). "Simple analytics of the government expenditure multiplier," *American Economic Journal: Macroeconomics*, 3: 1–35.

6

Monetary Policy with a Fixed Exchange Rate Regime

6.1 Introduction

The dollar peg has been the nominal anchor for monetary policy for many years in the GCC.[1] The pegged exchange rate regime provided certainty about future exchange rates and was overall successful in anchoring inflation at levels below those that are thought to hurt growth (see Chapter 2). However, in theory, the cost of fixing the exchange rate to the US dollar is that domestic interest rates can no longer deviate from foreign interest rates,[2] leaving little space for central banks to control money market liquidity, banks' extension of credit, and economic growth. In practice, in several instances, interest rates in GCC countries have nonetheless deviated vis-à-vis US rates. During the global crisis of 2008–10, several GCC countries that wanted to maintain higher interest rates because of domestic inflationary pressures were able to do so, even though interest rates had fallen dramatically in the US. Partly, this divergence was made feasible because investors' appetite for emerging market assets had decreased and inflows to the GCC unwound. In addition, the monetary authorities in the region employed a variety of instruments to influence liquidity conditions.

GCC central banks commonly manage short-term liquidity conditions through open market operations and standing facilities, liquidity and reserve requirements, issuance of certificates of deposits, repo operations, and macroprudential regulations. Following the tightening of liquidity conditions in the last quarter of 2008, the authorities implemented measures to keep financial systems stable (liquidity support, government guarantees of deposits). Central banks also infused liquidity into the financial system

[1] In Kuwait, a dollar peg was in place from 2003 to May 2007, while a basket peg with undisclosed weights was in place before and has been in place since.

[2] For instance, if interest rates are persistently lower than US interest rates, foreign investors can borrow in local currency and invest in the US. The large capital outflows put pressure on central bank reserves and eventually the central bank is forced to either depreciate the currency or align interest rates.

through repos in the interbank market and provided direct injections of liquidity into the banking system, supplemented by deposits from government institutions.

This chapter first looks at the experience of the GCC countries with their fixed exchange rate regimes (section 6.2) before discussing the pass-through of US interest rates to local rates (and therefore the constraints on monetary policy (sections 6.3 and 6.4). Finally, section 6.5 estimates the influence of interest rates and monetary aggregates on the economy using a monetary policy VAR, extended to take into account that interest rate policy is determined to a large extent by US dollar interest rates.

6.2 Experience with Inflation in the GCC Countries

Inflation in the GCC has historically been controlled thanks to the peg to the dollar. Inflation spiked after the oil price shocks and the First Gulf War, but was below 5 percent for all the GCC countries between 1995 and 2003 (see Figure 6.1). Thereafter, inflation rose as it had in the rest of the world. Although the increase in headline inflation was driven mostly by food and energy prices, core inflation started rising as well. Broadly speaking, three types of underlying inflationary challenges arose. First, many countries faced a combination of strong capital inflows, rapid credit growth, and tightening labor markets. This pointed to evidence of overheating as reflected in rising core inflation and strong growth in asset prices. Second, many commodity-exporting countries saw rising export earnings, pushing up aggregate demand and facilitating domestic credit growth. Third,

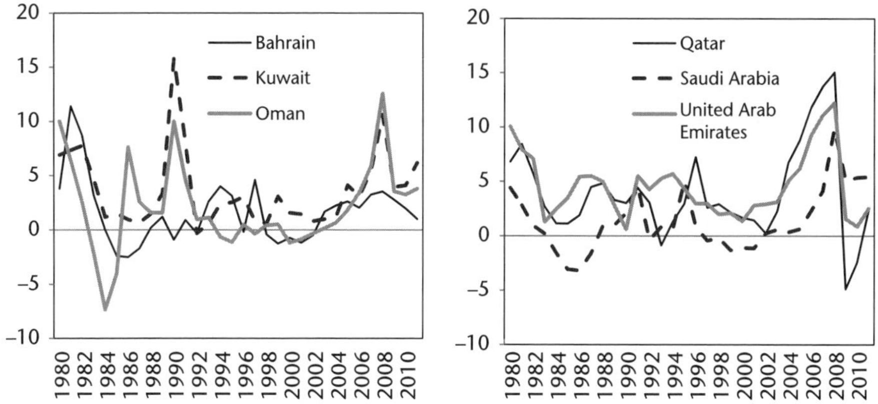

Figure 6.1. CPI inflation, in percentage points
Source: IMF

surging commodity and food prices boosted inflation across the global economy.[3] In fact, for the first time since 1973, countries were hit by a combination of record oil and food prices. In the GCC, capacity constraints, especially in housing, and the limited availability of raw materials exacerbated the situation.

Governments used a combination of monetary, trade, and fiscal responses to counter inflationary pressures. Monetary policy, the first line of defense, was constrained by the peg to the US dollar in the GCC. Nevertheless, monetary authorities attempted to limit overheating by increasing reserve requirements (for example, Oman, Qatar, and Saudi Arabia), imposing limits on credit-deposit ratios to prevent high credit growth (Kuwait and the UAE), and when possible by keeping policy rates high (Bahrain, Qatar, and Kuwait). Speculative inflows, taking advantage of interest rate differentials and expectations of appreciation of currencies, could have taken place, but this did not happen, except in the case of Kuwait—which then changed its exchange rate regime. On May 2007, Kuwait abandoned the Kuwaiti dinar peg to the US dollar in favor of a peg to an undisclosed currency basket, reverting to the exchange system before January 2003. The decision was motivated by the depreciation of the US dollar against other major currencies and the potential impact of increasing inflationary pressures from imported goods.

GCC countries also implemented policies aimed at addressing the local sources of inflation. In Bahrain, the Ministry of Housing and Works coordinated with the real estate bank to increase social housing. The Kuwaiti government increased its capital spending on housing to alleviate shortages, reduced import duties on food items, and increased food subsidies. Oman introduced a wheat subsidy of about $65 per ton in February 2008, capped rent increases, and implemented measures to increase the production capacity of cement. In Qatar, port facilities, which limited the processing of imported materials, were expanded. Private builders were awarded undeveloped land in Doha's suburbs at token rents to increase the supply of housing, and a waiver of customs duties was granted on imports of cement, gravel, and steel from outside the GCC. The Qatari government also imposed a freeze on rents and on the prices of steel, cement, sand, and gabbro stones. A two-year moratorium on the demolition of old housing was decided and the diesel subsidy was extended. The Saudi government waived passport, driver's license, and work permit fees for domestic helpers, lowered import duties by 50 percent or more on 180 items, and increased subsidies on several food items. In the United Arab Emirates, maximum retail prices were introduced on some food items

[3] Global food price inflation almost doubled in 2007. While food inflation in advanced countries was below 3 percent, the figure was almost 10 percent for developing countries (IMF 2008).

and customs duties were removed on cement and steel imports. Cooperative societies were allowed to directly import foodstuffs, and government-owned investment companies were expected to increase the availability of low-cost housing units.

It is difficult to assess the impact of those policies at the frequency used normally to interpret inflation data and monetary policy (six months to a year) because the cycle of inflation ended abruptly with the post-Lehman global recession. In 2009, fuel prices plummeted some 40 percent and global food prices declined almost 15 percent. With global demand squeezed, world inflation of 2.5 percent was less than half its 2008 peak of 6 percent. By the end of 2010, the global average annual inflation rate over the period 2005–10 had shrunk to around 7.5 percent for food and fuel. Inflation in the GCC countries fell as the global economy collapsed and triggered capital outflows, reduced credit, an appreciated US dollar, and lower imported inflation.

6.3 Behavior of GCC Monetary Policy vis-à-vis the United States

Although monetary policy is constrained by the peg to the US dollar, policy rates[4] and interbank rates in the GCC are not identical to US rates. Interbank rates, which may better reflect the monetary policy stance since a range of instruments is used in the region,[5] have mirrored US rates but with significant deviations in Kuwait, Qatar, Oman, and the UAE, particularly since the onset of the global crisis in 2007.

Bova (2012) casts light on the way the GCC rates behaved with respect to the US-Libor rate for the period from January 1993 to May 2009. She finds that the GCC rates were all cointegrated with the US rate, and that the long-run coefficient was very close to one, which constitutes a validation of a long-term interest parity condition.[6] Through a decomposition of the variance of

[4] These are precisely the central bank overnight rate for Bahrain; the repo and discount rate for Kuwait; the overnight central bank and certificates of deposit (CD) rates for Oman; the QCB lending and deposit rates for Qatar, the reverse repo for Saudi Arabia; the CD rate for the UAE.

[5] The use of interbank rates, however, raises problems of interpretation inasmuch it makes it difficult to distinguish whether changes in the rates are simply due to market dynamics (capital flows, interbank market conditions), or more specifically to monetary policy interventions.

[6] Due to lack of data on expected exchange rates, the study only tests for the validity of the covered interest parity condition. A cointegration relationship and an error correction model (ECM) are also estimated for the interest rate spreads in order to evaluate long- and-short-run dynamics. Finally, the study carries out a decomposition of the variance of the interbank rates and GMM estimates to evaluate the relative impact of the US rate and domestic variables—CPI inflation, the spot and forward exchange rate ratios, and the stock market index—on monetary policy.

the interbank rates and GMM estimates, the study also provides some evidence in support of the hypothesis that deviations from the US rate have been determined by monetary policy interventions, although the deviations are not large enough to undermine the validity of the fixed exchange rate regime.[7]

Interest rates also converged within the GCC before 2008 and diverged during the crisis. Espinoza, Prasad, and Williams (2011) found some evidence of interest rate convergence using the widely used measure of beta-convergence (e.g. Baele et al. 2004), and estimated a half-life of two to five months.[8] They also found the cross-sectional variation among interest rates in GCC countries had declined, notwithstanding a widening in this variance with the emergence of the global financial crisis.

6.4 Interest Rate Pass-Through

The response of lending and deposit rates to interbank rates can be quantified by estimating the interest rate pass-through. In this section, the pass-through is estimated country by country using cointegrated VARs. The pass-through can depend upon a number of factors such as: the structure of the financial system (e.g., the extent of the regulation of the financial system, ceilings on interest rates, and geographical and product-line restrictions); the degree of competition between intermediaries; the usage of variable-rate products (both deposits and loans) by the banking system; the existence of lottery systems for deposits; negative real interest rates for deposits over prolonged periods; the response of portfolio substitution to the policy rate; and the transparency of the monetary policy operations.

In addition, in some countries, deposit rates are stickier than lending rates while in others the reverse is true. For instance, in the Euro area, overnight and three-month deposit rates with pass-through reach at most 40 percent, even in the long run. The low pass-through in the Euro area can be attributed partly to the way these deposits are administered and partly to the low elasticity of deposits to interest rates. In contrast to what was found for the Euro area, Mizen and Hofmann (2002) found that, for the UK, pass-through

[7] The speed at which each GCC rate adjusts to its long-run relationship with the US rate can be estimated via an error correction model. Estimates indicate that the Bahraini rate is the quickest to adjust to deviations from the long-run relationship (less than two months), followed by Qatar (less than four months), Saudi Arabia (more than four months), and the United Arab Emirates (about six months). Kuwait and Oman have the slowest adjustment (about a year). For all economies but the UAE, the speed of adjustment is estimated to have slowed in the years corresponding to the financial crisis.

[8] The first measure, beta-convergence, evaluates whether interest rates in countries with relatively high spreads have a tendency to decrease rapidly, relative to those in countries with low spreads. The second measure, sigma-convergence, which draws from the growth literature, tests whether the cross-country standard deviation of interest rates had a declining trend.

from policy rates to deposit rates is larger than that for lending rates. In addition, pass-through may vary by types of loans. Pass-through to consumer lending rates is found to be the weakest, reflecting a variety of factors—weak competition, inelastic demand, asymmetric information, and credit rationing (Bondt 2002; Bondt et al. 2003). In the US, credit card rates remain the stickiest. Pass-through was found at only 30 percent during the 1990s, albeit higher than the almost negligible level during the 1970s (Sellon 2002). A more recent study (Kwapil and Scharler 2010) compared the pass-through in deposit and lending rates in the US and in the Euro area. Their study finds that for the US, the long-run pass-through is complete for most categories of deposit rates and on average 0.57 for lending rates. In the Euro area, the average long-run pass-through to deposit rates amounts to 0.32 and the pass-through for the weighted average lending rates lies at 0.48.

We estimate the pass-through from interbank rates over the period 2004–11, for both deposit and lending rates, to assess the effect of monetary policy on the credit and deposit markets. For each country, the interbank rate is used as a proxy for the policy stance. The weighted average deposit and lending rates are used[9] (see Figure 6.2) for deposit and lending rates in Bahrain, Kuwait, Oman, and Qatar. Data for lending rates and deposit rates were not available for Saudi Arabia and the UAE. Some stylized facts can be obtained from GCC-wide panel estimates (not reported here), which show that the interest rate pass-through is 0.30 and 0.50 for lending and deposit rates, respectively; i.e., a reduction of 100 basis points (bps) in the policy rate led to a reduction of almost 50 bps in the banks' deposit rates and 30 bps in their lending rates. Retail rates used in the estimates include rates on existing and new loans and deposits, so actual transmission to new deposit and loan rates might be somewhat higher.

We analyze, country by country, the short-term dynamics and long-term transmission of interbank rates to bank rates using a simple cointegrated VAR. The cointegrated VAR is constructed around two variables, the interbank rate (*IB*) and the bank interest rate under study (*R* represents alternatively the deposit rate and the lending rate). More precisely, the following model is estimated on monthly data covering the period January 2004–December 2010:

$$\begin{cases} \Delta IB_t = \alpha^1 + \sum\limits_{1 \le s \le 11} \beta_s^1 \Delta IB_{t-s} + \gamma_s^1 \Delta R_{t-s} + \lambda^1 (IB - R)_{t-12} + \varepsilon_t^1 \\ \Delta R_t = \alpha^2 + \sum\limits_{1 \le s \le 11} \beta_s^2 \Delta IB_{t-s} + \gamma_s^2 \Delta R_{t-s} + \lambda^2 (IB - R)_{t-12} + \varepsilon_t^2 \end{cases}$$

[9] For Bahrain, the deposit rate is the average time deposit rate (three-month maturity) and the lending rate is the average lending rate (total, including overdraft approvals). For Kuwait and Oman, the rates are the weighted average deposit and lending rates across maturity. For Qatar, the deposit rate is the one-year time deposit rate, and the lending rate is for loans of maturity less than three years.

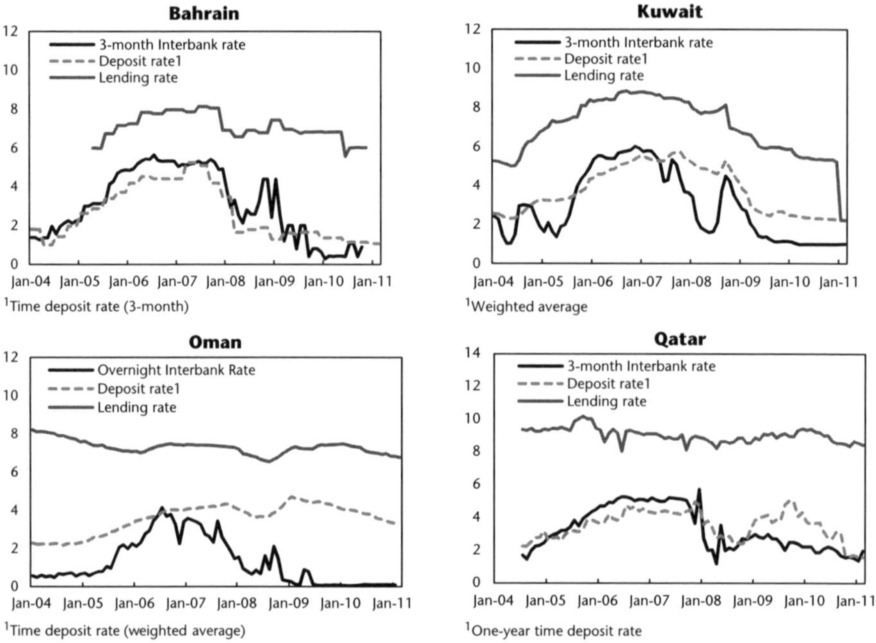

Figure 6.2. Interbank and retail interest rates (in percent)
Source: Haver Analytics and country authorities

The cointegrated VAR is estimated with twelve lags.[10] The long-term relationship is presented in Table 6.1, and the impulse response functions showing short-term adjustments are shown in Figure 6.3. The figure shows the orthogonalized impulse response functions for the two cointegrated VAR models (interbank rate and lending rate; interbank rate and deposit rate). Shocks are identified thanks to a Choleski decomposition where it is assumed that shocks originate first from interbank rates (i.e., the interbank rate is ordered first in the cointegrated VAR). The shock to the interbank rate has been normalized to a permanent one percentage point shock.

Deviations from full pass-through in the long-term relationship (i.e., coefficients lower than 1) are more likely due to regulations in the financial system (caps on interest rates, limits on portfolio shares based on products or

[10] The BIC and the AIC criteria suggested using a very long lag structure (more than 36 lags) but this is not compatible with the number of observations in the dataset. Since these criteria tend to overestimate the number of lags needed, the model was restricted to the twelve lags that are typically needed with monthly data. For Kuwait, the lending rate–interbank rate cointegrated VAR was estimated with only four lags, and the deposit rate–interbank rate cointegrated VAR was estimated with six lags, because VARs with longer lags were unstable. The deposit rate–interbank rate VARs for Oman (six lags) and for Bahrain (nine lags) were also estimated with a shorter lag structure for the same reason.

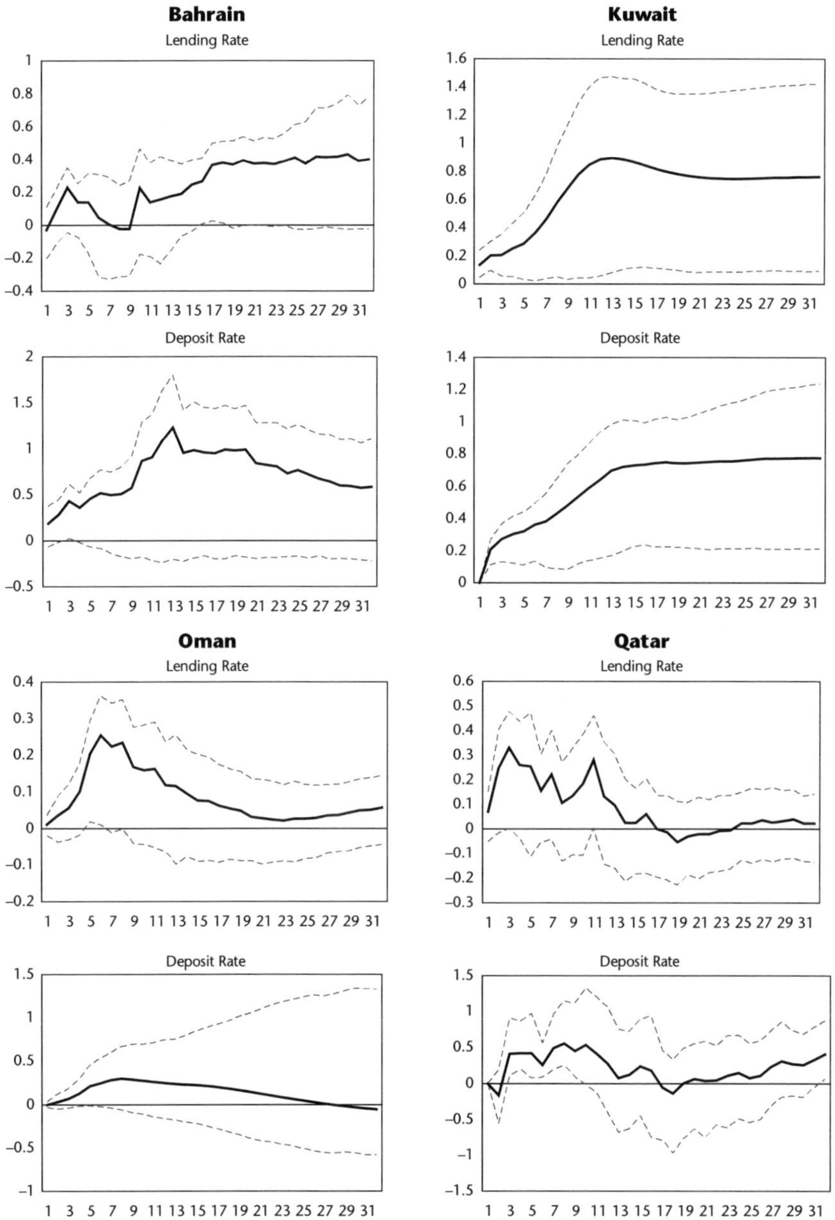

Figure 6.3. Dynamic adjustment of deposit and lending rates to shocks in the interbank rates

Note: Orthogonalized impulse response of deposit and lending rates to a shock in the interbank rate. The interbank rate is ordered first in the Choleski decomposition and the shocks in the interbank rate have been normalized to a permanent 1 percentage point shock. The error bands are the 90% Efron percentile error bands, computed using 500 bootstrap replications (see Efron and Tibshirani 1993).

geographical factors), lack of competition, and to portfolio substitution to the policy rate, which may matter in equilibrium. Slow pass-through in the short term can also be caused by a lack of competition between intermediaries and by the limited use of variable-rate products.

Table 6.1 shows that the long-term relationship between interbank rates and bank lending and deposit rates is strongest for Bahrain and Kuwait. In Bahrain, a 100 basis points increase in the interbank rate is associated in the long run with a 63 basis points increase in the deposit rate and a 29 basis points increase in the lending rate. In Qatar, the relationship is weaker, though still significant for the deposit rate, while there is no relationship between rates in Oman. As expected, because competition for funds drives lending rates in the region, deposit rates are more clearly related to interbank rates compared to lending rates, which are strongly affected by the level (or rather lack of) competition.

Table 6.1. Cointegration vector

Long-term sensitivity to interbank rate	Deposit Rate	Lending Rate
Bahrain	0.63	0.29
Kuwait	0.80	0.74
Oman	–0.05	0.03
Qatar	0.20	0.01

Source: Authors' calculations

Figure 6.3 also shows that lending-rate adjustment is relatively slow in Bahrain, with rates adjusting fully after twenty months. In Kuwait, the adjustment of deposit rates and lending is also slow, with only half of the adjustment captured in the first six months after the shock. In Oman and in Qatar, shocks to the interbank rates do have an immediate effect on deposit and lending rates (albeit with a small sensitivity, of around 0.1 to 0.3) but most of the impact vanishes after ten months.

In Oman, regulations in the banking sector are a likely cause of weak pass-through. Oman's regulations include a ceiling on personal lending and an interest rate cap. Limits to real estate lending, and both absolute and interest rate ceilings on personal loans assigned against salary, are also present in Qatar, where pass-through is weak, especially in the long run. In Kuwait, the lending rates operate within a mandated ceiling benchmarked to the policy discount rate. Limits on consumer credit also exist in Bahrain.

Overall, the cointegrating VAR models show that the limits to the pass-through come essentially from distortions that are active over the long run, suggesting that regulations such as caps on interest rates or on portfolio shares are the main frictions limiting the impact of policy rates. However, the time-varying estimates have documented increases in pass-through over time, reflecting policy efforts to liberalize the banking sector.

Table 6.2. Forecast Error Variance Contribution

Forecast Error Variance Contribution of interbank rate, 12 months ahead	Deposit Rate	Lending Rate
Bahrain	0.52	0.30
Kuwait	0.87	0.54
Oman	0.10	0.16
Qatar	0.38	0.28

Source: Authors' calculations

The Forecast Error Variance Decomposition of the cointegrated VAR model (Table 6.2) allows us to summarize the contribution of shocks to interbank rates to deposit and lending rates. We present the contribution at a horizon of one year. The contribution of shocks to interbank rates is high, except in Oman, where there is no long-term relationship. Shocks to interbank rates would account for 30 to 57 percent of the variance of deposit and lending rates in the region. The countries in which the long-term relationship is the strongest (as shown in Table 6.1) are also the countries for which shocks to interbank rates matter the most, but interbank rates also contribute significantly to the variance of deposit and lending rates via short-term effects (as witnessed by the variance decomposition in Qatar).

6.5 Monetary Transmission in the GCC—A Panel VAR Approach

The monetary transmission mechanism is the process by which monetary policy decisions influence economic outcomes such as output, employment, and inflation. Traditionally, four key channels of monetary policy transmission are identified: interest rates, credit aggregates, asset prices, and exchange rate channels. An expansionary monetary policy is expected to lead to a lowering of the cost of loanable funds, which in turn raises investment and consumption demand that eventually gets reflected in aggregate output and prices. Monetary policy also affects the supply of loanable funds, i.e., the credit channel. A contractionary monetary policy that decreases excess bank reserves also curtails banks' lending capacity. Changes in interest rates could also induce movements in asset prices generating a wealth effect, which is commonly known as the asset price channel. Finally, high interest rates can induce an appreciation of domestic currency, leading to a reduction in net exports and, hence, in aggregate demand and output (this is the exchange rate channel). The main channels of transmission in the GCC are likely to be the interest rate, credit, and asset price channels—under a fixed exchange rate regime the exchange rate channel is inactive.

We investigate the impact of monetary policy shocks in the region using a panel VAR on macroeconomic data for the six countries of the GCC. A VAR approach seems the most appropriate because it allows us to identify monetary policy shocks and to study their dynamic transmission through the economy.

In a fixed exchange regime, monetary shocks have two origins. First, US monetary policy affects local interest rates, credit, asset prices, and activity and it is therefore important to investigate the effect of the US Fed interest rate policy. Second, given that GCC monetary authorities use many tools in the region, shocks to monetary aggregates can also be interpreted as GCC monetary policy shocks (either as money supply shocks or as accommodation of money demand shocks).

A large empirical literature has investigated the impact of monetary policy using VAR models (e.g., Christiano, Eichenbaum, and Evans 1999, for the US; Sims 1992, for several advanced economies). VAR models allow us to disentangle, the impact of an increase in interest rates on growth from the reverse causation stemming from the decision of a central bank to increase interest rates because growth is high. VAR models help "explain the correlation" between interest rates and growth by making specific *identifying* assumptions—for instance, that monetary policy shocks have no immediate effect on growth. With this assumption, any contemporaneous correlation between policy rates and growth must be due to the response of policy to growth.

This strategy for identifying US monetary policy shocks follows the literature on the US economy (e.g., Christiano, Eichenbaum, and Evans 1999; Hanson 2004; see more details in section 6.5.2) and we take a similar route. We extend the VAR model of the US economy by including macroeconomic data on the GCC (non-oil growth and inflation), and we add the identifying assumption that GCC shocks do not influence contemporaneously US variables. This approach has been used for instance by Miniane and Rogers (2007) to assess whether capital controls reduce the transmission of US monetary policy shocks to other advanced and emerging economies.

Monetary VARs have been used on quarterly or even monthly data in advanced economies, but macroeconomic data in the GCC exist only at an annual frequency. The annual frequency of the data poses two serious challenges. The first one is that of sample size in VAR models that would include many variables (eight variables in total since we include variables for the US and for the GCC). Macroeconomic data before 1980 is of little use given its uncertain quality and the structural break of the 1970s. As a result, the annual dataset is too small to estimate a model country-by-country. This is why a panel VAR is our preferred model, although it is based on the restrictive assumption (especially given the analysis presented earlier in this chapter) of homogeneity of coefficients in the different equations estimated.

The second problem is that the identification of US monetary policy shocks is typically based on the assumption that the US economy does not react to monetary shocks within the unit time period, which is why the preferred time unit in the literature has been a quarter or even a month. We therefore investigate both VARs based on annual data and VARs based on quarterly data with annual GCC data interpolated into quarterly data.

6.5.1 Data

An eight-variable panel VAR was estimated on non-oil real GDP (the "GCC Y" variable), government expenditure (GCC G), CPI inflation (GCC P), and broad money (GCC M2) in the GCC, from 1980 to 2010.[11] In addition, we used the Fed Funds Rate (FFR) as an indicator of imported monetary policy, and US GDP (US Y), the US Personal Consumption Deflator (US P), as well as the IMF agriculture commodity price index (COM P) to identify US monetary shocks. The data come from IMF (2011) and the US Bureau of Economic Analysis (2011). All variables but the Fed Funds Rate were expressed in logarithm and found to be integrated of order 1 (I(1)) in log level but stationary in difference (including prices in the US and in the GCC) according to the Levin, Lin, and Chu (2002) panel unit root test.

6.5.2 Annual Data Panel VAR

The annual data VAR is estimated on log levels (except for the Fed Funds Rate) using OLS, as is common in the literature (e.g. Christiano, Eichenbaum, and Evans 1999). The VAR is estimated with three lags, since the size of the panel (162 observations) allows us to maintain enough degrees of freedom. The

Table 6.3. Correlation Matrix of Innovations

	COM P	US Y	US P	FFR	GCC G	GCC Y	GCC P	GCC M2
COM P	1.00							
US Y	–0.27	1.00						
US P	0.56	–0.10	1.00					
FFR	0.15	0.39	–0.12	1.00				
GCC G	0.17	–0.13	0.12	0.00	1.00			
GCC Y	0.03	0.09	0.15	–0.06	0.09	1.00		
GCC P	0.01	–0.02	0.02	–0.09	0.04	0.02	1.00	
GCC M2	–0.07	0.07	0.08	–0.01	0.01	0.18	–0.15	1.00

[11] Data for Oman and the UAE starts in 1981; data for Qatar starts in 1983.

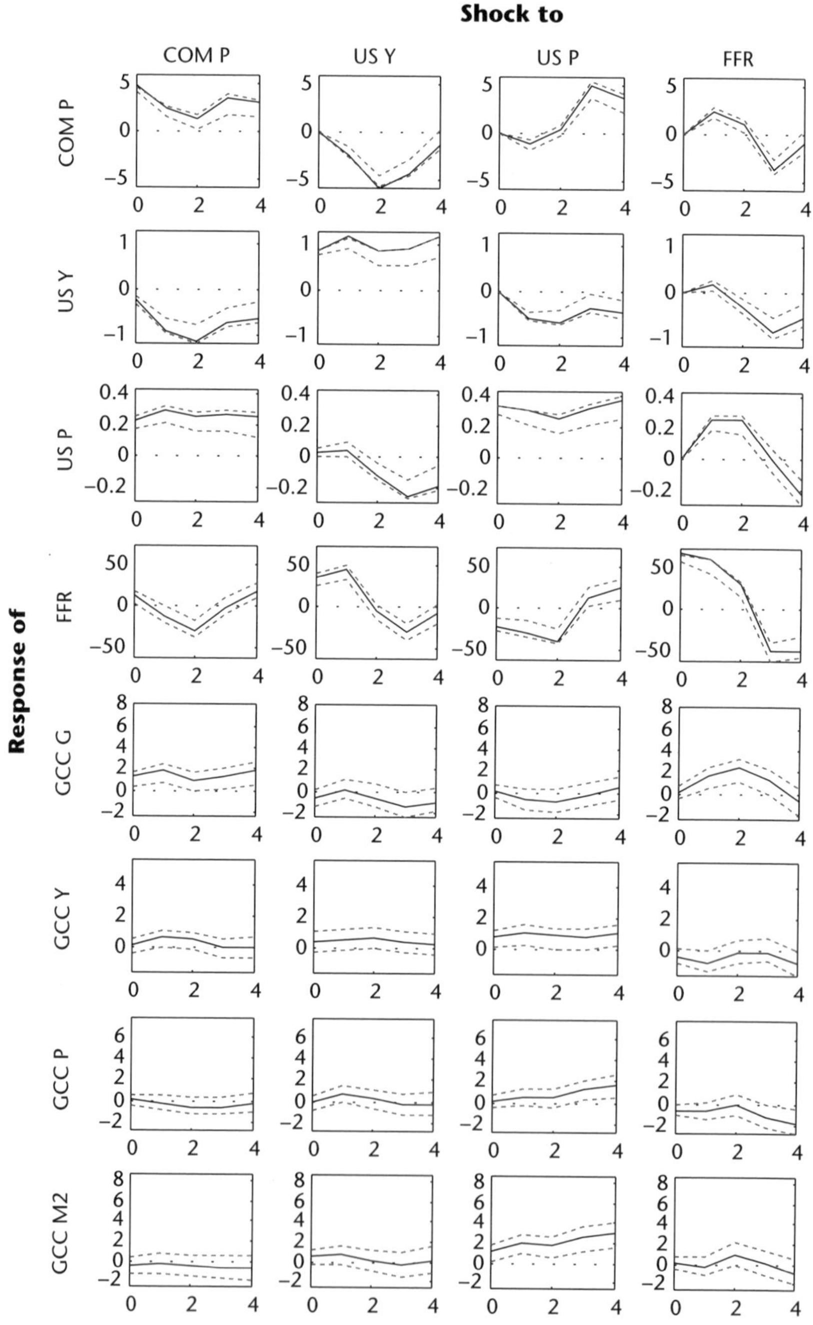

Figure 6.4. Annual data panel VAR

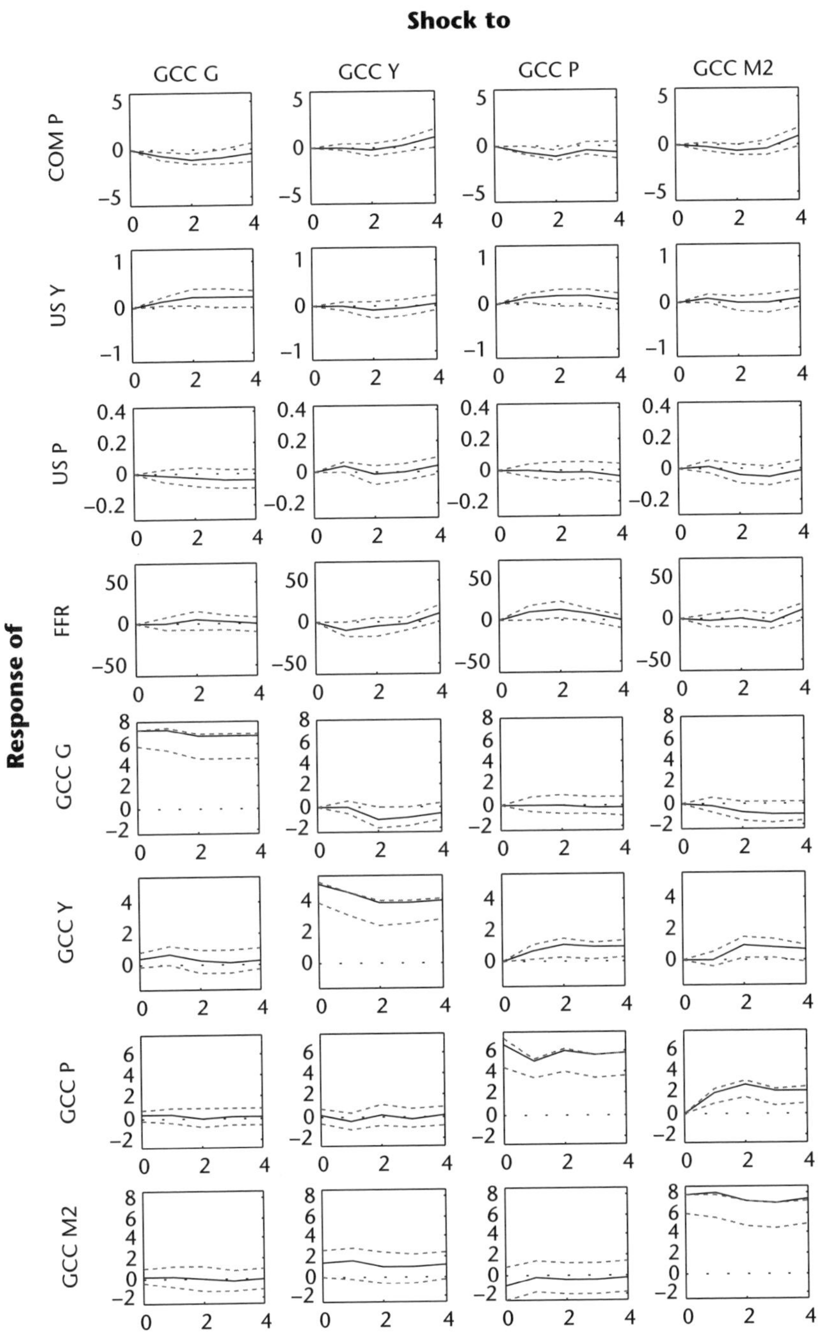

Figure 6.4. (Continued)

Table 6.4. OLS estimates of the annual VAR

	(1)	(2)	(3)	(4)	(5)	(6)	(7)	(8)
Equation	COM P	US Y	US P	FFR	GCC G	GCC Y	GCC P	GCC M2
$(\text{COM P})_{-1}$	0.350***	–0.0731***	–0.00344	–2.026	0.0114	0.0638	–0.0335	–0.155
	(0.106)	(0.0185)	(0.00898)	(1.593)	(0.212)	(0.121)	(0.0483)	(0.117)
$(\text{COM P})_{-2}$	–0.530***	0.0315**	–0.0118	–0.509	–0.132	–0.155	–0.0179	–0.308***
	(0.0881)	(0.0154)	(0.00746)	(1.380)	(0.184)	(0.105)	(0.0418)	(0.101)
$(\text{COM P})_{-3}$	0.122*	0.0194	0.0120**	1.196	0.130	0.122	–0.0267	–0.00277
	(0.0689)	(0.0120)	(0.00583)	(1.053)	(0.140)	(0.0800)	(0.0319)	(0.0774)
$(\text{US Y})_{-1}$	–3.487***	1.059***	–0.0719	28.65***	0.399	0.809	–0.0736	1.321*
	(0.678)	(0.118)	(0.0573)	(9.158)	(1.220)	(0.697)	(0.278)	(0.673)
$(\text{US Y})_{-2}$	–2.128***	–0.727***	–0.144**	–76.37***	–2.122	–2.602***	–0.471	–3.631***
	(0.657)	(0.115)	(0.0556)	(10.11)	(1.346)	(0.769)	(0.306)	(0.743)
$(\text{US Y})_{-3}$	4.220***	0.715***	0.316***	53.12***	2.163**	1.937***	0.467*	2.082***
	(0.500)	(0.0872)	(0.0423)	(8.113)	(1.081)	(0.617)	(0.246)	(0.596)
$(\text{US P})_{-1}$	–0.499	–1.521***	1.169***	–38.51**	2.129	0.399	–0.375	0.925
	(1.169)	(0.204)	(0.0989)	(18.72)	(2.494)	(1.424)	(0.567)	(1.376)
$(\text{US P})_{-2}$	–2.171	1.392***	–0.422**	18.17	–2.612	0.0724	0.802	1.774
	(2.044)	(0.357)	(0.173)	(33.21)	(4.423)	(2.525)	(1.006)	(2.440)
$(\text{US P})_{-3}$	4.131***	–0.0509	0.0799	2.875	0.00965	–0.813	–0.307	–1.914
	(1.283)	(0.224)	(0.109)	(21.16)	(2.818)	(1.609)	(0.641)	(1.555)
$(\text{FFR})_{-1}$	0.0288***	0.00365**	0.00316***	0.794***	0.00379	–0.00316	0.00681*	0.0109
	(0.00836)	(0.00146)	(0.000707)	(0.116)	(0.0154)	(0.00879)	(0.00350)	(0.00849)
$(\text{FFR})_{-2}$	–0.00281	–0.00240*	–0.00233***	–0.171	–0.00329	0.00646	–0.00213	0.0131
	(0.00797)	(0.00139)	(0.000674)	(0.111)	(0.0148)	(0.00842)	(0.00336)	(0.00814)
$(\text{FFR})_{-3}$	–0.0527***	–0.00389***	–0.00194***	–0.504***	–0.0100	–0.0162**	–0.00732***	–0.0280***
	(0.00551)	(0.000962)	(0.000466)	(0.0876)	(0.0117)	(0.00666)	(0.00266)	(0.00644)
$(\text{GCC G})_{-1}$	–0.0339	0.0109	–0.000676	–0.801	0.898***	0.186***	0.0266	0.0582
	(0.0395)	(0.00689)	(0.00334)	(0.647)	(0.0862)	(0.0492)	(0.0196)	(0.0476)

$(GCC\ G)_{-2}$	0.0845	–0.0240**	0.00178	–0.0118	–0.146	–0.0763	–0.0295	–0.106*
	(0.0532)	(0.00928)	(0.00450)	(0.873)	(0.116)	(0.0664)	(0.0265)	(0.0641)
$(GCC\ G)_{-3}$	–0.0609	0.0162**	–0.00153	0.866	0.200**	–0.119**	0.00703	0.0898*
	(0.0411)	(0.00717)	(0.00348)	(0.673)	(0.0896)	(0.0511)	(0.0204)	(0.0494)
$(GCC\ Y)_{-1}$	–0.103	0.0409***	0.000226	1.756*	0.260*	0.715***	0.00379	0.119
	(0.0634)	(0.0111)	(0.00537)	(1.030)	(0.137)	(0.0783)	(0.0312)	(0.0757)
$(GCC\ Y)_{-2}$	–0.0289	–0.0428***	–0.00415	–1.512	–0.268	0.302***	–0.0211	–0.260***
	(0.0756)	(0.0132)	(0.00640)	(1.245)	(0.166)	(0.0947)	(0.0377)	(0.0915)
$(GCC\ Y)_{-3}$	0.132**	0.00164	0.00393	–0.220	0.0150	–0.0189	0.0144	0.134**
	(0.0552)	(0.00963)	(0.00467)	(0.903)	(0.120)	(0.0687)	(0.0274)	(0.0663)
$(GCC\ P)_{-1}$	0.209	–0.0630*	0.0196	3.111	0.398	–0.237	1.521***	0.167
	(0.194)	(0.0339)	(0.0164)	(2.957)	(0.394)	(0.225)	(0.0896)	(0.217)
$(GCC\ P)_{-2}$	–0.536	0.161***	–0.0370	2.245	–0.356	–0.255	–0.728***	-0.259
	(0.348)	(0.0607)	(0.0294)	(5.191)	(0.691)	(0.395)	(0.157)	(0.382)
$(GCC\ P)_{-3}$	0.366*	–0.107***	0.0185	–5.372	0.0537	0.642**	0.183*	0.161
	(0.218)	(0.0381)	(0.0185)	(3.367)	(0.449)	(0.256)	(0.102)	(0.247)
$(GCC\ M2)_{-1}$	–0.0356	0.0170	0.00162	–0.657	0.0434	0.125	0.0172	0.901***
	(0.0720)	(0.0126)	(0.00609)	(1.159)	(0.154)	(0.0881)	(0.0351)	(0.0852)
$(GCC\ M2)_{-2}$	–0.0200	–0.0415**	–0.0166**	0.357	0.0407	–0.113	–0.000106	0.0418
	(0.0934)	(0.0163)	(0.00790)	(1.516)	(0.202)	(0.115)	(0.0460)	(0.111)
$(GCC\ M2)_{-3}$	0.0642	0.0220*	0.0154***	0.206	–0.0514	–0.00696	–0.0151	0.0243
	(0.0678)	(0.0118)	(0.00573)	(1.112)	(0.148)	(0.0846)	(0.0337)	(0.0817)
Constant	11.57***	0.601***	–0.107	39.70*	–2.345	–0.509	0.710	0.573
	(1.318)	(0.230)	(0.111)	(21.08)	(2.808)	(1.603)	(0.639)	(1.549)
Observations	162	162	162	168	168	168	168	168

Standard errors in parentheses

*** $p < 0.01$, ** $p < 0.05$, * $p < 0.1$

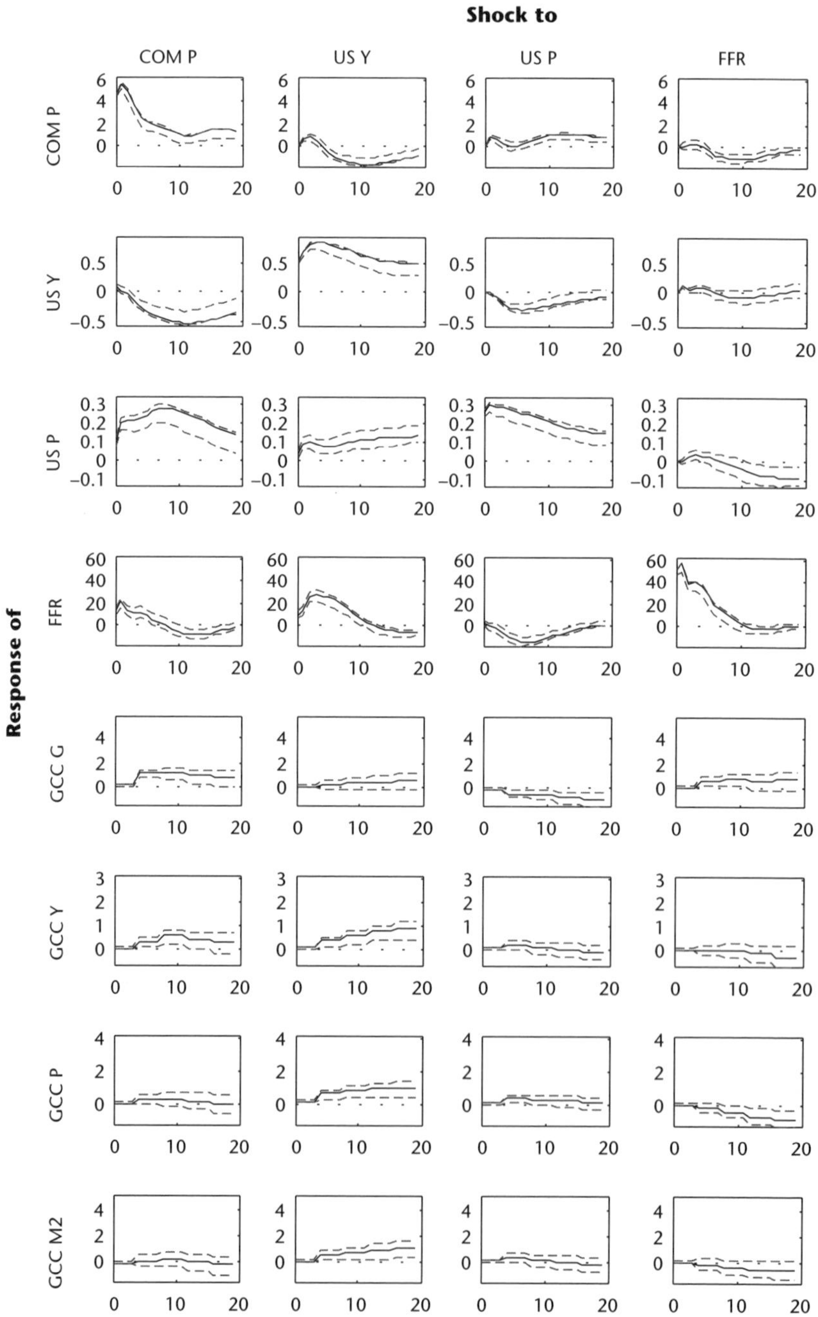

Figure 6.5. Quarterly data panel VAR

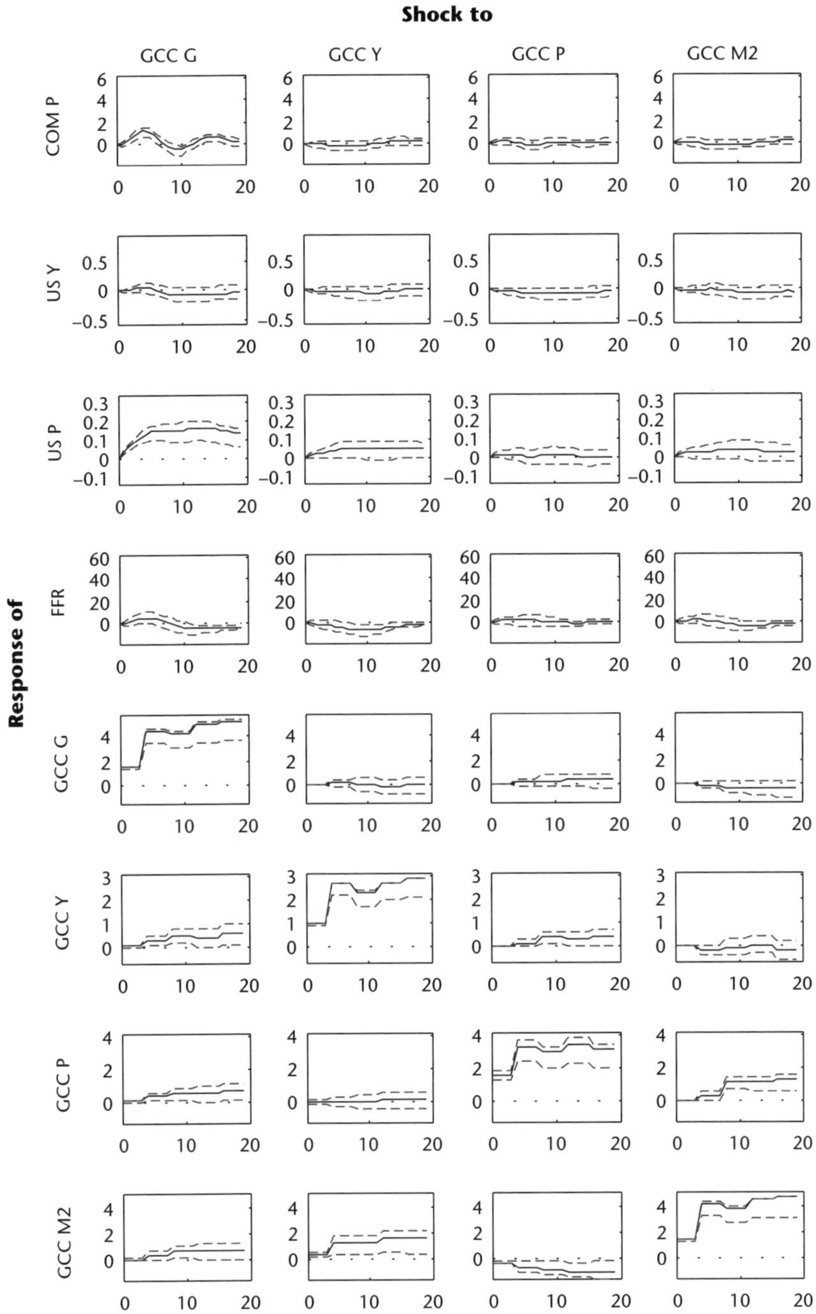

Figure 6.5. (Continued)

identification procedure is based on the Choleski decomposition of the correlation matrix of the reduced-form residuals. This correlation matrix (Table 6.3) shows that shocks to world commodity prices are negatively correlated with shocks to economic activity in the US. In addition, world commodity prices are positively correlated with US inflation, US policy rates, and government spending in the GCC. Shocks to growth and to the Fed Funds Rate are also strongly correlated, and there seems to be some contemporaneous correlation between growth in the US and growth in the GCC.

In the Choleski identification procedure, the commodity price index is ordered first, followed by US GDP, US prices, and then the Fed Funds Rate. We also assume that the GCC variables are ordered after the US variables, because it is unlikely that the macroeconomic situation of the GCC affects the US contemporaneously. This ordering is also the one chosen by Miniane and Rogers (2007). The ordering of GCC variables is akin to that of US variables in the monetary VAR literature: GDP is ordered first, followed by the CPI and the monetary aggregate M2. In addition, we added a variable capturing government spending (GCC G), and ordered it first among the GCC variables because government spending is planned ahead within a budget (see also Chapter 5).

The orthogonalized impulse response functions of the annual data VAR are shown in Figure 6.4. The error bands (excluding 10 percent of the simulations on each side, and therefore yielding statistical significance at the 90th percentile) were constructed using 500 bootstrap replications, following the method of Runkle (1987). Shocks to the Fed Funds Rate of around 50 basis points reduce growth and prices in the US in year 3 but have no effect on activity, prices, or broad money in the GCC. Permanent increases by 8 percent of broad money (M2, see the last column in Figure 6.4) increased prices by 2 percent and non-oil GDP by slightly less than 1 percent.

However, we find that the VAR impulse responses suffer from a "Price Puzzle", the counterintuitive finding that increases in policy rates are followed by more inflation. A Price Puzzle is thought to indicate that US monetary policy has not been well identified (Zha 1997; Sims 1998). The inclusion of the IMF agriculture commodity price index as the first variable in the VAR is known to prevent the occurrence of the Price Puzzle in quarterly or monthly VAR, and the interpretation since Sims (1992) has been that commodity prices help forecast inflation and therefore are used by the Fed to take decisions on monetary policy. Therefore, forgetting this variable could lead us to misestimate the systematic component (and therefore the shock component) of monetary policy (Zha1997; Sims 1998).[12]

[12] Hanson (2004) has argued that this interpretation is not supported by the data because the commodity prices that most reduce the Price Puzzle are not those that forecast better future inflation.

The Price Puzzle remained present in our baseline model with the IMF agricultural price index, and the result did not change when using a different commodity price variable (the IMF global commodity price index), a different US price index (the US CPI), or when estimating the model in growth rates as opposed to log levels. These results confirm that it is difficult to identify a US monetary policy shock using annual data. The (reduced-form) OLS estimates of the VAR (Table 6.4) may in fact be more informative than the orthogonalized impulse responses because to a large extent the US variables (and the Fed Funds Rate) are exogenous in the GCC equations. Table 6.4 shows that the Fed Funds Rate is negatively related to non-oil GDP, CPI, and M2 in the GCC, but the relationship is stronger with the third lag of the Fed Funds Rate.

6.5.3 Quarterly Data Panel VAR

We turn now to the results of the quarterly data panel VAR. The annual data for the GCC was interpolated using cubic spline interpolation[13] and the VAR model was estimated with four lags (as suggested by the Aikake and Schwarz information criteria—see also the robustness exercises later in this section). The orthogonalized impulse response functions (IRFs) for the baseline VAR (with the same ordering as the annual data VAR) are shown in Figure 6.5. Although the VAR was estimated using the interpolated quarterly data, the IRFs for the GCC variables have been converted into annual IRFs because their quarterly dynamics is due to their own interpolations.

The quarterly US-GCC VAR model is free of the Price Puzzle issue and the impulse responses resemble closely those obtained for the US in the literature (Hanson 2004). This result increases our confidence that the US monetary shocks are better identified in the quarterly VAR. An increase in the US policy rate by 100 basis points reduces after ten quarters US activity and US prices by around 0.1 percent. The reduction in US activity is marginally insignificant at the 90th percent level. The monetary policy shock also has a strong effect on world commodity prices (a reduction by 2 percent), and probably as a result of this, on GCC prices which are reduced by 0.8 percent ten quarters after the shock (this result is statistically significant at the 90th percent level). Non-oil GDP in the GCC is also reduced by around 0.1 percent and M2 by 0.6 percent but these impulse response functions are not significantly different from 0. Shocks to M2 (last column) increase prices in the GCC with an elasticity of around 0.3, but the effect on economic activity is insignificant. These results suggest that monetary policy as run by GCC central banks, with a focus on

[13] Data for broad money which is available at the quarterly frequency was also interpolated from annual data to keep a consistent method for GCC data.

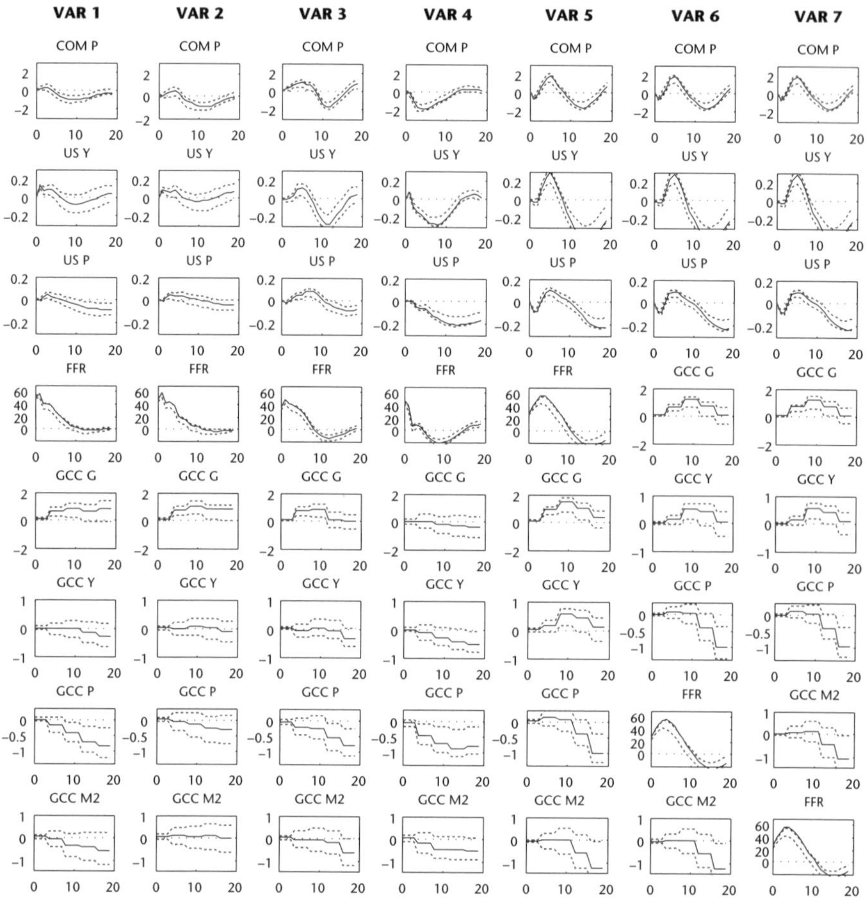

Figure 6.6. Robustness to VAR specification composition

Note: VAR 1: Baseline VAR; VAR 2: 5 lags; VAR 3: 8 lags; VAR 4: 1980–94 sample; VAR 5: 1995–2010 sample; VAR 6: Fed Funds Rate ordered second to last; VAR 7: Fed Funds Rate ordered last

monetary aggregates given the limits of the peg, is important for price stability but has a limited effect on economic activity.

The VAR also provides some interesting results regarding the impact of the other variables, although this is not the primary objective of the analysis. Shocks to world commodity prices boost government spending, certainly because there is a strong relationship between oil revenues and government spending in the region. In turn, shocks to government spending increase non-oil GDP, with an elasticity of around 0.1 after ten quarters. This elasticity would imply a short-term multiplier of around 0.15–0.2, slightly lower than what was found in the simpler models analyzed in Chapter 5. Shocks to US GDP have positive spillovers on GCC non-oil GDP, with an elasticity of 0.9 after ten quarters. Finally, according to the forecast error variance decomposition, the main drivers of non-oil GDP are commodity prices, government spending, and US growth (see Chapter 5 for a country-by-country analysis of these interactions). As is often found in monetary VARs, monetary policy shocks contribute relatively little to the variance of economic activity.

We tested the robustness of the responses of a shock to the Fed Funds Rate for different modifications to the baseline VAR. The VARs were estimated dropping one country at a time, to provide information about the importance of the homogeneity assumption of the panel. The IRF was found to be robust to the exclusion of data from the UAE, Qatar, Bahrain, or Oman, but excluding data from Saudi Arabia or Kuwait resulted in different and counter-intuitive IRF for GCC prices. Saudi Arabia and Kuwait are the largest economies of the GCC. We therefore think the specifications that include these two countries in the sample are representative of the GCC economy for the purpose of this analysis.

The second set of robustness exercises consists in changing the number of lags in the model, the time period for the estimation, and the ordering of the variables with particular reference to the Fed Funds Rate (Figure 6.6). The IRF to a shock in the Fed Funds Rate is almost unchanged when adding one lag to the model (VAR 2). A Price Puzzle however emerges again when the model includes eight lags (VAR 3), though after three years the impact of monetary tightening on prices in the US and in the GCC is again negative.

The identification of a US monetary policy shock seems also less robust when the data is restricted to the second part of our sample (1995–2010, VAR 5). In that period, there is a remaining although minor, Price Puzzle, as the US monetary policy shock is followed by a small increase in US prices.[14] More significantly, over that period, the US monetary policy shock is counterintuitively followed by an increase in US growth, world commodity prices, and probably as a result GCC growth, for the first two years after the shock. The VAR estimate over the earlier period (1980–94, VAR 4) is more in line with theoretical priors. World commodity prices, US inflation, US growth, GCC growth, GCC inflation, and broad money all decrease after the US monetary policy shock, roughly in line with what was found over the entire sample.

Finally, the estimated impact of US monetary policy shocks on GCC prices did not seem to depend much on the specific position of the Fed Funds Rate (see VAR 6 and VAR 7), although the different ordering did generate an

[14] Hanson (2004) noted that the Price Puzzle was also stronger over the period 1959–79.

unappealing impact of US monetary policy on global prices, US growth, and as a result GCC growth.

6.6 Summary and Policy Implications

In the GCC, monetary policy is constrained by the exchange rate regime. This is why central banks in the region use various instruments to affect liquidity conditions and thus interbank rates. However, the pass-through of changes in the local interbank rates to local deposit and lending rates in the four countries analyzed—Bahrain, Kuwait, Oman, and Qatar—is less than complete (although the long-term relationship between interbank rates and bank lending and deposit rates is stronger in Bahrain and Kuwait). Nevertheless, a panel VAR model suggests that there is a strong and statistically significant impact of US monetary policy on broad money, non-oil activity, and inflation in the GCC region. A 100 basis points increase in the Fed Funds Rate decreases broad money growth by 0.6 percentage point and non-oil activity by 0.1 percent ten quarters after the shock. Global commodity prices are also reduced by 2 percent, which contributes to lower inflation in the GCC (–0.8 percent).

The low pass-through of interest rates is not surprising, given the shallow nature of money markets in the GCC countries. Policy signals will transmit quickly and more efficiently onto market rates if the financial system is developed and competitive. A thin market would typically display a high degree of volatility in interest rates, making it difficult for market participants to disentangle noise from policy signals, and this may reduce the pass-through. The existence of arbitrary limits on lending and interest rate ceilings would limit the transmission of interest rate movements. This is why continued efforts to develop domestic financial markets should be the key focus of increasing interest rate pass-through and strengthening monetary policy transmission.

References

Baele, L., Ferrando, A., Hördahl, P., Krylova, E., and Monnet, C. (2004). "Measuring financial integration in the Euro area." ECB Occasional Paper No. 14. Frankfurt am Main: European Central Bank.

Bondt, Gabe de (2002). "Retail bank interest rate pass-through: New evidence at the Euro level." ECB Working Paper No. 136, April. Frankfurt am Main: European Central Bank.

Bondt, Gabe de, Mojon, B., and Valla, N. (2005). "Term structure and the sluggishness of retail bank rates in Euro Area countries." ECB Working Paper No. 518, April. Frankfurt am Main: European Central Bank.

Bova, E. (2012). "Interest rate spread in the GCC: The role of monetary policy intervention." Mimeo, IMF.

Christiano, L. J., Eichenbaum, M., and Evans, C. L. (1999). "Monetary policy shocks: What have we learned and to what end?" *Handbook of Macroeconomics*, 1: 65–148.

Efron, B. and Tibshirani, R. J. (1993). *An Introduction to the Bootstrap*. New York: Chapman & Hall.

Espinoza, R., Prasad, A., and Williams, O. (2011). "Regional financial integration in the GCC," *Emerging Markets Review*, 12: 354–70.

Hanson, M. S. (2004). "The price puzzle reconsidered," *Journal of Monetary Economics*, 51: 1385–413.

International Monetary Fund (IMF) (2008). "Food and Fuel Prices—Recent Developments, Macroeconomic Impact, and Policy Responses: An Update." SM/08/182, June.

—— (2011). *World Economic Outlook*, September. Washington DC: International Monetary Fund.

Kwapil, C. and Scharler, J. (2010). "Interest rate pass-through, monetary policy rules, and macroeconomic stability," *Journal of International Money and Finance*, 29: 236–51.

Levin A., Lin, F., and Chu, C. (2002). "Unit root tests in panel data: Asymptotic and nite-sample properties," *Journal of Econometrics*, 108: 1–24.

Miniane, J. and Rogers, J. H. (2007). "Capital controls and the international transmission of U.S. money shocks," *Journal of Money, Credit and Banking*, 39: 1003–35.

Mizen, P. and Hofmann, B. (2002). "Base rate pass-through: Evidence from banks' and building societies' retail rates." Bank of England Working Paper No. 170. London.

Runkle, D. E. (1987). "Vector autoregressions and reality," *Journal of Business and Economics Statistics*, 5: 437–42.

Sellon Jr, G. (2002). "The changing U.S. financial system: Some implications for monetary transmission mechanism," *Federal Reserve Bank of Kansas City Economic Review*, First Quarter.

Sims, C. (1992). "Interpreting the macroeconomic time series facts: The effects of monetary policy," *European Economic Review*, 36: 975–1000.

Sims, C. (1998). "Comment on Glenn Rudebusch's 'Do measures of monetary policy in a VAR make sense?'" *International Economic Review*, 36: 933–41.

Zha, T. (1997). "Identifying monetary policy: A primer," *Federal Reserve Bank of Atlanta Economic Review*, 82: 26–43.

7

Nonperforming Loans and Financial Stability

7.1 Introduction

The global crisis exposed the vulnerabilities of the banks in the GCC countries to varying degrees. The favorable macroeconomic environment in the years preceding the global crisis had been conducive to high credit growth and lower nonperforming loans (NPLs) of banks. Although the direct exposure of the GCC banks to the subprime market was low, the global financial crisis and the fall in oil prices after the collapse of Lehman Brothers triggered a spiral of falling asset prices and liquidity and credit tightening. This interaction weakened the financial system's balance sheets and prompted government intervention in the financial sector. In 2009, NPLs increased sharply and credit stagnated, raising worries that the recovery could be slowed down by credit constraints.

The low levels of NPLs in the GCC before the crisis were to a large extent the result of the good economic fortune of the region, and the downturn in the Gulf economies meant that credit risk could worsen. NPLs had reached very high levels in the GCC before the boom years and NPL ratios in double digits were not uncommon.[1] We present in Table 7.1 some summary statistics on NPLs in the GCC banking system, based on a Bankscope database that covers around eighty banks in the GCC (see Table 7.3 for coverage).

[1] Nonperforming loans increased in most GCC countries in 2009 to 3.9 percent in Bahrain, 9.7 percent in Kuwait, 2.8 percent in Oman, 1.7 percent in Qatar, 3.3 percent in Saudi Arabia, and 4.6 percent in the UAE. (Khamis and Senhadji 2010).

Table 7.1. Summary statistics on nonperforming loans, 1995–2008

	Bahrain	Kuwait	Oman	Qatar	Saudi Arabia	UAE
No. Banks	26	15	16	9	20	32
No. Obs	161	120	99	84	163	219
NPL ratio in 2008 (unweighted)	2.9	5.5	1.2	1.7	1.4	2.4
NPL ratio (historical data)						
25th percentile	2.1	3.4	3.5	1.3	1.7	1.7
Median	5.9	6.7	6.5	3.1	3.1	4.3
75th percentile	14.8	12.5	11.3	11.5	7.3	9.6

Source: Bankscope and authors' calculations

The GCC countries had experienced particularly high levels of NPLs in the 2000–2 period, when low oil prices and deflated stock markets hurt liquidity and balance sheets (Figure 7.1).

Although impaired loans fluctuated with the macroeconomic conditions, banks' individual situations mattered as well. Figure 7.2 shows for Bahrain and Oman (and the same is true across the GCC) that although in good times NPLs are low across the board, in bad times, NPLs increase much faster for banks with higher initial levels of NPLs.

Financial soundness indicators (FSIs) post-crisis show that the banking sector appears now generally sound, but there are risks associated with banks' direct and indirect exposure to real estate and stock markets. As FSIs are available with a lag, they tend however to be backward-looking and the average masks the distribution across banks. Nonetheless, stress tests for some GCC countries (e.g. Kuwait, see IMF 2010) suggest that the banking system is resilient to various credit and market events and it would take a significant increase in NPLs before the need arises for recapitalization of any bank in these countries.[2]

The crisis highlighted the importance of linking the macroeconomic conditions to the health of the banking system. The main goal of macroeconomic stress tests, which have become more common with the financial crisis, is to identify structural vulnerabilities in the financial system in order to assess its resilience to shocks (Drehmann 2008), in particular losses in the loan books. Credit risk increases as the economic situation deteriorates and interest payments rise, a result found in many credit risk models (see for instance IMF 2006).

This chapter focuses on the relationship between macroeconomic variables and NPLs (credit risk) in GCC banks' books. This is to the best of our knowledge the first attempt to model NPLs in the GCC countries, using bank-level

[2] Recent IMF stress tests conducted by staff for Kuwait and Bahrain show that the respective banking systems are adequately capitalized and that it would take a significant increase in NPLs before the need arises for recapitalization of any bank (see IMF Article IV reports for Kuwait and Bahrain).

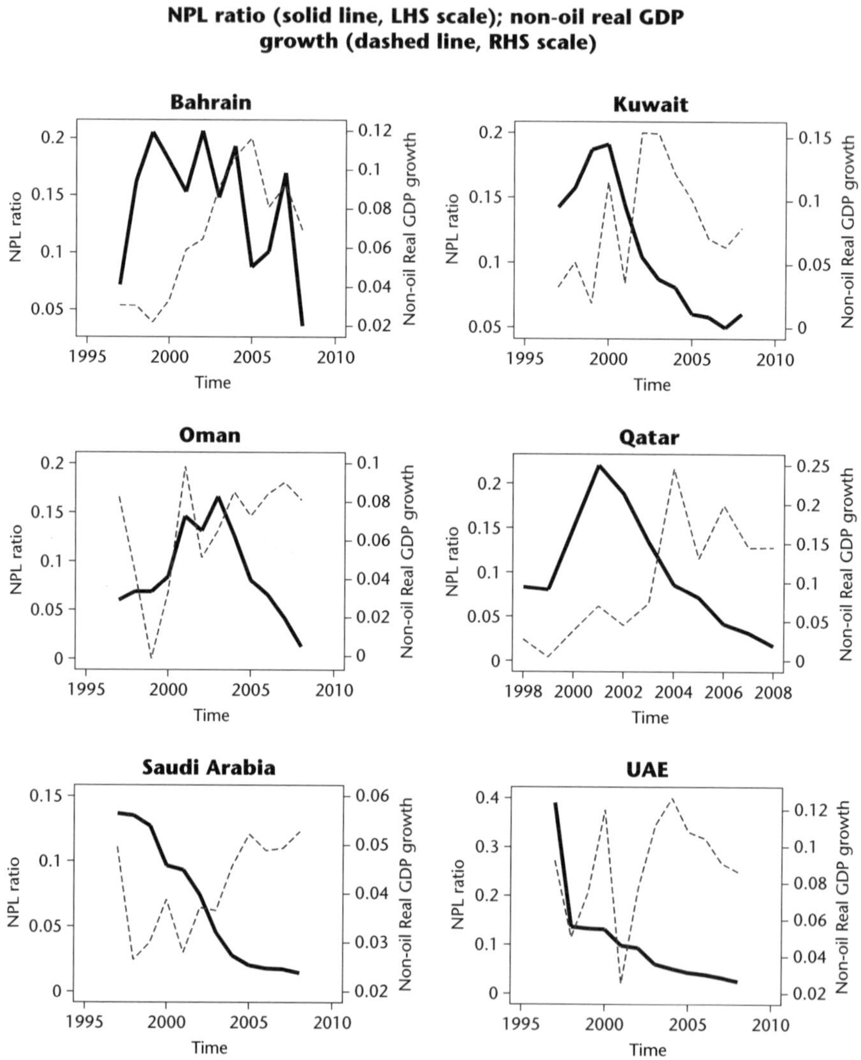

Figure 7.1. NPL ratio and economic activity in the GCC
Source: Bankscope and authors' calculations

data. This additional level of disaggregation strengthens the accuracy of estimation and allows a discussion of the impact of macro-variables and of bank-specific characteristics. It also allows a discussion of meaningful here nonlinearities, in particular the finding that banks with higher levels of NPLs are also more sensitive to macroeconomic shocks. The model estimates elasticities that are a key input for stress-testing banks' balance sheets in the GCC.

The study conducts this analysis using bankwise data from Bankscope. According to a dynamic panel estimated over 1995–2008 on around eighty

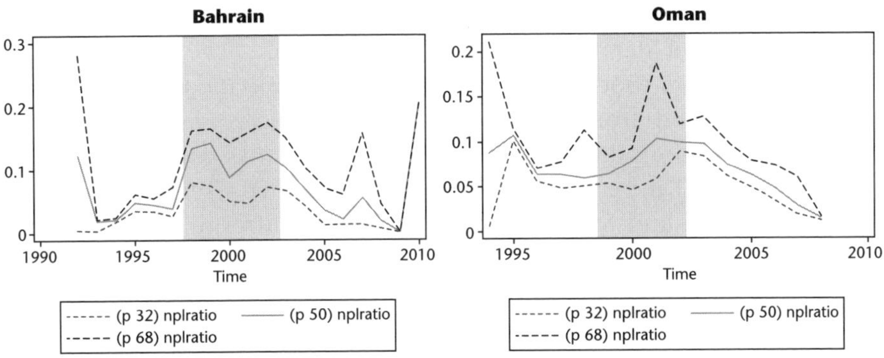

Figure 7.2. Bank heterogeneity and the business cycle

Note: Periods of lowest growth in shaded area

Source: Bankscope and authors' calculations

banks in the GCC region, the NPL ratio worsens as economic growth becomes lower and interest rates increase. Larger banks and banks with lower expenses would also have lower NPLs. Finally, high credit growth in the past could generate higher NPLs in the future. According to all models, NPLs are very persistent, which would suggest that the response of credit losses to the macroeconomic cycle could take time to materialize, although it would also imply that NPLs would then cumulate to high levels. The model implies that the cumulative effect of macroeconomic shocks over a three-year horizon is indeed large.

Conversely, a deterioration in banks' balance sheets may feed back into the economy because banks will tighten credit conditions, especially if there remain uncertainties on the valuation of projects and of assets. As in most countries, the impact of the crisis on the GCC was magnified through the bank lending channel. In response to adverse changes in their capital base, banks became more reluctant to lend and some were forced to deleverage. This chapter therefore concludes on the feedback effect of high NPLs on the real economy.

7.2 Determinants of Nonperforming Loans

Our focus in this section will be on the determinants of NPLs. A reader who is interested in the general context and practices of stress-testing can find several other surveys. For example, the special feature of the Financial Stability Report of the European Central Bank (2006) provides a brief introduction into macro stress-testing as well as an overview of EU country-level macro stress-testing practices.[3] A detailed introduction to stress-testing and an overview of the related literature is given in Sorge (2004).

Financial system shocks can emanate from firm-specific factors (idiosyncratic shocks) and from macroeconomic imbalances (systemic shocks). Economic conditions directly affect loan losses in banks portfolios (Keeton and Morris 1987) and credit risk because of deteriorated asset prices (Mueller 2000; Anderson and Sundaresan 2000; Collin-Dufresne and Goldstein 2001).[4] Credit risk tends to be accumulated during upturns but losses are realized during the contractionary phase of the business cycle (Kent and D'Arcy 2000; Rajan and Dhal 2003).

Economic growth is however not the only factor driving credit risk. Interest rates can have a stronger effect on NPLs than growth (Fuentes and Maquieira 2003), and changes in unemployment, housing prices, and exchange rates also trigger losses, independently from growth (IMF 2006). The money multiplier and reserve adequacy have also been found to matter (Bercoff, Giovanni, and Grimard 2002).

In addition to macroeconomic factors, bank-specific characteristics may signal or cause risky lending. For instance, bank size, capital ratio, and market power have been linked to the NPL ratio of individual banks (Salas and Saurina 2002). Understanding the determinants of risk-taking behavior of banks has been a subject of much attention in the banking literature. Risk-taking tends to be affected by a number of factors, including, among others, moral hazard, agency problems, ownership structure, and regulatory actions.

Because of moral hazard induced by deposit insurance, banks may increase their risk positions and more so as capital declines. But Duan et al. (1992) did not find that risk-shifting was widespread in the US, perhaps because risk-taking driven by moral hazard is limited by regulation and market discipline. The debate on the effect of government intervention on banks' risk-taking behavior is large and need not be summarized here (Levine 2004 provides a short survey of the literature).

Additional bank specificities are also likely to be correlated with credit risk. For instance, Hughes et al. (1995) model risk preferences and operating

[3] Macro stress-testing refers to a range of techniques used to assess the vulnerability of a financial system to exceptional but plausible macroeconomic shocks.

[4] It is important to bear in mind for macro stress-testing that not only credit exposures but also default probabilities and recovery rates may change in the simulated macro stress scenario, compared to estimates derived from a benign sample period. In fact, Sorge (2004) documents several empirical studies that provide evidence of the sensitivity of default probabilities and recovery rates to macroeconomic variables. For example, Carey (1998) provides evidence of significant differences in default rates and loss severity between "good" and "bad" years. Altman et al. (2002) document the increase in default rates and decrease in recovery rates in the US during the recession of 1990–1 and the downturn of 2001–2, and contrasts it with the low levels recorded during the expansion years 1993–8. In this chapter, we leave the issue of recovery rates aside as we did not have access to recovery rates data for the GCC.

efficiency of banks: risk-averse managers' utility is a function of both profits and risk. In order to improve loan quality, the managers increase monitoring and incur higher costs, affecting the measure of operating efficiency. Therefore, a less efficient bank may in fact hold a low-risk portfolio. Indeed, Hughes et al.'s (1995) empirical test rejects the hypothesis that banks are risk-neutral.

On the other hand, there may be a positive link between bank risk and operating efficiency because risks are costly to manage. Overall, while studies examining the interplay between capital and portfolio risk have been considered in the literature (Shrieves and Dahl 1992; Jacques and Nigro 1997), little work has been forthcoming on the examination of the relationship between capital and credit risk and its interaction with operational efficiency.

7.3 A Panel Model for GCC Banks

We investigate the determinants of NPL ratios in GCC banks using panel data of individual banks' balance sheets from Bankscope. Although some of the data goes as far back as 1995, for most of the banks, data was available only from 1998 (the list of banks is available in Table 7.3). As in much of the literature on credit risk, the dependent variable is the logit transformation of the NPL ratio (i.e., log(NPL/(1-NPL)) where NPL is the Nonperforming Loans ratio), as this transformation ensures that the dependent variable spans over the interval] $-\infty; +\infty$ [(as opposed to between 0 and 1) and is distributed symmetrically in the GCC (see Figure 7.3).

The macroeconomic explanatory variables include non-oil real GDP growth, stock market returns, interest rates, world trade growth, the VIX index (proxying for global risk aversion and tight financing conditions), and a 1997–8 dummy for the Asian crisis. Non-oil real GDP is the appropriate variable to use, for both theoretical and econometric reasons. In the GCC countries, NPLs are driven by the state of the non-oil economy: indeed, the government and large oil and petrochemical companies (whose revenues depend directly on oil) are government-owned in the region and do not default on loans. To the extent that oil revenues spill over to the non-oil economy, via public spending, household revenues, and downstream activity, etc., this effect will be captured well by non-oil real GDP growth. Econometrically, oil prices are constant across GCC countries and therefore bring less country-specific information on the state of the economy.

Unemployment was not used because in the GCC, the importance of the foreign labor force means that unemployment is very stable and very low (Saudi Arabia is an exception as its domestic labor force is larger). Housing prices were not used either owing to paucity of a consistent data series in the

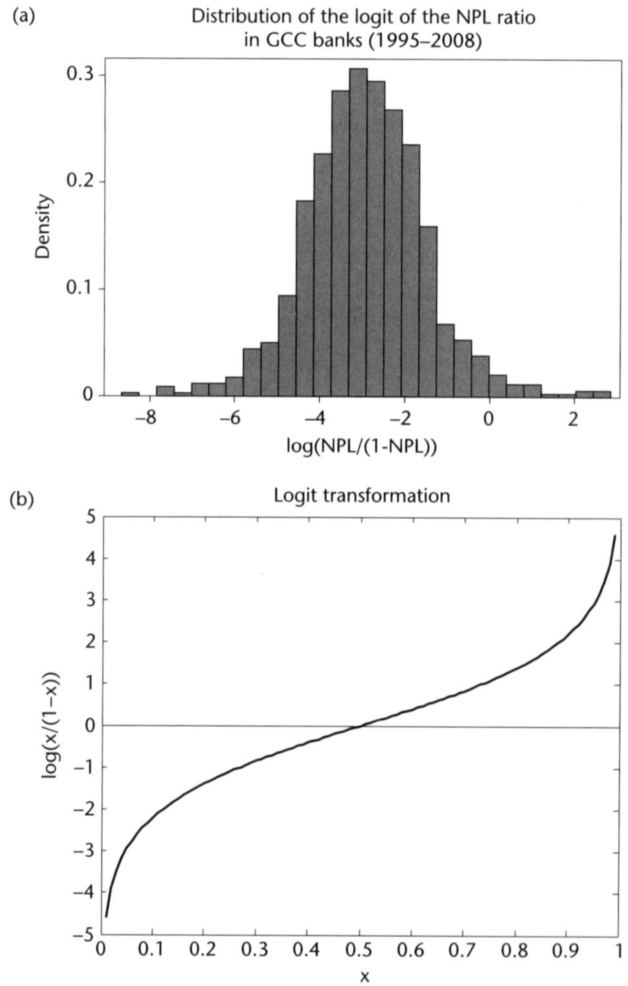

Figure 7.3. Logit transformation of the NPL ratio

GCC. Finally, because the GCC countries peg their currencies to the dollar, there seems to be no reason to include the exchange rate in a model of NPLs. The regressions also control for firm-level variables. In particular, we look at the risk factors suggested by the literature: the capital adequacy ratio, different measures of efficiency (the expenses/asset ratio, the cost/income ratio, and the return on equity), size (we use the logarithm of equity), the lagged net interest margin, and lagged credit growth (deflated by the CPI).

Several econometric specifications of the dynamic panel are estimated, including OLS, fixed effects, difference GMM (Arellano and Bond 1991), and system GMM (Blundell and Bond 1998), which may be a better specification when the auto-regressive coefficient is close to

1 (in which case difference GMM is inefficient). The forward orthogonalization procedure of Arellano and Bover (1995) was also used to reduce observation losses due to differencing. Finally, to reduce the number of instruments, the collapsing method of Holtz-Eakin, Newey, and Rosen (1988) was used. The macroeconomic variables were considered as strictly exogenous (i.e., can be instrumented by itself as a one-column "IV-style" instrument; see Roodman 2006), while the lagged bank-level variables were modeled as predetermined (and need to be instrumented GMM-style in the same way as the lagged dependent variable). The results are presented in Table 7.2.

The number of instruments was kept below forty in all GMM specifications. The Arellano-Bond AR(1) test for autocorrelation of the residuals rejects the hypothesis that the errors are not autocorrelated, which is expected since differencing generates autocorrelation of order 1. The Arellano-Bond AR(2) p-values are above 5 percent. This is needed in order not to reject the hypothesis that the errors in the levels equation are uncorrelated, an assumption that ensures that the orthogonality conditions and the Arellano-Bond specifications are correct. The Hansen test of overidentifying restrictions also suggests that the instruments are appropriate.

Our analysis shows that both macroeconomic variables and bank-specific variables contributed to the build-up in NPLs in the GCC countries. Non-oil GDP and interest rates were dominant in the first category, and the size of capital, credit growth, and efficiency (non-interest expenses/assets) were found to be the significant bank-specific variables.

Starting with firm-specific variables, the NPL ratio exhibits a strong autocorrelation, estimated to be between 0.6 (the fixed-effect model suffers from a downward Nickell-bias) and 0.9 (the OLS estimate is upward-biased). As a result, NPLs should be expected to worsen relatively slowly when affected by a shock, but in the same vein, it would be reasonable to anticipate long-lasting increases in NPLs. A high coefficient on the lagged NPL ratio also implies that the system GMM is a more efficient estimator than the difference GMM, which is why our preferred specification is that presented in Table 7.2, column 4 (or column 5, a specification which is nearly identical).

The capital adequacy ratio was not found to be significant even in the fixed-effect regression and in the GMM specifications, and was dropped from the model. This result matches those found for other countries and suggests that regulation is effectively preventing capital from reaching low levels and influencing risk-taking. Nevertheless, efficiency was found to be significant and with the expected sign. The two alternative measures of efficiency (the cost to income ratio and return on equity) were not significant and were also dropped from the model. The net interest margin was also found to be insignificant. Finally, the past expansion of a bank's balance sheet was also found in

Table 7.2. Macroeconomic and firm-specific determinants of NPLs

Model specification	(1)	(2)	(3)	(4)	(5)
	OLS	FE	Arellano-Bond 2-step collapsed	System GMM collapsed	System GMM fwd. orth. collapsed
$\ln(NPL/(1\text{-}NPL))_{-1}$	0.898***	0.676***	0.714***	0.881***	0.865***
	[37.31]	[15.27]	[12.04]	[11.50]	[12.08]
$\ln(equity)_{-1}$	−0.0543**	−0.364***	−0.359***	−0.102	−0.102
	[−2.468]	[−4.439]	[−3.107]	[−1.193]	[−1.221]
$(expenses/avg.\ assets)_{-1}$	0.0483*	0.0868*	0.154**	0.114**	0.106**
	[1.803]	[1.931]	[2.524]	[2.576]	[2.141]
loans $growth_{-2}$	0.104**	0.0946*	0.0993*	0.137	0.145
	[2.364]	[1.709]	[1.913]	[1.499]	[1.490]
non-oil GDP growth	−1.948***	−0.974	−1.893**	−2.156*	−2.090*
	[−2.597]	[−0.812]	[−2.337]	[−1.887]	[−1.711]
interest $rate_{-1}$	0.0241*	0.0535**	0.0044	−0.0053	0.0001
	[1.778]	[2.197]	[0.376]	[−0.163]	[0.00291]
VIX	0.0131***	0.0115***	0.0119***	0.0140***	0.0132***
	[3.162]	[2.825]	[4.228]	[2.982]	[3.040]
Constant	−0.599**	0.488		−0.342	−0.402
	[−2.275]	[0.997]		[−0.527]	[−0.592]
Observations	426	426	347	426	426
R-squared	0.84	0.69			
Number of banks		79	67	79	79
No. of instruments			34	38	38
Hansen test p-value			0.27	0.48	0.52
A-B AR(1) test p-value			0.00	0.00	0.00
A-B AR(2) test p-value			0.17	0.18	0.19
t-statistics in brackets					

*** $p < 0.01$, ** $p < 0.05$, * $p < 0.1$, t-statistics in brackets

two specifications to worsen NPLs, even after controlling for macroeconomic variables.

Indeed, the macroeconomic conditions were found to be important and with the expected sign in all models. A temporary decrease by 3 percentage points in non-oil GDP growth would increase NPLs by 0.3 to 1.1 percentage points, depending on the initial level of NPLs (the model is nonlinear and therefore one can only interpret the coefficients using marginal effects at different points of the distribution of NPLs). The effect of a 300 basis points increase in interest rates would be similar. Since the AR coefficient of the logit transformation of NPL is high (between 0.6 and 0.9), these shocks cumulate to a large extent (Figure 7.4).

World trade growth and the Asian crisis dummy were not found to be significant, but the VIX index was highly significant in all specifications. External

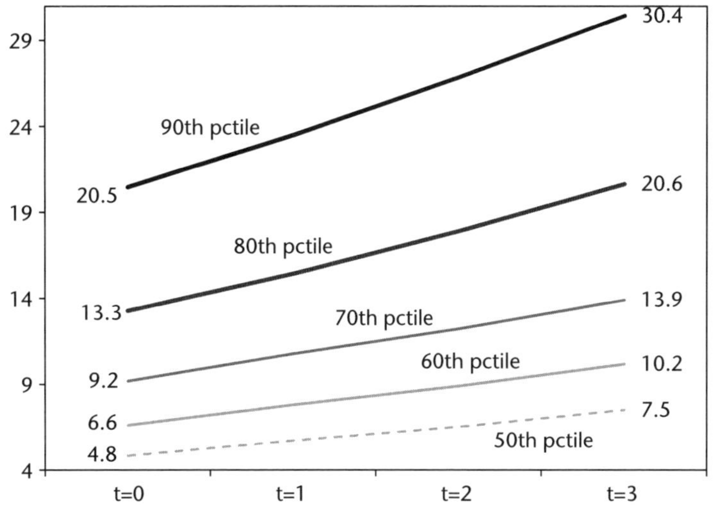

Figure 7.4. Dynamics of NPLs with maintained macroeconomic shocks

Note: Effect of a 3 percentage point fall in non-oil real GDP and a 300 basis points increase in interest rates

financing conditions, in addition to interest rates, seem therefore to matter more than the global trade cycle in driving credit risk in the GCC. We also investigated, using interaction terms, whether banks that have higher expenses or that expanded faster are more sensitive to decreases in activity, but we found no significant effect. It is likely that the nonlinearity embedded in the logit transformation already captures some of these effects since banks that expanded quickly or are inefficient also are likely to start from a higher base of NPLs.[5]

7.4 Concluding on the Systemic Importance of Credit Risk

Our empirical results support the view that both macro-factors and bank-specific characteristics determine the level of nonperforming loans. In particular, we find strong evidence of a significant inverse relationship between real (non-oil) GDP and nonperforming loans. The study also showed that global financial market conditions have an effect on NPLs of banks. This implies that regulators and central banks in the GCC have to be wary about

[5] Results are overall similar when looking at post-2001 data, with the coefficients robust to the smaller sample. Lagged credit growth becomes significant in all specifications, suggesting that balance sheet expansion drives future NPLs, but non-oil growth loses significance in the GMM specifications as data covers a smaller part of the business cycle.

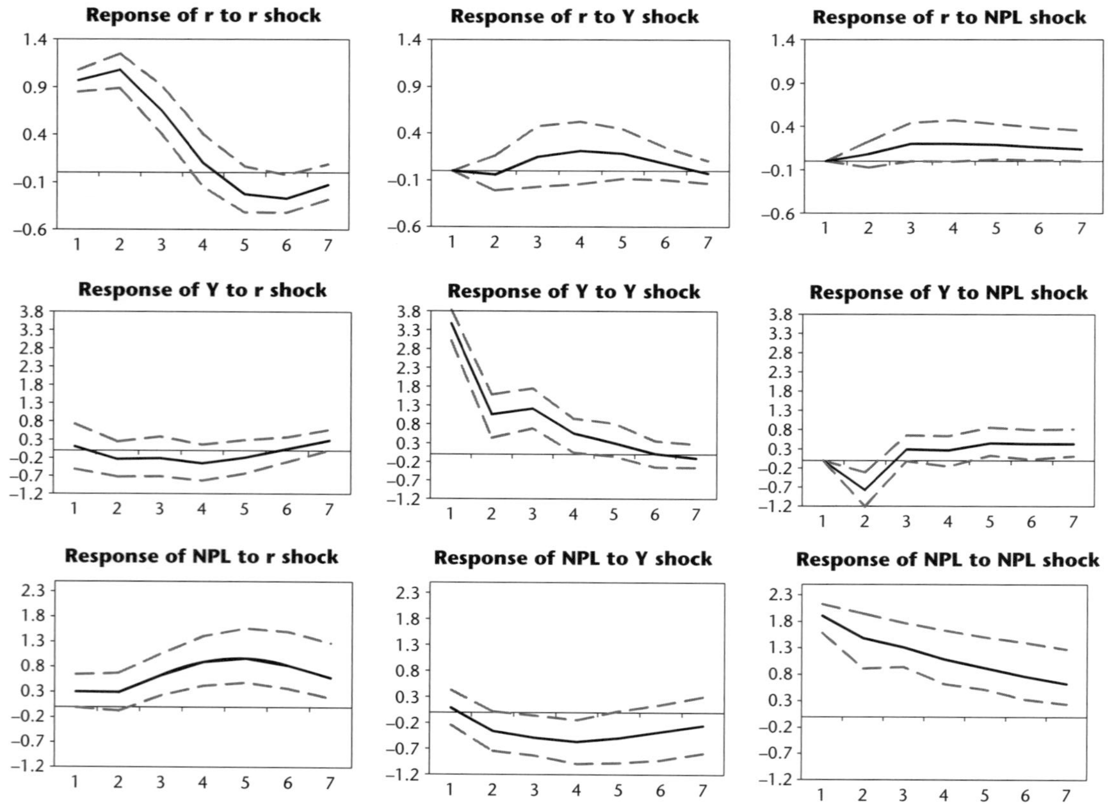

Figure 7.5. Feedback effect—panel VAR impulse response functions

increasing NPLs during periods of low growth and tight financing. Among bank control factors, efficiency and past expansion of the balance sheet were found to be significant.

As banks' balance sheets have remained affected in the aftermath of the 2009 recession, worries have been raised that credit growth may remain sluggish—as was indeed the case in past episodes in MENA (Barajas et al. 2011)—hampering the speed of the recovery. Indeed, there are four channels via which banking stress can affect economic growth: (i) individual exposures can spread to the wider financial system, triggering lower economic activity in the financial sector; (ii) credit and market risk lead to higher lending interest rates; (iii) losses may prompt asset sales, which further depress asset prices; and (iv) increased risk aversion leads to tighter credit conditions, resulting in lower credit growth (Kida 2008). Econometric models have confirmed the existence of a feedback between credit losses and the macroeconomy in the US (Keeton 1999) and Europe (Ciccarelli et al. 2010).

An exploratory panel VAR we estimated, using macroeconomic data, also found that this channel is plausible in the GCC.[6] The results (Figure 7.5) show that higher interest rates increase NPLs and higher GDP reduces the NPL ratio (row 3, columns 1 and 2). The feedback effect of higher NPLs suffered by the banking sector is shown in the last column of the second row: a one-standard deviation increase in the change in the NPL ratio (an increase by 2 percentage points) reduces GDP growth by around 0.7 percentage point after two years. However, default shocks do not occur often and the forecast error variance decomposition shows that only 5 to 7 percent of the non-oil GDP growth variance can be explained by NPLs shocks. Overall, according to the panel VAR, there could be a strong, albeit short-lived feedback effect from losses in banks' balance sheets on economic activity.

[6] The variables in the VAR are the interest rate, the log of non-oil real GDP, and the NPL ratio. The Levin-Lin-Chu test could not reject the presence of a unit root in the sample. The variables were demeaned using the Helmert procedure as in Love and Zicchino (2006). The identification procedure is based on a Choleski decomposition with the interest rate ordered first, followed by non-oil real GDP, and the NPL ratio ordered last. This ordering is predicated by the pegged exchange rate regime (interest rates follow dollar rates and are mostly unaffected by domestic conditions) and the assumption that causality initially runs from growth to NPLs. In particular, the Choleski decomposition assumes that the NPL ratio cannot instantaneously affect non-oil GDP.

Appendix

Table 7.3. Bankscope coverage in the GCC

Country	Bank	Country	Bank
Qatar	Ahli Bank QSC	Bahrain	Commercial Bank of Bahrain B.S.C.
Qatar	Commercial Bank of Qatar (The) QSC	Bahrain	Gulf International Bank BSC
Qatar	Doha Bank	Bahrain	National Bank of Bahrain
Qatar	International Bank of Qatar	Bahrain	Shamil Bank of Bahrain B.S.C.
Qatar	Qatar Development Bank Q.S.C.	Bahrain	TAIB Bank B.S.C. (2)
Qatar	Qatar International Islamic	Bahrain	United Gulf Bank (BSC) EC
Qatar	Qatar Islamic Bank SAQ	Kuwait	Al Ahli Bank of Kuwait (KS
Qatar	Qatar National Bank	Kuwait	Bank of Kuwait & The Middl
Oman	Ahli Bank SAOG	Kuwait	Burgan Bank SAK
Oman	Bank Dhofar SAOG	Kuwait	Commercial Bank of Kuwait
Oman	Bank Muscat SAOG	Kuwait	Gulf Bank KSC (The)
Oman	Bank Muscat SAOG (2)	Kuwait	Industrial Bank of Kuwait
Oman	Bank of Oman, Bahrain and Kuwait SAOG	Kuwait	Kuwait Finance House
Oman	Commercial Bank of Oman S.A.O.G. (Old)	Kuwait	Kuwait International Bank
Oman	Majan International Bank SAOC	Kuwait	National Bank of Kuwait S.A.K.
Oman	National Bank of Oman (SAOG)	UAE	Abu Dhabi Commercial Bank
Oman	Oman Arab Bank SAOG	UAE	Abu Dhabi Islamic Bank - P (2)
Oman	Oman Development Bank SAOG	UAE	Bank of Sharjah
Oman	Oman International Bank	UAE	Commercial Bank International P.S.C.
Saudi Arabia	Al Rajhi Bank-Al Rajhi Banking & Investment Corporation	UAE	Commercial Bank of Dubai P.S.C.
Saudi Arabia	Arab National Bank	UAE	Dubai Bank (2)
Saudi Arabia	Bank Al-Jazira	UAE	Emirates Bank International PJSC
Saudi Arabia	Bank AlBilad	UAE	Emirates Industrial Bank
Saudi Arabia	Banque Saudi Fransi	UAE	Emirates NBD PJSC
Saudi Arabia	National Commercial Bank (The)	UAE	First Gulf Bank
Saudi Arabia	Riyad Bank	UAE	Invest Bank P.S.C.
Saudi Arabia	Samba Financial Group	UAE	Mashreqbank
Saudi Arabia	Saudi British Bank (The)	UAE	National Bank of Abu Dhabi
Saudi Arabia	Saudi Hollandi Bank	UAE	National Bank of Dubai Public Joint Stock Company
Saudi Arabia	Saudi Investment Bank (The)	UAE	National Bank of Fujairah
Saudi Arabia	United Saudi Bank	UAE	RAKBANK-National Bank of Ras Al-Khaimah (P.S.C.) (The)
Bahrain	Ahli United Bank (Bahrain) B.S.C.	UAE	National Bank of Umm Al-Qaiwain
Bahrain	Bahrain International Bank	UAE	Sharjah Islamic Bank
Bahrain	Bahrain Islamic Bank B.S.C. (2)	UAE	Union National Bank
Bahrain	Bahraini Saudi Bank (The)	UAE	United Arab Bank PJSC
Bahrain	BBK B.S.C.		

References

Anderson, R. and Sundaresan, S. (2000). "A comparative study of structural models of corporate bond yields: An explanatory investigation," *Journal of Banking and Finance*, 24: 255–69.

Arellano, M. and Bond, S. (1991). "Some tests of specification for panel data: Monte Carlo evidence and an application to employment equations," *Review of Economic Studies*, 58: 277–97.

Arellano, M. and Bover, O. (1995). "Another look at the instrumental variables estimation of error components models," *Journal of Econometrics*, 68: 29–51.

Altman, E. I., Resti, A., and Sironi, A. (2002). "The link between default and recovery rates: Effects on the procyclicality of regulatory capital ratios." Bank for International Settlements Working Paper No. 113.

Barajas, A., Chami, A., Espinoza, R., and Barajas, H. H. (2011). "Further fallout from the global financial crisis: Credit crunch in the 'periphery'," *World Economics*, 12: 153–76.

Bercoff, J., di Giovanni, J., and Grimard, F. (2002). "Argentinean banks, credit growth and the tequila crisis: A duration analysis." Unpublished.

Blundell, R. and Bond, S. (1998). "Initial conditions and moment restrictions in dynamic panel data models," *Journal of Econometrics*, 87: 11–143.

Carey, M. (1998). "Credit risk in private debt portfolios," *Journal of Finance*, 53: 1363–87.

Collin-Dufresne, P. and Goldstein, R. (2001). "Do credit spreads reflect stationary leverage ratios?" *Journal of Finance*, 56: 1929–57.

Ciccarelli, M., Maddaloni, A., and Peydró, J. L. (2010). "Trusting the bankers: A new look at the credit channel of monetary transmission." European Central Bank Working Paper Series No. 1228.

Drehmann, M. (2008). "Stress tests: Objectives, challenges and modeling choices," *Riksbank Economic Review*, 2: 60–92.

Drehmann, M. (2009). "Macroeconomic stress testing banks: A survey of methodologies," in M. Quagliariello (ed.), *Stress Testing the Banking System: Methodologies and Applications*. Cambridge: Cambridge University Press, 37–67.

Duan, J. C., Moreau, A. F., and Sealey, C. W. (1992). "Fixed-rate deposit insurance and risk-shifting behaviour at commercial banks," *Journal of Banking and Finance*, 16: 715–42.

European Central Bank (2006). "Country level macro stress-testing practices," *Financial Stability Review* (June), 147–54.

Fuentes, R. and Maquieira, C. (2003). "Institutional arrangements, credit market development and loan repayment in Chile." School of Business and Economics, Universidad de Chile.

Holtz-Eakin, D., Newey, W., and Rosen, H. S. (1988). "Estimating vector autoregressions with panel data," *Econometrica*, 56: 1371–95.

Hughes, J. P., Lang, W., Mester, L. J., and Moon, C.-G. (1995). "Recovering technologies that account for generalized managerial preferences: An application to non-risk-neutral banks." Federal Reserve Bank of Philadelphia Working Paper.

International Monetary Fund (2006). "Spain: Financial sector assessment program. Technical note: Stress-testing methodology and results." IMF Country Report No. 06/216. Washington DC: International Monetary Fund.

International Monetary Fund (2010). "Kuwait: Financial system stability assessment—update." IMF Country Report No. 10/239.

Khamis, M. and Senhadji, A. (2010). "Impact of the global financial crisis on the Gulf Cooperation Council Countries and challenges ahead: An update." Washington DC: International Monetary Fund.

Jacques, K. and Nigro, P. (1997). "Risk-based capital, portfolio risk and bank capital: A simultaneous equations approach," *Journal of Economics and Business*, 49: 533–47.

Keeton, W. R. (1999). "Does faster loan growth lead to higher loan losses?" *Federal Reserve Bank of Kansas City Economic Review*, 84 (2): 57–75.

Keeton, W. R. and Morris, C. S. (1987). "Why do banks' loan losses differ?" *Federal Reserve Bank of Kansas City Economic Review, 72 (5):* 3–21.

Kent, C. and D'Arcy, P. (2000). "Cyclical prudence: Credit cycles in Australia." Bank for International Settlements Working Paper No 1.

Kida, M. (2008). "A macro stress testing model with feedback effects," *Reserve Bank of New Zealand*, Discussion Paper Series, DP2008/08. Wellington, May.

Levine, R. (2004). "The corporate governance of banks: A concise discussion of concepts and evidence." World Bank Policy Research Working Paper No. 3404.

Love, I. and Zicchino, L. (2006). "Financial development and dynamic investment behavior: Evidence from panel VAR," *Quarterly Review of Economics and Finance*, 46: 190–210.

Mueller, C. (2000). "A simple multi-factor model of corporate bond prices." Doctoral dissertation, University of Wisconsin-Madison.

Rajan, R. and Dhal, S. C. (2003). "Nonperforming loans and terms of credit of public sector banks in India: An empirical assessment," *Reserve Bank of India Occasional Papers*, 24: 81–121.

Roodman, D. (2006). "How to do xtabond2: An introduction to 'Difference' and 'System' GMM in Stata." Center for Global Development Working Paper No. 103.

Salas, V. and Saurina, J. (2002). "Credit risk in two institutional regimes: Spanish commercial and savings banks," *Journal of Financial Services Research*, 22: 203–24.

Shrieves, R. and Dahl, D. (1992). "The relationship between risk and capital in commercial banks," *Journal of Banking and Finance*, 16: 439–57.

Sorge, M. (2004). "Stress-testing financial systems: An overview of current methodologies." Bank for International Settlements Working Paper No. 165.

8

Financial Markets in the GCC Countries

8.1 Introduction

As the global economic crisis took hold, the GCC countries' financial systems found themselves affected through contagion despite the relatively low direct exposure to subprimes and to advanced economies' sovereign debts. Symptoms of excessive risk-taking had appeared before the crisis with soaring capitalization of the equity market, high credit growth, booming real estate markets, and large flows into financial markets. More generally, the financial crisis shed light on the extraordinary vulnerability of the global financial system to valuation losses and to disruptions in wholesale funding of banks. GCC financial sector imbalances came to the fore, given these countries' participation in global equity and credit markets.

Thus the heightened risk to financial institutions in the GCC that the global crisis has unveiled, as well as the current discussions of regulators on systemic risk and capital surcharge, both underscore the importance of understanding the exposures of financial institutions to each other in the region and their exposure to distressed global markets. This chapter gives an overview of financial markets in the GCC and investigates the interconnectedness among listed banks in two of the largest financial markets in the GCC: Saudi Arabia and the UAE.[1]

Using two different statistical methodologies on daily data of expected default frequencies (EDF) of listed banks in Saudi Arabia, the UAE, of financial sectors in Europe, and the US, we assess the performance of and interconnectedness among banks in the GCC as well as their exposure to spillovers

[1] Saudi Arabia is by far the largest stock market in the region, and the UAE has the second largest banking sector after Bahrain.

from the global crisis during the period 2008–10. The first method used is the Conditional Value at Risk (Co-VaR) quantile regression model of Adrian and Brunnermeier (2011). Quantile regressions are useful because they allow estimation of a predicted value for the probability of default of a bank (represented by the EDF), conditional on another bank being under stress (i.e. conditional on the other bank's EDF being at a certain "tail" quantile). This predicted conditional probability of default is therefore a measure of contagion. The second method is the one proposed by Segoviano (2006) and Segoviano and Goodhart (2009), who recommend modeling the joint density of asset valuation to deduce the probability of a bank being in distress (i.e., the probability that the value of one asset is lower than a prespecified default threshold) conditional on the event that another bank is in distress. The joint density is constructed using nonparametric methods, from a prior copula that is updated with the information on individual probabilities of default.

In addition to the financial crisis that started with the Lehman Brothers collapse, the period under study (2008–10) covers local and regional events that shook the financial markets of the GCC (in particular the Dubai world debt distress episode in the UAE). We investigate local and regional interconnectedness amongst banks by identifying the local banking systems' most vulnerable and most systemically important banks, as well as measuring international spillovers by identifying the advanced economies whose financial sectors were the most systemically important to the GCC banking systems. We find evidence of both inter-country and intra-country interconnectedness between banks in the UAE and Saudi Arabia. Moreover, we find that UAE banks were more exposed than Saudi banks to international spillovers during the global crisis.

The rest of this chapter is structured as follows. Section 8.2 highlights some important facts on the GCC stock markets, including market capitalization, liberalization, and volatility in light of regional and global events. Section 8.3 reviews the GCC banking sector and presents data on expected default probabilities for listed banks in Saudi Arabia and UAE. Section 8.4 discusses the estimation methods and section 8.5 presents the estimation results. Section 8.6 concludes.

8.2 Background on GCC Stock Markets

Stock markets in the GCC have grown fast over the last decade, driven by high and stable economic growth, stock market reform, privatization, and financial liberalization.[2] Taken together, GCC stock markets constituted

[2] GCC equity markets were established around the mid-1970s. The first market to be established was the Kuwait Stock Exchange in 1977 followed by Tadawul All Share Index (TASI) in Saudi Arabia in 1984. The most recently established markets are the Dubai Financial Market (DFM) and the Abu Dhabi Securities Market (ADSM) in 2000.

Table 8.1. Foreign investment ceiling for listed stocks in the GCC markets

Bahrain	49% in general; 10% for a single entity; some banks and insurance companies are 100% open to foreign ownership; 100% in general for GCC nationals
Kuwait	100% in general; 49% some banks
Oman	Up to 70% with some restrictions at company level; restrictions may differ for GCC nationals
Qatar	25% in general
Saudi Arabia	25% for GCC nationals, other foreign investors may access market via mutual funds managed by Saudi banks
United Arab Emirates	49% in general, different restrictions may apply to individual companies; 100% for GCC nationals with company's approval

Source: Standard & Poor's Global Stock Markets Factbook, 2011

63 percent of the MENA region stock markets based on market capitalization in 2011. Saudi Arabia is by far the largest market in the region (with a capitalization of $339 billion in 2011), and Bahrain and Oman are the smallest ($17 and $20 billion, respectively, in 2011). Kuwait was the second-largest market before 2003 when Qatar and UAE alternated in second place. The latest data shows Qatar ($125 billion) ranking second and the UAE ($94 billion) third.[3]

The GCC stock markets are classified by Morgan Stanley Capital International (MSCI) as frontier markets, a subset of emerging markets categorized as relatively small and illiquid. Qatar, the UAE, and Saudi Arabia have submitted in the past bids to the MSCI to upgrade their status to emerging markets, as this would increase demand (institutional investors in particular have limits on the share of their portfolios that can be allocated to frontier market assets). The bids by Qatar and the UAE have been unsuccessful so far, mainly due to the existing restrictions on foreign ownership, although there have been recent efforts to reduce these restrictions. Most companies in Qatar cap overseas ownership at 25 percent (Table 8.1). Under UAE law, foreign companies must have UAE nationals as their sponsors and are limited to a maximum 49 percent ownership of businesses, except in free zones. "The MSCI UAE Index meets all requirements besides specific market accessibility issues related to custody and clearing and settlement", MSCI said in the statement. Delivery-versus-payment started in the UAE in 2011, which was cited in 2010 as a reason for not upgrading the market.

[3] Market capitalization of listed companies based on World Development Indicators database.

8.2.1 GCC Stock Markets' Integration: Global and Regional Spillovers

Despite varying degrees of foreign participation, several studies have found that GCC stock markets are integrated both regionally and internationally. Saadi Sedik and Williams (2012) also found that the transmission of shocks from the S&P 500 to the UAE was the largest among the GCC markets. Spillovers from regional equity markets were also found to be significant but the magnitude of the effects was on average smaller than that from mature markets. Sbeiti and Alshammari (2010) similarly show evidence for regional integration among the GCC stock market indices, which are found to exhibit strong ties and to move together in the long run. Espinoza, Prasad, and Williams (2010) look at price differentials for stocks cross-listed within the GCC and cross-listed in London and Frankfurt stocks and find that stock markets in the GCC are fairly integrated regionally, compared with either GCC integration with the European markets or compared with regional integration in other emerging and frontier markets (Hong-Kong-Singapore and Caribbean markets). However, they note that financial integration is hampered by market illiquidity.

We present here some additional evidence on GCC stock markets integration with regional and global markets. We investigate whether volatility from US and regional markets had a significant effect on conditional volatility of stock prices in Gulf equity markets. Valuations in the GCC markets have not recovered since September 2008, and the combined market capitalization losses in the GCC stock exchanges were $250 billion between September 1, 2008 and March 2012 (Table 8.2). Volatility in the stock markets increased after September 2008. The average correlation of the GCC equity markets with the global markets turned positive in the period after September 2008, as compared to a negative correlation during the period between January 1, 2007 and September 9, 2008 (Table 8.3). These trends are also shown in Figure 8.1 which plots the six GCC stock market indices and the S&P 500 index during the period 2007–12. This time period covers not only major events at the start and during the global crisis (such as the Lehman collapse and the onset of the Greek crisis) but also major local events such as the Dubai World default in the UAE, commercial banks' recapitalization in Qatar, and the Algosaibi default in Saudi Arabia.[4]

[4] Qatar Investment Authority, the country's sovereign wealth fund, injected $2.8 billion of capital into the banking system in three tranches between 2009 and 2011. In November 2009, the Dubai government announced a moratorium on the debt of Dubai World, a government-owned investment company. Debt was worth $59 billion at the time, and Dubai World announced its plans to restructure debt related to part of its business, mainly real estate. In response to that, both Moody's and Standard & Poor's Investors Services heavily downgraded the debt of various Dubai government-related entities. Algosaibi & Brothers Co., a Saudi investment company, defaulted on billions of dollars of debt at end 2010.

Table 8.2. Market capitalization losses

	Sept. 1, 2008 to end-Mar. 2012 (US dollar billions)
Bahrain	12
Kuwait	90
Oman	7
Qatar*	–1
Saudi Arabia	42
Dubai	59
Abu Dhabi	43

Note: * Market Capitalization Gain
Source: Zawya and authors' calculations

Table 8.3. Correlations of stock market indices with S&P 500

	Jan. 1, 2007 to Sept. 9, 2008	Sept. 10, 2008 to end-Dec. 2010	Jan. 1, 2011 to end-Mar. 2012
Bahrain	–0.54	–0.26	0.20
Kuwait	–0.57	–0.04	0.44
Oman	–0.69	0.77	0.39
Qatar	–0.63	0.85	0.26
Saudi Arabia	–0.45	0.88	0.75
Dubai	–0.47	0.12	0.57
Abu Dhabi	–0.59	0.36	0.27

Source: Bloomberg and authors' calculations

Market volatility increased after the crisis, but seems to have settled down since the beginning of 2011 (Table 8.4).

8.3 Banking System

The banking sector constitutes a major part of the financial system in the GCC. Bank operations are domestically oriented, relying mainly on lending and private deposits. Foreign assets and liabilities form a relatively small share of the total size of the balance sheet. Saudi Arabia's banking sector is the most closed—only 5.7 percent of liabilities originate abroad—while Bahrain has the most open banking industry: up to 48 percent of liabilities are foreign (Table 8.5).

Two key structural features that are common to the GCC members are worth noting: public ownership and concentration in banking. Public and quasi public-sector ownership varies but ranges from 13 percent in Kuwait, to 30 and 35 percent in Oman and Saudi Arabia, and reaches over 52 percent in the UAE (end 2007 data). Oman and Saudi Arabia's relatively high public-sector ownership is mostly attributed to quasi government ownership, while in the UAE public ownership of domestic banking assets is mostly attributed

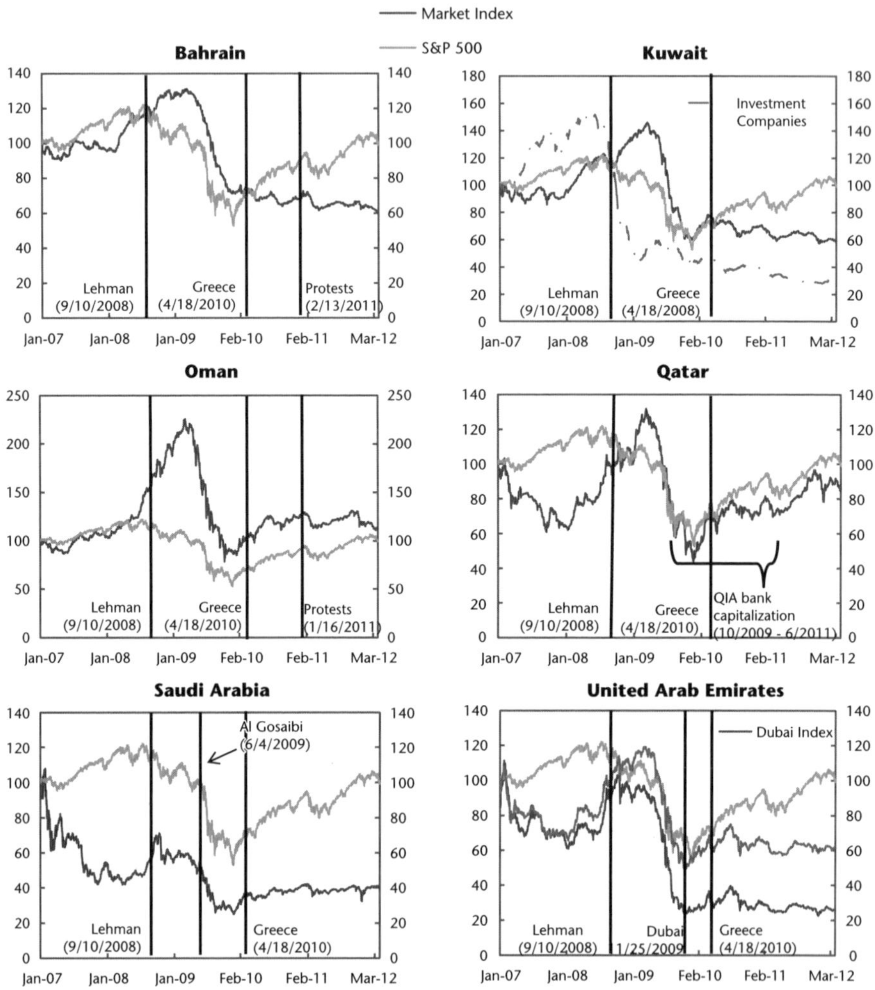

Figure 8.1. GCC: Market indices, January 2007–March 2012
Note: Index, January 1, 2007=100
Source: Bloomberg

to direct ownership by the government (41.5 percent) (Al-Hassan, Khamis, and Oulidi 2010).

The GCC banking sector is also concentrated with a few domestic banks dominating the market: in all countries, the five largest banks (which are domestic banks) account for 50–80 percent of total banking sector assets. The UAE and Bahrain are the most competitive markets, whereas Oman, Kuwait, and Qatar are the most concentrated.

We now turn our attention to Saudi and Emirati commercial banks and we analyze the dynamics and extent of contagion to these banking systems at

Table 8.4. Stock market volatilities

	Jan. 1, 2007 to Sept. 9, 2008	Sept. 10, 2008 to end-Dec. 2010	Jan. 1, 2011 to end-Mar. 2012
Bahrain			
Standard deviations	0.52	0.76	0.49
Average returns	0.05	–0.08	–0.07
Kuwait			
Standard deviations	0.51	0.94	0.46
Average returns	0.08	–0.10	–0.01
Oman			
Standard deviations	1.12	1.60	0.66
Average returns	0.12	–0.09	–0.06
Qatar			
Standard deviations	1.21	2.00	0.80
Average returns	0.08	–0.03	–0.02
Saudi Arabia			
Standard deviations	1.29	1.40	0.78
Average returns	0.05	–0.04	–0.03
Dubai			
Standard deviations	1.37	2.31	1.08
Average returns	0.04	–0.14	–0.05
Abu Dhabi			
Standard deviations	1.07	1.48	0.57
Average returns	0.05	–0.09	–0.04

Source: Bloomberg and authors' calculations

Table 8.5. GCC: Loans, deposits, and foreign assets and liabilities, 2011

	GCC Banks: Deposits and Loans (in percent)			GCC Banks: Foreign Assets and Liabilities (in percent)		
	Loans to GDP	Deposits to GDP	Loan to Deposit		Foreign Assets/ Total Assets	Foreign Liabilities/Total Liabilities
Bahrain	98.2	95.9	102.4	Bahrain	44.5	48.2
Kuwait	61.8	55.0	112.4	Kuwait	18.5	8.3
Oman	47.8	44.6	107.4	Oman	12.5	10.9
Qatar	78.5	54.5	144.1	Qatar	16.8	26.9
Saudi Arabia	47.8	49.9	95.7	Saudi Arabia	13.5	5.7
UAE	87.3	72.5	120.4	UAE	15.1	21.1

Source: Authors' calculations

the time of the global crisis. The banks included for Dubai are the four largest listed banks in terms of their total assets, constituting 92 percent of total banking system assets in Dubai and about 46 percent of UAE GDP in 2010. All five listed banks for Abu Dhabi are also included.[5] We also include seven listed Saudi banks, constituting about 60 percent of the total banking system.[6]

Daily data on Expected Default Frequencies (EDFs) of financial sectors in advanced economies are normally obtained from Moody's KMV database. Since this database does not include any Saudi or Emirati bank, we have constructed EDFs using Merton's structural approach to assessing default risk (Merton 1974). A bank's probability of default is defined as the probability that asset valuation falls below equity at some horizon *T*.

Asset valuation is modeled[7] as a Geometric Brownian Motion with trend μ_V and volatility σ_V, which is why the probability of default is given by the formula:

$$\begin{aligned} P(V_T < E) &= P(\ln(V_T) < \ln(E)) \\ &= \Phi\left(\frac{\ln(V_0) + (\mu_V - 1/2\sigma_V^2)T - \ln(E)}{\sigma_V\sqrt{T}}\right) \\ &= \Phi\left(\frac{\ln(V_0/E) + (\mu_V - 1/2\sigma_V^2)T}{\sigma_V\sqrt{T}}\right) \end{aligned}$$

where $\Phi(.)$ is the cumulative density function of the normal distribution. Intuitively, the probability of default is an increasing function of the current leverage ratio plus the expected growth of asset valuation over the horizon *T*, divided by the standard deviation of asset valuation for the same horizon *T*.[8]

Figure 8.2 shows that EDFs for Dubai banks started to rise quickly after the Lehman collapse (September 2008), and peaked for all banks in early 2009. The second peak (for all banks except one) happened around the Dubai

[5] Abu Dhabi's banks' total assets constituted 63 percent of UAE GDP in 2010. For the purpose of this section, the above identified banks in Abu Dhabi and Dubai are interchangeably used as UAE banks or UAE banking system.

[6] The remaining five banks could not be included due to lack of data for the first four, and the last is not listed.

[7] As with other frontier markets, asset returns do not follow a random walk in the GCC. Therefore, the Geometric Brownian Motion assumption seems ill-suited. We acknowledge that this problem is a serious one, which may explain why EDFs are high in our estimates (see, e.g., Figure 8.2). However, since the objective of the chapter is to discuss co-movement and contagion as opposed to specific levels of EDFs, we think the methodology remains broadly appropriate. The estimation of the volatility of equity and of asset valuation is however made more difficult because when asset returns do not follow a random walk, the volatility estimate becomes a function of the time window used. We estimated σ_E over a one-year window, using year-on-year returns, to limit the volatility of the estimate.

[8] We cannot compute annual volatility as 365 times estimates of the volatility of assets' daily returns. We deviate from this random walk assumption (as it generates huge volatility of assets in countries like Saudi Arabia), and estimate instead the volatility of assets on year-on-year returns.

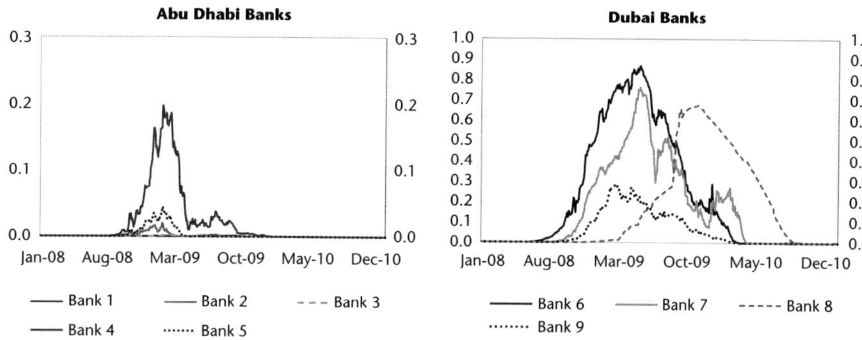

Figure 8.2. Expected default frequencies of local UAE banks, 2008–10
Source: Authors' calculations

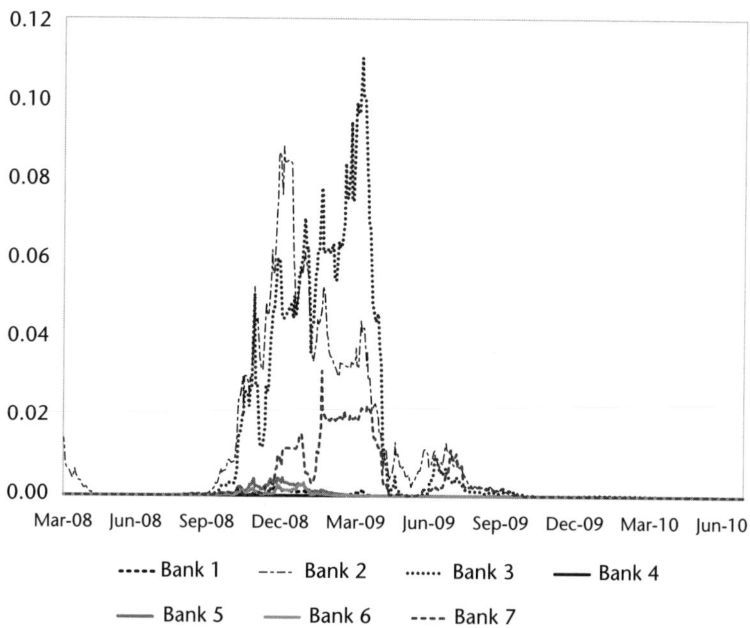

Figure 8.3. Expected default frequencies of Saudi banks, 2008–10
Source: Authors' calculations

World default (November 2009). Default probabilities of Abu Dhabi banks are overall significantly lower when compared to those of Dubai banks across the whole period. For Abu Dhabi banks, the data identify a Lehman effect and a minor Dubai World effect only for one bank.

Saudi banks instead exhibited fairly low EDFs across the period 2008–10, with major peaks following Lehman and some signs of minor distress for a couple of banks following Dubai World in November 2009 (Figure 8.3).

8.4 Econometric Methods

The analysis is divided into two parts. The first part focuses on international spillovers from financial sectors in Europe and the United States to the UAE and Saudi Arabia banking systems. The analysis identifies the advanced economies whose financial sectors were the most important to GCC banking systems, in terms of the threat of distress these sectors pose to banks. For this part, we use the Conditional Value at Risk (Co-VaR) methodology.

The second part analyzes local and regional interconnectedness among banks in the UAE and Saudi Arabia, by identifying each local banking system's most vulnerable and most systemically important banks, and by investigating whether spillovers exist between each banking system. We use the Co-VaR methodology for this part, as well as the distress dependence methodology. Including the international "Lehman collapse" and internal "Dubai World default" and Al Gosaibi events in the analysis allows for disentangling domestic from international pressures.

8.4.1 Conditional Value at Risk (Co-VaR) Methodology

The Co-VaR methodology, proposed by Adrian and Brunnermeier (2011) calculates predicted pairwise conditional default probabilities through quantile regressions. More specifically, for each bank in Saudi Arabia and the UAE, we separately regress its EDFs on the EDFs of the other banks in the system as well as on the EDFs of advanced country financial sectors, and focus on relationship at the 90th quantile level. In other words, we estimate the conditional 90th EDF quantile for each bank (conditional on the EDF of any other bank in the system).

Using the estimated coefficients, the predicted EDFs from the 90th quantile regression of bank i given the EDF of bank j define the value at risk (VaR) of bank i given bank j. Then, for each pair bank i and bank/financial sector j:

- We compute *particular* predicted values which define the conditional VaR ($\text{Co-VaR}_{i/j}$): the VaR of bank i conditional on bank j being in distress, which we take as the EDF of bank/financial sector j being at its 90th percentile value.
- We also compute the change in Co-VaR for bank i which we define as the difference between the VaR of bank i conditional on the distress of bank/financial sector j and the VaR of bank i conditional on the median state of bank/financial sector j (i.e., bank/financial sector j not being in distress).

Focusing on international spillovers, the Co-VaR thus measures, for each advanced economy's financial sector, the value at risk of a banking system conditional on the distress of financial sectors in Europe. In addition, the change in Co-VaR captures the marginal contribution of a particular financial sector (in a noncausal sense) to the overall systemic risk in the UAE or Saudi Arabia.

8.4.2 Distress Dependence Methodology

We also use the distress dependence methodology of Segoviano (2006) and Segoviano and Goodhart (2009), who conceptualize the banking system as a portfolio of banks, and compute banking system stability measures. Since banks are either directly (through the interbank deposit market) or indirectly (through lending to common sectors) linked, and their distress changes with the economic cycle, the banking system's joint probability of default (i.e., the probability that all banks in the system suffer large losses simultaneously) may experience larger nonlinear increases than those experienced by the probabilities of distress of individual banks. Estimating the aggregate banking system's stability thus requires adequately capturing banks' default dependence and measuring how it changes over time.

The nonparametric methodology proposed in Segoviano (2006) is based on updating a prior multivariate distribution $q(x,y)$ for asset valuation x and y (assuming there are only two banks) using information on the individual probabilities of default of bank x and bank y. The posterior multivariate distribution $p(x,y)$ is the distribution closest to $q(x,y)$,[9] such that the marginal density for x satisfies the condition that bank x probability of distress (i.e., the probability that asset values fall below a given threshold T_d^x) is equal to the empirically observed EDF_x. A second, symmetric, condition is that the marginal density for y satisfies the condition that bank y probability of distress is equal to EDF_y. The final condition is that $q(x,y)$ indeed be a distribution, always positive and summing to 1. Using calculus of variation, the algorithm of Segoviano (2006) minimizes the distance between $p(x,y)$ and $q(x,y)$ under these three constraints (if there are two banks only—the method is easily generalized to more banks).

Using EDF data for Emirati and Saudi banks, we construct a set of indicators assessing the level of distress from a bank or group of banks on others in the system. The measure we focus on is the Bank Stability Index (BSI) which computes the expected number of bank defaults in a banking system, conditional on the default of at least one bank in the system.[10]

[9] The criteria used is the Kullback cross-entropy criteria, which is the weighted average relative distance between p and q, using p(x,y) as weights.

[10] Another measure that comes out from this analysis is banks' Joint Probability of Default (JPoD): the probability that all the banks in the system experience large losses and default simultaneously.

8.5 Results

8.5.1 International Spillovers

For the GCC, as for most emerging and frontier markets, global developments are the main sources of risk. Figure 8.4 shows that the Co-VaR with the larger advanced economies is higher. Since value at risk is higher for distress events that are probable and/or that would trigger large losses, the Co-VaR model singles out risk coming from a Greek banking distress (a probable event) and from US/UK markets (where losses would be largest). The probability of bank distress in Germany or France is considered to be lower. The Co-VaR with Turkey is relatively high and reflects regional exposure.

The general interpretation of the results should therefore be that the distress in the global financial system has spillover effects on the UAE banking system. It is, however, worth noting that the ranking of advanced economies changes depending on the time period covered. As expected, the United States was the prime source of risk when narrowing the estimation window around Lehman.

For Saudi Arabia, Spain, Turkey, and Greece's financial sectors are identified as affecting the value at risk of the banking system the most with respect to both Co-VaR and Δ Co-VaR measures. The ranking of the USA depends on the measure used, but under both measures, the US financial sector ranks among the top seven advanced economies with the largest potential spillovers to the Saudi banking system (Figure 8.5). While the magnitudes of distress are quite low, the relative ranking of advanced economies can be indicative of the relative exposure of Saudi banks to these countries' financial systems and hence to contagion risks.

Emirati banks are much more exposed to distress in global markets than Saudi banks. Since foreign asset exposure is relatively similar, the source of

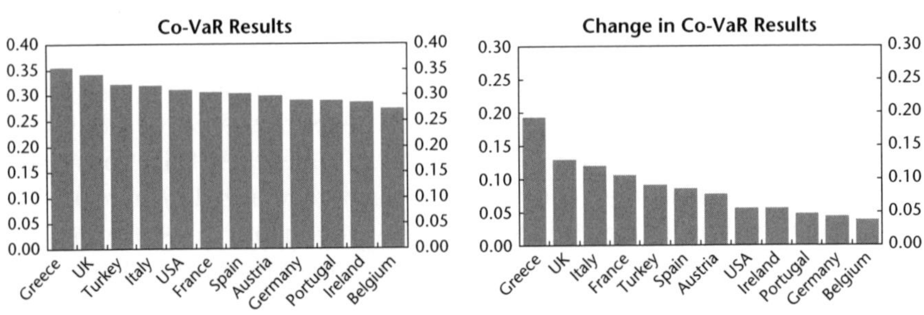

Figure 8.4. International spillovers to UAE banks: Effect of distress in Europe and the United States, 2008–10

Source: Authors' calculations

However, the likelihood of such an event happening is very low, due to the predominance of domestic banks with access to significant potential government support. Indeed, when we run the model for UAE and SA banking systems, we find the JPoD to be equal to zero during 2008–10, despite exhibiting minor spikes around the global crisis.

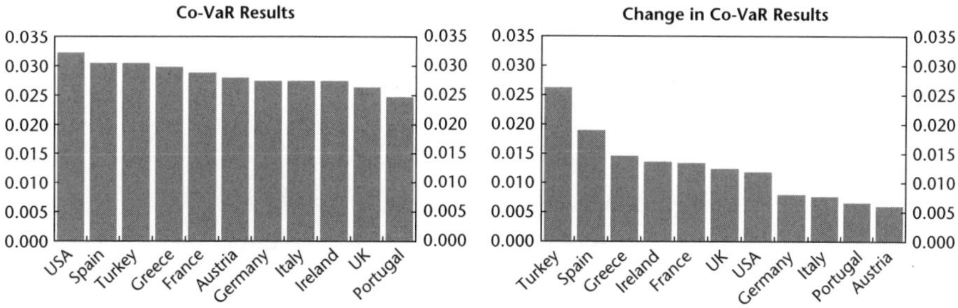

Figure 8.5. International spillovers to Saudi Arabian banks: Effect of distress in Europe and the United States, 2008–10
Source: Authors' calculations

such vulnerability in the UAE is probably due to funding risks (Table 8.5). The global crisis did indeed highlight the risks coming from banks' dependence on external funding. Banks in the US and in other advanced economies, facing liquidity shortages at home, reduced their international exposure, which put pressure on emerging market banks. In addition, the profitability of UAE banks was squeezed during the global meltdown and the related collapse of the real estate and construction sectors. On the contrary, real estate loans in Saudi Arabia are marginal, and prudential regulations require banks to get the central bank's approval for foreign exposure.

8.5.2 Local Spillovers within and Between UAE and Saudi Arabia

Using first the Bank Stability Index (BSI) measure, we show how banks' local interconnectedness in the UAE and in Saudi Arabia evolved over the crisis period 2008–10. Since September 2008, the UAE BSI, which shows the number of banks expected to default if one bank defaults, exhibited two peaks: a major peak around the global financial crisis post- Lehman collapse (January–September 2009) and a minor one around the Dubai World distress (December 2009–February 2010). The BSI then converged to one (i.e., no risks of contagion), its pre-crisis level, by mid-2010. The BSI for Saudi banks showed smaller and less prolonged signs of distress around the global crisis compared to UAE banks. The BSI was consistently below two and quickly converged to one by end-2009 (Figure 8.6).

Second, we report two matrices of bilateral exposures of banks to each other in each banking system (Tables 8.6 and 8.7). We measure these exposures by banks' predicted pairwise conditional default probabilities or Co-VaR.[11] In the UAE, a few banks show a high probability of default, conditional on stressing

[11] In this section, we focus only on the Co-VaR measure, as results from the change in Co-VaR were very similar.

Table 8.6. Co-VaR estimates for UAE banks 2008–10

	Bank 1	Bank 2	Bank 3	Bank 4	Bank 5	Bank 6	Bank 7	Bank 8	Bank 9	Vulnerability
Bank 1	–	0.87	0.87	0.94	0.88	0.96	0.82	0.93	1.00	0.91
Bank 2	0.67	–	0.61	0.73	0.61	0.53	0.52	0.60	0.56	0.60
Bank 3	0.76	0.72	–	0.73	0.63	0.65	0.65	0.67	0.65	0.68
Bank 4	0.26	0.27	0.26	–	0.37	0.36	0.20	0.27	0.33	0.29
Bank 5	0.00	0.00	0.00	0.00	–	0.00	0.00	0.00	0.00	0.00
Bank 6	0.01	0.01	0.01	0.01	0.01	–	0.01	0.01	0.01	0.01
Bank 7	0.00	0.00	0.00	0.00	0.00	0.00	–	0.00	0.00	0.00
Bank 8	0.18	0.20	0.14	0.16	0.22	0.20	0.12	–	0.15	0.17
Bank 9	0.04	0.03	0.04	0.03	0.04	0.03	0.03	0.03	–	0.03
Importance	0.24	0.26	0.24	0.33	0.34	0.34	0.29	0.31	0.34	–

Note: Each cell in the table reports the predicted 90th percentile default probability of the bank listed in the rows conditional on the bank listed in the columns being in distress (i.e., at its 90th percentile value). For instance, column 1 row 2 suggests that the predicted 90th percentile default probability of Bank 2, conditional on Bank 1 being in distress, is 0.67. For each column, the average represents the systemic importance of the bank in the column (the average of default probabilities of any other bank, conditional on column bank being in distress). For each row, the average value represents the vulnerability of the bank in the row (the average of its conditional default probabilities, given that each of the other banks in the system is separately in distress).

Source: Authors' calculations

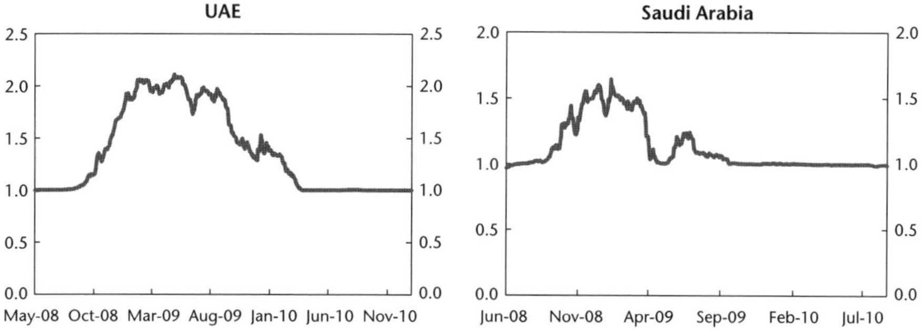

Figure 8.6. Bank stability index of local banks, 2008–10
Source: Authors' calculations

Table 8.7. Co-VaR estimates for Saudi Arabian banks 2008–10

	Bank 1	Bank 2	Bank 3	Bank 4	Bank 5	Bank 6	Bank 7	Vulnerability
Bank 1	–	0.00	0.00	0.00	0.00	0.00	0.00	0.00
Bank 2	0.06	–	0.08	0.08	0.08	0.08	0.08	0.07
Bank 3	0.08	0.09	–	0.12	0.11	0.12	0.07	0.10
Bank 4	0.00	0.00	0.00	–	0.00	0.00	0.00	0.00
Bank 5	0.00	0.00	0.00	0.00	–	0.00	0.00	0.00
Bank 6	0.00	0.00	0.00	0.00	0.00	–	0.00	0.00
Bank 7	0.02	0.02	0.02	0.04	0.03	0.03	–	0.03
Importance	0.03	0.02	0.02	0.04	0.04	0.04	0.03	–

Source: Authors' calculations

any other bank in the system (vulnerability index, last column of Table 8.6). However, there is no concentration of risk in any individual bank. Instead the average conditional default probability for banks in the system is similar whether Bank 1 or any other bank is stressed (indicator of "importance" in Table 8.6). Risk is relatively more concentrated in Saudi Arabia, although the levels of risk are much lower. Three banks (Banks 4, 5, and 6) are systemically important banks since the average impact of their distress on any other bank in the system is higher than average (Table 8.7). In addition, Banks 2 and 3 are by far the weakest banks in the system in terms of their average exposure to distress in other banks in the system.

Finally, we investigate intra-regional spillovers between Emirati and Saudi banks, which we find to be strong. Each bar in Figure 8.7 shows the systemic importance of each bank in UAE and Saudi Arabia for the Saudi banking system (top panel) and the UAE banking system (bottom panel). For instance, looking at the first bar of the top panel, systemic importance is measured here as the average default probability of all banks in Saudi Arabia, conditional on distress of Bank 1 in the UAE. Indeed some of the results here, in particular the effect of Saudi banks on each other and of Emirati banks on each other,

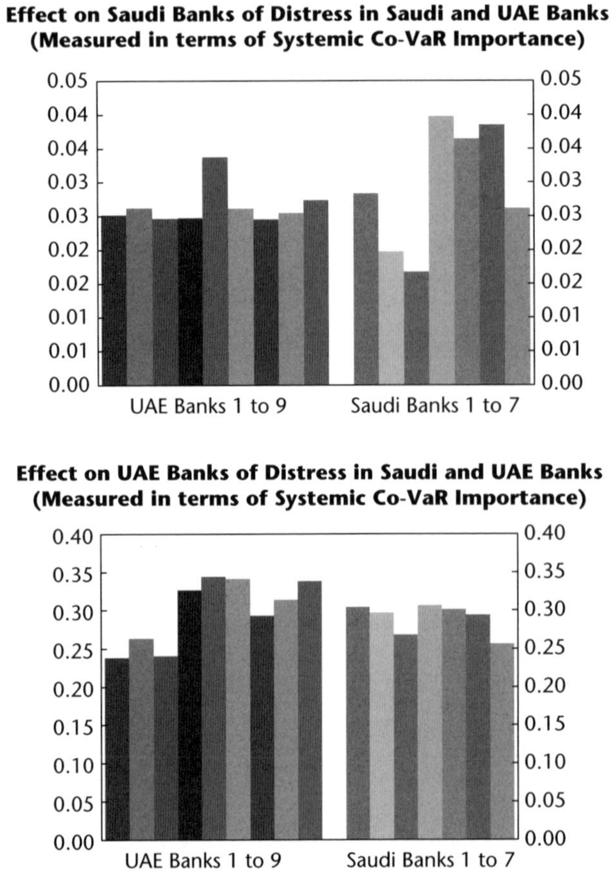

Figure 8.7. Intra-regional spillovers between UAE and Saudi Arabian banks, 2008–10
Source: Authors' calculations

are the same as the ones reported in the tables above on local spillovers. We report them again here to show the relative response of Emirati or Saudi banking systems to distress in its own banks or in neighboring banks. While in both countries the most systemically important banks are local banks, we find that some Saudi banks are systemically more important to the UAE banking system than some other UAE banks, and that similarly distress in some UAE banks has a larger effect on Saudi banks than distress originating in Saudi banks.[12]

[12] These results are based on the Co-VaR measure. Similar results, not reported here, were obtained using the change in Co-VaR measure.

8.6 Conclusion

The GCC financial sector has developed significantly over the last decade and thus far has been resilient to the current global crisis. Notwithstanding the strength of the financial system, our analysis identified risks to the banking sector's financial stability in the context of the current global crisis and of regional stress events such as the Dubai World default. We find that while the degree of international spillovers from the global crisis has varied throughout the region, with Dubai banks more exposed than Abu Dhabi and Saudi banks, local and intra-regional interconnectedness between banks remain strong. Notwithstanding that, our analysis shows that on aggregate, markets currently do not anticipate bank defaults or systemic events either in the UAE or Saudi banking system, though banks are perceived as affected by spillovers from advanced financial markets. A direct policy implication arises from our analysis: managing liquidity and credit risks in robust risk assessment culture, among others, would help insulate the banking system from contagion risks and strengthen financial stability.

References

Adrian, T. and Brunnermeier, M. K. (2011). "CoVaR." NBER Working Paper No. w17454. Cambridge, Mass.: National Bureau of Economic Research.

Al-Hassan, Khamis, M., and Oulidi, N. (2010). "The GCC banking sector: Topography and analysis." IMF Working Paper No. 10/87. Washington DC: International Monetary Fund.

Espinoza, R., Prasad, A., and Williams, O. (2010). "Regional financial integration in the GCC." IMF Working Paper No. 10/90. Washington DC: International Monetary Fund.

Merton, R. C. (1974). "On the pricing of corporate debt: The risk structure of interest rates," *Journal of Finance*, 29: 449–70.

Saadi Sedik, T. and Williams, O. (2012). "Do Gulf Cooperation Countries' equity markets waltz or tango to spillovers?" *Macroeconomics and Finance in Emerging Market Economies*, 5: 213–27.

Sbeiti, W. and Alshammari, T. (2010). "Integration of stock markets in the GCC countries: An application of the ARDL bounds testing model," *European Journal of Economics, Finance & Administrative Sciences*, 20 (May): 35.

Segoviano, M. A. (2006). "The consistent information multivariate density optimizing methodology." Financial Markets Group, London School of Economics, Discussion Paper 557. London: London School of Economics.

Segoviano, M. A. and Goodhart, C. (2009). "Banking stability measures." IMF Working Paper WP/09/04. Washington DC: International Monetary Fund.

9

The Importance of the GCC for the Wider Region

9.1 Economic Openness and Spillovers

The book thus far has analyzed the GCC macroeconomic stabilization and longer-term structural challenges. The importance of researching the GCC countries however is not only limited to a deeper understanding of the region itself since there are significant implications for developments in the GCC on the wider MENA region, as well as on many countries in South Asia. The GCC region is very open and extensively connected internationally. We conclude the book by discussing the economic relationships of the GCC with the rest of the world.

For decades, the GCC region has been a stable source of sizeable private as well as public foreign-exchange flows to neighboring countries. While the many expatriate workers hosted in the Gulf have steadily repatriated a significant portion of their earnings to their home countries, the GCC countries have used their natural resource windfalls to provide foreign aid as well as directly invest in a large number of countries and, to a lesser extent, to support their exports. As a result, growth linkages between the GCC countries and the wider MENA region are significant. The global crisis has indeed shown the importance of the GCC as a stabilizing economy in the region: high and resilient levels of financial flows have helped mitigate the impact of the global crisis on many countries since 2008.

This conclusion goes into the details of the spillover channels, summarizing the literature on the complementarity between migration, trade, and FDI and discussing the data and the determinants of international linkages between the GCC countries and the MENA region. Although financial flows from the GCC to its neighbors have been relatively stable during the recent crisis, the literature as well as the historical GCC data show that economic conditions in source countries matter for the volumes of the different financial flows (remittances, trade, FDI, and foreign aid) to recipients. These results confirm the importance given to economic developments in the GCC for the MENA region. The panel regressions presented at the end of this chapter show that growth in the GCC is indeed a very significant explanatory variable for growth in MENA.

9.1.1 The Importance of Migration and Remittances

The large numbers of migrant workers in the GCC is probably one of the main reasons why the GCC region is such an important source of foreign exchange flows for neighboring and South Asian countries. According to the World Bank Bilateral Matrix, the 2010 stock of immigrants from neighboring Arab and South Asian countries in the GCC constituted for most GCC countries over 90 percent of their total number of immigrants. Looking at the source countries, large shares of their emigrants are in the GCC: 84 percent of Yemeni emigrants are in the GCC, and the share remains above 40 percent for Egypt, Sri Lanka, India, and Pakistan, and over 25 percent for Syria, Jordan, and Sudan.

Reflecting the pattern of migrants, remittances from the GCC are an important source of income for many Arab and South Asian countries, and constituted, based on the World Bank bilateral remittances data, a large share of total remittance receipts in these countries. Accounting for about half of total GCC remittance outflows in 2010, India was the largest single recipient, but given the size of India's economy these flows represented just 1.4 percent of its GDP. Remittances from the GCC constituted about 80 percent of total remittance receipts in Yemen and over a quarter of remittance receipts in a large number of neighboring Arab and Asian countries. Looking at individual GCC countries, the largest source of remittances for Yemen was Saudi Arabia, whereas the largest source for Syria was Kuwait and the largest source for India was the UAE. (Figure 9.1).

The resilience of remittance outflows from the GCC to the global crisis during 2008–10 is worth noting. While total world remittance outflows experienced their first ever recorded decrease between 2008 and 2009, contracting at about 7 percent (compared to 14 percent growth between 2007 and 2008), GCC outflows continued their strong, though lower, growth in 2008–9 at 13 percent, compared to 22 percent in 2007–8. A similar pattern emerges when looking at total world remittance inflows. Remittance inflows to countries that are known to receive most of their flows from the GCC (such as in Figure 9.1) continued to grow, albeit at smaller rates, between 2008 and 2009, when remittance

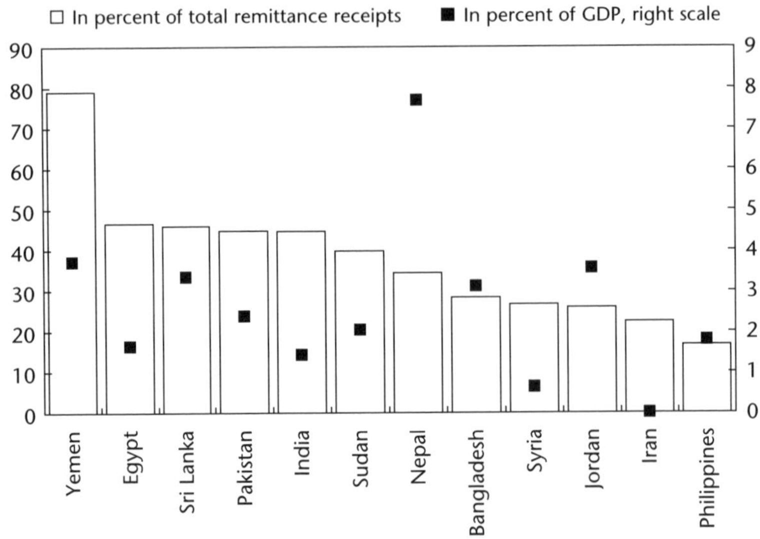

Figure 9.1. Remittances from the GCC in 2010
Source: World Bank

inflows to the rest of the world contracted for the first time ever. This indeed reflects the resilience of GCC economies' growth rates to global distress.

9.1.2 International Trade

A well-established literature has shown the role of migrants, especially skilled ones, in contract enforcement and information transmission needed to develop international trade between home and host countries. Using a panel dataset of bilateral trade between the US and forty-seven trading partners from 1970 to 1986, Gould (1994) found a strong positive effect of immigrant networks on US exports to, as well as imports from, immigrants' home countries. Similarly, Head and Ries (1998) estimated an extended trade gravity model using bilateral trade data between Canada, a main immigration destination, and 136 trading partners, and found, among other things, that a 10 percent increase in immigrants is associated with a 3 percent increase in Canadian imports from immigrants' home countries, and that these effects are larger for more independent (skilled) migrants. Rauch and Trinidad (2002) do not focus on a specific immigration destination but instead show the large effect of ethnic Chinese business networks on global bilateral trade patterns.

Although trade with the MENA region has represented only a small share of total GCC imports and exports (only 3 percent of GCC imports originated from non-GCC MENA countries, Figure 9.2), for many countries, trade with

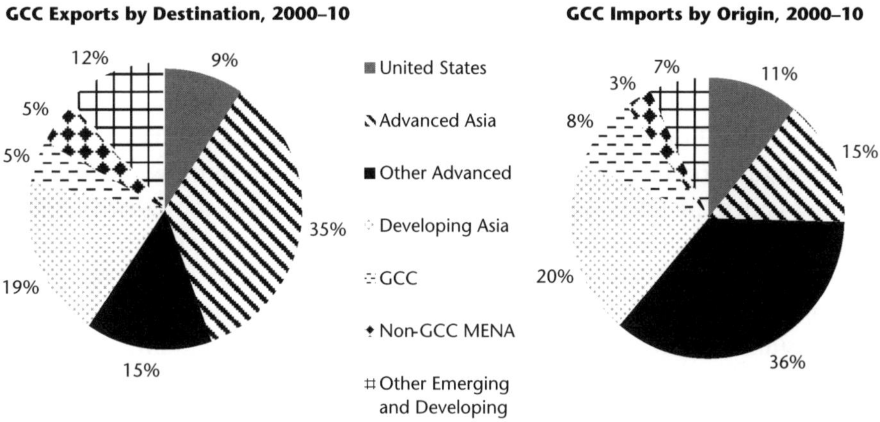

Figure 9.2. Geographical distribution of GCC merchandise trade, 2000–10
Note: Advanced Asia includes Japan, Republic of Korea, Hong Kong, Singapore, Taiwan
Source: IMF Direction of Trade Statistics

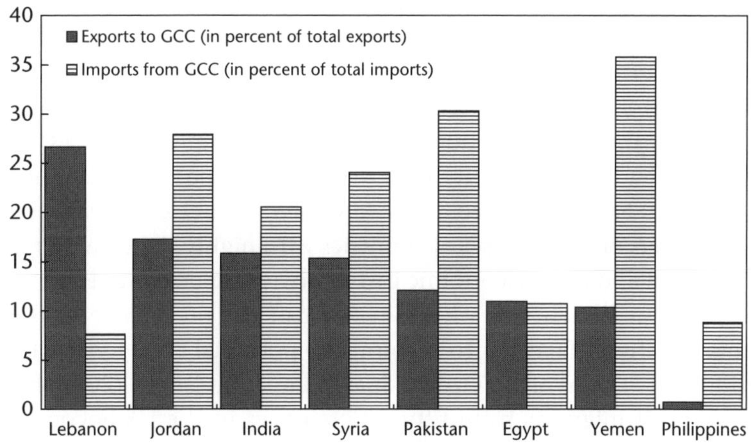

Figure 9.3. Merchandise trade with the GCC, 2011
Source: IMF Direction of Trade Statistics

the GCC has been the highest relative to the size of their economies. In line with the gravity models of international trade, bilateral trade data show that the countries where trade with the GCC represents the largest share of their own exports and imports tend to be within close geographical proximity. However, the migrant networks also matter. Countries where the GCC accounts for more than 15 percent of outgoing exports are Jordan, India, Lebanon, and Syria, and more than 10 percent Yemen, Egypt, and Pakistan. Imports from the GCC into neighboring countries are also significant but they mainly comprise oil (Figure 9.3).

9.1.3 Complementarity between Migration and FDI[1]

Large migrant networks can also bring in foreign capital to the labor-exporting economies. This hypothesis of complementarity between migration flows and FDI flows, however, challenges the standard trade substitutability effect, which argues for a negative relationship between labor outflows and capital inflows (since the former increases the relative return of labor and therefore decreases the attractiveness of the domestic economy to foreign investors).

The complementarity hypothesis is that the presence of an educated diaspora provides foreign investors with a much-needed knowledge of the domestic consumer and of the local labor and input markets (including consumer preferences, regulations, etc.). This helps break contractual and informational barriers to long-term inward foreign investments in the labor-exporting country. In addition to the resulting financial remittance transfers from overseas professionals, skilled emigration can thus lead to improved development in labor-exporting countries, and in this particular setting, the argument is that educated migrants either attract foreign investors or themselves make investments in their native countries. Unskilled migrants can also increase FDI by revealing workforce characteristics (such as worker productivity) and decreasing cross-border information costs, thereby reducing uncertainty about the profitability of FDI. Furthermore, migration could also provide unskilled migrants with the necessary human and physical capital to invest in their home countries, an opportunity that would not be possible without migration. In the MENA region specifically, the migration channel can be one of the main drivers of FDI for a set of countries with highly skilled emigrants but where political and macroeconomic instability is a deterrent to FDI.

The empirical evidence has been in favor of the prevalence of the complementarity effect. Taking into account the potential endogeneity between migration and FDI, Javorcik, Ozden, Spatareanu, and Neagu (2011) find that the presence of migrants from fifty-six countries in the US encouraged US FDI flows into those countries, with a stronger effect for skilled (educated) migrants. Kugler and Rapoport (2007) show the existence of contemporaneous substitutability and dynamic complementarity between migration and FDI, with a stronger relationship for migrants with highest schooling attainments. In the short run, the trade substitutability effect prevails as increased immigration and the resulting factor price changes reduce the incentives for

[1] This section only focuses on FDI outflows within the GCC and from the GCC to its Arab neighbors, where the relationship is most important and comparable data available. Data are based on several issues of the *Investment Climate in Arab Countries Report*, which is published annually by the Arab Investment & Export Credit Guarantee Corporation. This is not say that GCC countries' outward FDI is only focused on Arab countries. For instance, according to data by the Central Bank of Pakistan, about 17 percent of total inward FDI in 2010–2011 originated from the GCC (the UAE in particular).

FDI. In the long run however, the migrant network effect comes into play and dictates a positive relationship between (mainly skilled) emigration and positive future FDI. Kugler and Rapoport (2007) argue that the migration-FDI effect can be interpreted as a reduction in the domestic economy risk premium required on foreign investments. Gao (2003), Federici and Giannetti (2010), and Ivlevs and de Melo (2008), among others, also find empirical evidence in support of a positive association between emigration from developing countries and FDI.

The GCC region has been a major source of FDI in the MENA (over the period 1985–2009, the UAE was by far the largest investor in the region). However, intra-GCC FDI constitutes about 91 percent of total FDI outflows in Bahrain and about 61 percent in Kuwait. On the other hand, Oman has predominantly invested in Algeria, while Saudi Arabia's investment destinations have been more diversified across all countries in the region.

For the recipient countries, GCC FDI constitutes the lion's share of their total inward Arab FDI (over 80 percent in many cases). For countries like Jordan, Lebanon, and Sudan, GCC FDI inflows amounted to more than 1 percent of their GDP. It is worth noting that the geographical distribution as well as amount of outward FDI from the GCC to Arab countries has fluctuated over the years. For instance, Saudi outward FDI to Arab countries in both 2009 and 2010 was about a third of its value in 2006. While Lebanon received about 16 percent of total Saudi FDI to Arab countries in 2005, its share rose to about 88 percent in 2007. Similarly, Yemen's share dropped from 31 percent in 2006

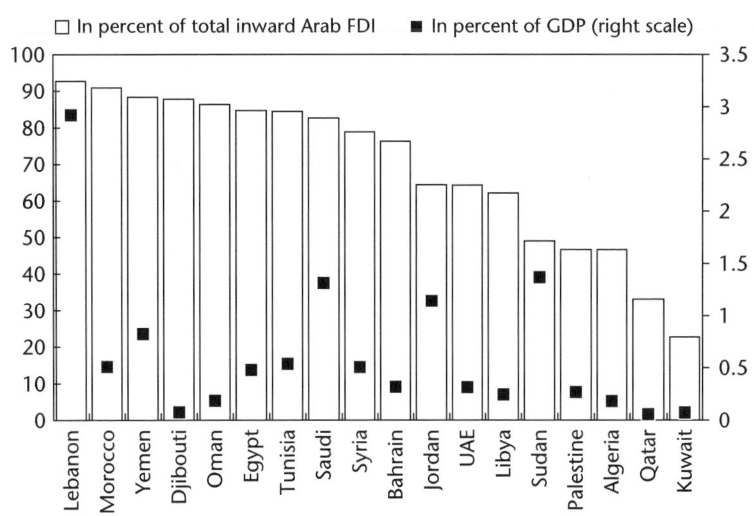

Figure 9.4. GCC outward FDI, 1985–2009

Source: The Arab Investment & Export Credit Guarantee Corporation to about 0 percent in 2009. Steady recipients have been Sudan, Syria, Egypt, and Jordan (Figure 9.4). Overall, the correlation between the 2010 stock of GCC migrant workers from Lebanon, Syria, Jordan, Egypt, Sudan, and Yemen and the cumulative value of FDI invested by the GCC in these countries over 1985–2009 was 0.90, confirming the complementarity channel.

9.1.4 Foreign Aid

Throughout the last three decades, the GCC countries have provided large amounts of foreign aid to many countries around the globe, with Saudi Arabia being the top Arab aid donor, followed by Kuwait, the UAE, and more recently Qatar.[2] Arab aid is mostly exogenous to recipient countries' economic conditions, as it is mainly driven by oil export revenues, hence inheriting the volatility of oil prices (Figure 9.5). Thus, Arab aid is positively correlated to the economic situation in the donor countries, a situation that mimics what has been found in the aid flow literature (e.g., Pallage and Robe 2001).

Arab aid is characterized as unconditional and highly concessional with low interest payments and long repayment and grace periods, and emphasizes

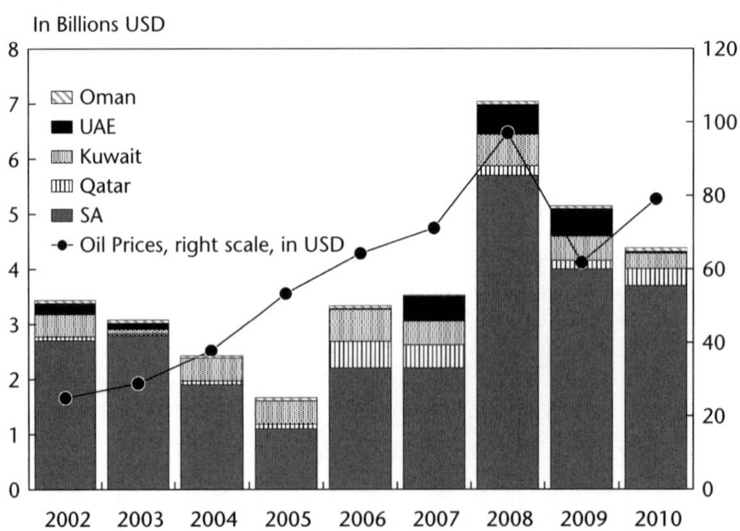

Figure 9.5. GCC aid outflows by source country, 2002–10
Source: Arab Monetary Fund

[2] Based on several issues of the *Joint Arab Economic Report*, an annual Arabic publication of the Arab Monetary Fund, which provides a chapter on "Developmental Arab Aid."

the importance of ownership of recipient governments of aid-financed development strategies and modalities of implementation. There are two major modalities of Arab aid: direct bilateral aid extended by Arab governments and aid granted through development funds (national and regional). In addition, Arab donors contribute to major international donor agencies and through charitable institutions. GCC bilateral assistance is mainly unconditional and grant-based. Even when involving loans, low interest rates and long repayment periods mean that the grant element is generally over 80 percent, compared to 40 to 45 percent for aid provided through the development funds. Bilaterally, the GCC have donated since 1970 a cumulative amount of $147 billion, constituting 95 percent of total Arab aid.[3] Saudi Arabia has ranked as the top donor by far. Contributing about 1 percent of its GDP over the past decade, Saudi Arabia has provided over $100 billion in bilateral foreign assistance since 1970, about 68 percent of total Arab aid. Kuwait has provided about 14 percent, followed by the UAE (9 percent) and Qatar (3 percent).

Since 1962 Arab development funds have provided about $104 billion in aid, mostly through regional, rather than national, development funds. For instance, Saudi Arabia contributed only about 10 percent of the total through its development fund, but has also made direct contributions to the regional funds (Figure 9.6). The bulk of this aid has been directed to Arab countries (61 percent), followed by Asian (22 percent), and African countries (15 percent). This aid has mostly been aimed at project financing, with

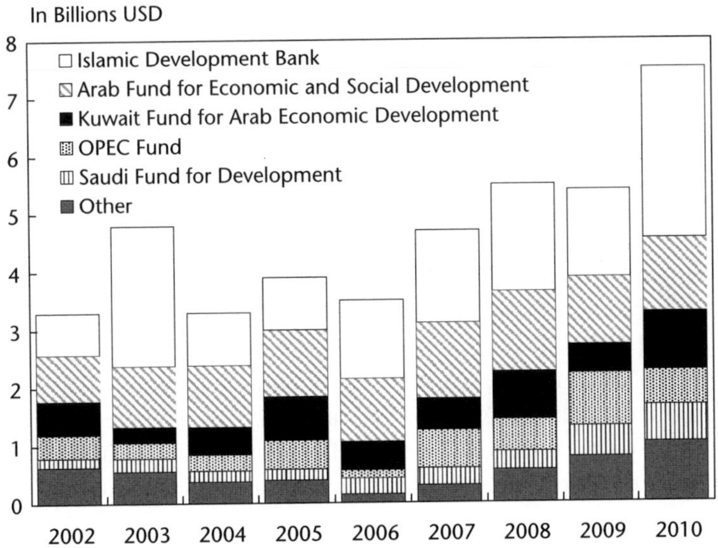

Figure 9.6. Arab aid through development funds, 2002–10

Source: Arab Monetary Fund

[3] Other Arab donors included Libya, Iraq, and Algeria.

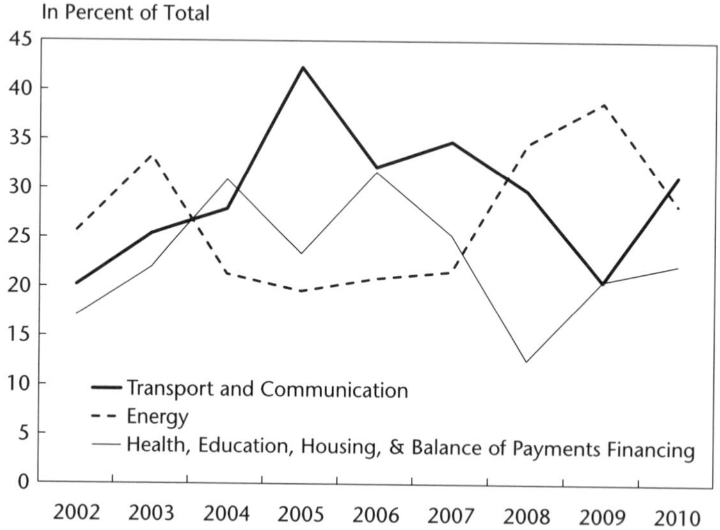

Figure 9.7. Sectoral distribution of Arab aid through development funds, 2002–10
Source: Arab Monetary Fund

transport, communication, and energy being the main sectors (Figure 9.7), and with an increasing focus on the private sector over the past decade. In addition to traditional transfer modalities such as concessional loans and grants, this category of assistance also operates through guarantees, technical assistance, and training.

9.2 Concluding on the Importance of the GCC

We conclude by estimating a growth spillover model that sheds light on the quantitative importance of GCC growth for economic developments in the neighboring MENA countries, given the spillover channels described earlier. The data is based on a panel model for sixteen countries of the MENA region,[4] for the period 1995–2008. The model is a fixed-effect model[5] with real GDP growth in MENA countries as a dependent variable (non-oil GDP growth for the oil producers). The independent variables are the average of non-oil GDP growth in the GCC, average G7 growth, Japan's growth (to capture the Asian crisis), oil prices, world trade growth, the Fed Funds Rate, and the VIX index.

[4] Afghanistan, Algeria, Djibouti, Egypt, Iran, Iraq, Jordan, Lebanon, Libya, Mauritania, Morocco, Pakistan, Sudan, Syrian Arab Republic, Tunisia, Yemen.
[5] The Breusch-Pagan test rejects at 90 percent the use of pooled OLS.

Table 9.1. Growth spillover model

	(1) FE	(2) FE	(3) FE	(4) FE	(5) FE	(6) FE	(7) OLS
VARIABLES							
Real GDP growth in individual MENA country (t-1)	–0.0337	–0.0337					
	[–0.348]	[–0.349]					
G7 real GDP growth	–0.0277						
	[–0.0423]						
GCC real GDP growth	0.556***	0.558***	0.477***	0.469***	0.300**	0.349***	0.415***
	[3.152]	[3.608]	[3.070]	[3.041]	[2.318]	[4.025]	[4.563]
Japan real GDP growth	–0.240	–0.238	–0.170				
	[–0.733]	[–0.747]	[-0.523]				
Oil price percentage change	0.0306**	0.0306**	0.0239*	0.0212*	0.00823	0.00865	0.0105
	[2.390]	[2.398]	[1.857]	[1.942]	[0.877]	[0.910]	[1.056]
World trade growth	–0.291	–0.297*	–0.232	–0.256*			
	[–1.175]	[–1.770]	[–1.398]	[–1.742]			
Fed Funds Rate	0.00377*	0.00373*	0.00203	0.00206	–0.00101		
	[1.861]	[1.777]	[0.880]	[0.904]	[–0.616]		
VIX index	–0.00100	–0.00100*	–0.000973*	–0.000792	–0.000534	–0.000380	–0.000363
	[–1.639]	[–1.670]	[–1.668]	[–1.637]	[–1.120]	[–0.935]	[–0.943]
Constant	0.0696**	0.0693**	0.0850***	0.0818***	0.0877***	0.0770***	0.0217*
	[2.008]	[2.154]	[2.841]	[2.790]	[2.957]	[3.472]	[1.653]
Observations	202	202	205	205	205	205	205
R-squared	0.248	0.248	0.271	0.270	0.254	0.253	0.117

Robust t-statistics in brackets

*** $p < 0.01$, ** $p < 0.05$, * $p < 0.1$

In addition, the lagged depended variable was also included, but it was not found to be significant.

A general-to-specific approach shows that growth in the GCC is the most significant variable explaining growth in the other MENA countries (see Table 9.1). The growth elasticity is around 0.4–0.5 and was found to be robust to the inclusion of control variables and to the use of pooled OLS, random effects, or fixed effects. Surprisingly, G7 growth and oil prices were not found to be significant and the coefficient for world growth was negative. The results are consistent with the findings of Ilahi and Shendy (2008), who also investigate the importance of remittances and financial flows and transmission channels.

The growing importance of the GCC countries, especially for the MENA region, has not been fully reflected in the number of comprehensive and quantitative analyses of these countries, despite the increasing availability of data. This book contributes to filling this gap. We have combined econometric analysis and theoretical modeling with anecdotal evidence and extensive data gathering, and hope that the findings will be useful to both academics and policy-oriented practitioners interested in a better understanding of the macroeconomics of the Gulf States.

With abundant resource wealth, pegged exchange rates, fiscal policy that is mostly discretionary, and pervasive subsidies, the macroeconomic experiences of GCC countries are indeed also worth analyzing because their successes as well as weaknesses offer many important lessons to countries around the world sharing one or more of these characteristics. Chapters 2 through 8 have covered these issues, looking at both long-term structural challenges and at short-term macroeconomic management. This concluding chapter showed that the importance of the GCC economies has increasingly spanned across their borders, as they have become increasingly interlinked with their Asian, Arab and non-Arab, neighbors through aid, trade, remittances, and FDI.

References

Federici, D. and Giannetti, M. (2010). "Temporary migration and foreign direct investment," *Open Economies Review*, 21: 293–308.

Gao, T. (2003). "Ethnic Chinese networks and international investment: Evidence from inward FDI in China," *Journal of Asian Economics*, 14: 611–29.

Gould, D. M. (1994). "Immigrant links to the home country: Empirical implications for U.S. bilateral trade flows," *Review of Economics and Statistics*, 76 (2): 302–16.

Head, K. and Ries, J. (1998). "Immigration and trade creation: Econometric evidence from Canada," *Canadian Journal of Economics*, 31: 47–62.

Ilahi, N. and Shendy, R. (2008). "Do the Gulf oil-producing countries influence regional growth?" *The Impact of Financial and Remittances Flows*, IMF WP/08/167. Washington DC: International Monetary Fund.

Ivlevs, A. and de Melo, J. (2008). "FDI, the brain drain and trade: Channels and evidence." CEPR Discussion Paper No. 7002. University of Nottingham.

Javorcik, B. S., Ozden, C., Spatareanu, M., and Neagu, C. (2011). "Migrant networks and foreign direct investment," *Journal of Development Economics*, 94: 231–41.

Kugler, M. and Rapoport, H. (2007). "International labor and capital flows: Complements or substitutes?" *Economic Letters*, 9: 155–62.

Pallage, S. and Robe, M. (2001). "Foreign aid and the business cycle," *Review of International Economics*, 9: 641–72.

Rauch, J. E. and Trinidade, V. (2002). "Ethnic Chinese networks in international trade," *Review of Economics and Statistics*, 84: 116–30.

Index

Abdalla, M., 49
Abreu, M., 32
Abu Dhabi 8, 10, 71, 146
  financial markets 150, 151, 153, 155–7, 165
Acemoglu, D., 36
Agénor, P. R., 3
Al-Hamidy, A., 2
Al-Jasser, M., 2
Aghion, P., 86
aid 11, 166–7, 172–6
Ali, A. A. G., 18
Altman, E. I., 140
Anderson, R., 138
appreciation 40, 51, 54, 56, 114, 121
Araujo, J., 4
Arellano, M., 140, 141, 142
Artadi, E., 25, 33
asset prices 7–9, 17,113, 121–2, 134, 138, 145
Aten, B., 16, 19

Baele, L., 116
Bahrain 1, 2, 5, 6, 7, 10, 171
  financial markets 149, 151, 153–5
  fiscal policy 86, 88, 89, 94, 101–4, 108, 109
  long-term growth 13–16, 18–29, 37
  migration 41, 43–46, 48–9, 51–2
  monetary policy 113–21, 133, 134
  loans/stability 134–7, 146
  spending, subsidies, and efficiency 65–6, 70–1
Baldwin-Edwards, M., 46
banks 2, 3, 7, 8–10, 22, 50, 65, 66, 78, 84, 108, 112–22, 131, 134–9, 141–3, 145–6, 149–65, 167–8, 170, 173
  central 3, 8, 65, 112–16, 122, 131
  credit 7, 112
  commercial 8, 87, 84, 152, 154
  distress 150, 160, 164
  interconnectedness 149–65
  lending 50, 120–1, 137
  sector 8, 9, 120, 135, 145, 149–50, 153–4, 165
  system 8–10, 113, 120, 134–5, 145, 149–50, 149–65
Barajas, A., 145
Barro, R., 25, 26, 30, 33, 35
Bercoff, J., 138
Bertola, G., 86
Billmeier, A., 35
Binder, M., 59
Blanchard, O., 91
Blundell, R., 140
Bond, S., 140, 141, 142
Bondt, G. de, 117
Bova, E., 115
Bover, O., 141
business cycle 91–2, 105, 138, 139, 143

capital:
  adequacy ratios 9, 135, 140–1
  depreciation 23, 31, 138
  expenditure 89–98, 109, 114
  human 15, 24–6, 29, 36, 54, 77
  inflow 1, 9, 113
  intensity 13, 23–4, 27, 67, 72
  outflow 112, 115
  physical 3, 15, 31, 33, 54, 170
  public 73–5
  stock 21–6, 29–30, 81
  type 29–30, 56
capitalization 9, 135, 149–53
Carey, M., 140
Caselli, F., 23, 25, 29, 30
Cherif, R., 4
Christiano, L. J., 122, 123
Chu, C., 123, 145
Ciccarelli, M., 145
Cobham, D., 4
cointegration 26, 58, 115, 118
Collin-Dufresne, P., 138
commodities 7, 41, 76–7, 113, 122–5, 131–2, 131
competitiveness 6–7, 21, 40, 61
complementarity 29, 166, 170–2
consumption 9, 15, 17, 33, 35, 57, 58, 72–6, 83, 90, 108, 121, 123
contagion 9, 10, 149–50, 154, 156, 160–1, 165
convergence 2, 31–2, 59, 116
Corden, W. M., 53, 57

correlation 9–10, 36, 56, 59–60, 68, 91, 95, 104, 122–4, 141, 152–3, 172
CoVar 150, 158–64
countercyclical 8, 31, 86–8, 91, 102, 105, 110
credit risk 134, 136, 138–9, 143, 165
crisis:
  Asian 139, 142, 176
  global financial 4, 7–10, 89, 106, 108, 112, 115–16, 131, 134–5, 137, 149–53, 156, 159–61, 165–7
  Greek 152
current account 3, 8
curse 6, 15, 28, 34, 37, 39, 40, 85, 110

D'Arcy, P., 138
determinants 4, 90, 167, 170
  long-term growth 13, 15–16, 19, 31
  migration 41, 56, 58, 60
  financial stability 137–9, 142
Dhal, D., 139
Dhal, S. C., 138
Dibeh, G., 4
distress dependence 158–60
diversification 1, 91
  long-term growth 14–15, 18, 20–1, 24
  migration 40, 50, 60–1
  spending, subsidies and efficiency 65–7, 70–2
Dixit, A., 51
Docquier, A., 44, 45
Doucouliagos, H., 36
Drehmann, M., 135
Duan, J. C., 138
Dubai 7, 9, 10, 51, 146
  financial markets 150–8, 161, 165
Dutch disease 6, 21, 34, 40–1, 50, 54–5, 60–1

economic cycle 4, 87–8, 95, 102, 137, 159
econometric estimate 15, 92, 109
economic union 2
Edwards, S., 35
education 14–15, 19, 24–5, 31, 33, 45–7, 49, 65–6, 73–4, 77, 79, 83, 109, 174
Efron, B., 119
Eichenbaum, M., 122, 123
elasticity 21, 25, 31, 49, 54–5, 60, 62, 76–7, 83, 92–3, 100–4, 116–7, 131–3, 137, 176
electricity 70–1, 74, 77
employment 13, 16, 18, 25, 40–2, 45–50, 61, 66–7, 74, 79–84, 91, 121, 138–9
equipment 15, 29–30, 56
Espinoza, R., 34, 86, 116, 152
Europe 30, 45, 145, 149, 152, 158, 160–1
Evans, C. L., 122, 123
exchange rate 2–8, 35, 138, 140
  fixed 90, 108, 112–32, 145, 176
  real 6, 7, 40–1, 51, 53–4, 56–61
exports 3, 5–8, 13–14, 17–19, 26, 28, 32–5, 37, 40–1, 56–8, 60–1, 69–74, 83, 86–9, 113, 166, 168–72
  hydrocarbon 19, 21, 52, 65, 72, 88–9
  non-oil 40, 50–2, 60, 71
  total 40, 50–1, 121, 169
exposure 7, 9, 134–5, 138, 145, 149–50, 160–1, 163

Fasano, U., 49, 89
FDI 11, 72, 166–7, 172, 176
Federici, D., 171
Feenstra, R., 29, 30
Felipe, J., 15
financial liberalization 34, 150
financial stability 137, 165
fiscal multiplier 90, 92, 101
fiscal policy 86, 95, 102
Fischer, S., 33
foreign aid 11, 166–7, 172–4
foreign workers 7, 13, 21, 40, 42, 45–6, 49, 53–5, 60–1, 83, 90, 139
Florax, R. J. G. M., 32
foreign direct investment 151, 170–1, 176
foreign reserves 87
Frankel, J., 2
Fuentes, R., 138

gas 4–5, 18, 21, 24, 71–3, 106
Gao, T., 171
Ghosh, A., 34
Giannetti, M., 171
Giorno, C., 91
Giovanni, J. di, 138
global crisis 7–10, 106, 108, 112, 115, 134, 149–50, 152, 156, 160–62, 165, 166–7
Goldstein, R., 138
Gould, D.M., 168
Goyal, R., 49
Grimard, F., 138
Groot, H. L. F. de, 32
Gross domestic product/GDP 2, 4, 6, 13–18, 20–3, 25–35, 37, 44–5, 50, 56, 69, 71, 74, 83–96, 100–101, 123–4, 131–2, 138, 139, 141–3, 145, 155–6, 167–8, 171, 173–5
growth, long-term 4, 6, 13, 15, 16, 20, 31, 77, 86
growth-accounting:
  model 15
  framework 15
  literature 25, 31
  exercise 15, 23, 25–6, 68
Gylfason, T., 60

Hakura, D., 31
Hall, R. E., 24

Hanson, M. S., 122, 130, 131, 133
Hasanov, F., 4
Head, K., 168
Heston, A., 16, 19
Hnatkovska, V., 34, 86
Hofmann, B., 116
Holtz-Eakin, D., 141
Hughes, J. P., 139
human development index 13, 19, 49
Hydrocarbon 18–21, 51, 88–9

Ilahi, N., 176
Ilzetzki, E., 90, 92, 95
Im, K., 58
IMF 4, 14, 16–20, 23–4, 26–8, 32, 51–2, 66, 78, 87, 92–4, 97, 107, 109–10, 113, 114, 123–5, 137, 138, 169
imports 2, 17, 35, 41–2, 53–4, 56–7, 60–1, 90, 109, 114–15, 123, 168–9
  capital goods 29–30, 89, 114
  and migration 60, 168
impulse response 92, 100, 102–3, 105, 118–19, 130–5, 144
incentive 7, 33, 44, 67, 72–3, 79–81, 171
inflation 32, 33
infrastructure 13, 19, 42, 44, 50, 56, 65, 67, 70, 74, 109
institutions 29–32, 35–7, 68, 83, 151, 173
  credit 50, 66
  financial 7, 10, 86, 149
  government/political/legal 29, 113
  quality of 15, 32, 34, 36, 70, 86
integration 1, 2, 3, 11, 26, 44, 152
interbank:
  liquidity 8
  market 8, 113, 159
  rates 2, 115–21
interconnectedness 149–50, 158, 161, 165
interest rate 2, 78, 90, 92–3, 95, 112–18, 120–2, 134, 137–9, 141–3, 145, 173
  ceiling/cap 116, 120, 134
  domestic/local 8, 87, 112, 122
  increase 8, 121–2, 132, 137, 142–5
  policy 8, 113
inverse Ramsey model 67, 73–4
investment 3, 7–10, 14–17, 23–6, 29, 33, 86, 88–90, 94, 115, 121
  companies 7, 10, 135, 146, 152–4
  foreign 151, 170–1
  non-oil 21, 25
  oil 21, 25
  public 67–76, 83, 88, 106
Islam, F., 88
Ivlevs, A., 171

Jacques, K., 139
Javorcik, B. S., 170
Johnson, S., 36
Jones, C. I., 24

Kao, C., 58
Kapiszewski, A., 42, 43
Keeton, W. R., 138, 145
Kent, C., 138
Khamis, M., 134, 154
Khan, M. S., 34
Kida, M., 145
Kose, M. A., 34, 86
Kugler, M., 170, 171
Kuwait 1, 2, 5, 6, 7, 8–11, 167, 171–3
  financial markets 150, 151, 153–5
  fiscal policy 87, 89, 94, 101–4, 106–7
  long-term growth 13–14, 16, 18–25, 27–9, 33–4, 37
  migration 43–6, 48–52
  monetary policy 112–21, 133, 134
  loans/stability 134–6, 146
  spending, subsidies, and efficiency 65–6, 70–1, 73
Kwapil, C., 117

labor force 1, 4, 13–15, 30, 40–3, 170
  female 42, 49, 79
  foreign 1, 7, 13, 40, 43, 52, 80, 90, 139
  growth of 41–2, 47, 54, 78
  indigenous/national 40, 52, 139
  education/skills of 15, 24, 29
Lee, H. Y., 35
Lee, J. W., 25
Leon, H., 34
Levin, A., 123, 145
Levine, R., 33, 138
Li, B., 4
Lin, F., 123, 145
linkage 1, 7, 10, 166–7
liquidity 7–8, 10, 86, 95, 112–13, 134–5, 151–2, 161, 165
Loayza, N., 34, 86
Love, I., 145
Lucas, R. E. B., 43

McCallum, J., 2
McDonald, R., 86
macroeconomic:
  cycle 137
  policy 4, 7, 29
  stability 31, 33–4, 86–110, 170
Makdisi, S., 35
Mankiw, N. G., 31
Maquieira, C., 138
Melo, J., 171
Mendoza, E. G., 35, 90
migrant 15, 16, 24, 40–5, 52–7, 60, 81, 167–72

migration 1, 33, 40–5, 49–51, 54–7, 59–61, 166–8, 170–1
Miniane, J., 122, 130
Mizen, P., 116
money market 3, 112, 134
Montiel, P. J., 56
Mookerjee, R., 35
monetary policy 3, 8, 87, 90, 112–17, 121–5, 131–33
monetary union 1–4
mortgage 9–10, 74, 83
Mountford, A., 92
Mueller, C., 138
Mundell, R. A., 3, 90

Nakibullah, A., 88
Nandini, D., 36
Nannicini, T., 35
nationalization 42, 49–50, 61
natural resource 6, 17, 39, 85, 166
Neagu, C., 170
Newey, W., 141
Nigro, P., 139
Nijkamp, P., 33
nonperforming loans 9, 134–46
non-oil GDP 14, 18, 21–2, 26–8, 30, 33, 50, 56, 69, 87–9, 93, 95, 101–9, 130–3, 142–5, 174
non-oil growth 18, 21, 87–8, 93–4, 95, 100, 102–4, 106, 122, 143
Norman, V., 51

Offermanns, C. J., 59
oil revenues 14, 18, 20, 33, 52, 58, 60, 65, 67, 68, 71, 73–4, 78, 83, 88–9, 91, 100–1, 103, 132, 139
Oman 1, 2, 5, 171–2
  financial markets 151, 153–5
  fiscal policy 87, 89, 94, 101–4, 106, 108, 110
  long-term growth 13–14, 16, 18–22, 24–29, 37
  migration 40–6, 50–2
  monetary policy 113–21, 123, 133–4
  loans/stability 134, 135–7, 146
  spending, subsidies, and efficiency 66–8, 71–2, 79
openness 29, 32, 33, 35, 56, 166
optimal policy 75
optimal taxation 67, 74
optimal spending 4
orthogonalization 100–5, 118–28, 141
outflow 41
Ozden, C., 170

Pallage, S., 172
Panel 1, 8, 9, 41, 58–9, 61, 76, 79, 81, 88, 90, 92–3, 95, 96, 98, 101, 117, 121–4, 128, 131–4, 137, 139–40, 144–5, 163, 167–8, 174
pass-through 113, 116–17, 120, 134
Peltonen, T. A., 9
Perotti, R., 91, 92
Pesaran, M. H., 58, 59
Phillips, S., 34
Plant, R., 43
Ploeg, F. van der 4, 34, 56, 86
Poelhekke, S., 34, 86
Poot, J., 33
Poplawski-Ribeiro, M., 4
Prasad, A., 34, 116, 152
private sector 6, 17, 40, 42, 45–9, 61, 65, 67, 70, 72, 74–5, 78–84, 90, 174
probability of default 150, 156, 159, 161
pro-cyclical 88, 92, 102–3, 110
productivity 6, 13, 15, 16, 23, 25, 27, 29, 33, 37, 54, 56, 68–9, 71, 75, 170
  total factor 15, 25, 27, 29, 37, 69
Psacharopoulos, G., 24
public investment 67–70, 75, 76, 83, 88, 106
public sector 33, 42, 45–9, 53, 55, 67–8, 74, 78–80, 82–3, 90, 153

Qatar 1–2, 5, 8–9, 11, 13–16, 18–22, 24–6, 29, 32–4, 36–7, 40, 42–52, 65–6, 68, 70–3, 87, 89, 94, 101–4, 106–7, 113–21, 123, 133, 134–6, 146, 151–5, 171–3

Rajan, R., 138
Ramey, G., 34, 86
Ramey, V., 34, 86
Rapoport, H., 170, 171
Rauch, J. E., 168
real exchange rate 6–7, 40–1, 51, 53–4, 56–61
remittances 7, 11, 41–5, 51, 55–7, 59, 90, 166–8, 176
Renelt, D., 33
reserves 2, 3, 5, 8, 19, 65, 71, 73, 87, 112, 114, 121, 138
resource curse 6, 15, 28, 34, 37, 40, 110
Ricci, L. A., 35
Ries, J., 168
Rigobon, R., 35
rights 2, 31, 36
  of migrants 41–3
Robe, M., 172
Rodriguez, F., 35
Rodrik, D., 35
Rogers, J. H., 122, 130
Romer, C., 92
Romer, D., 31, 91
Roodman, D., 141
Rose, A., 2

Rosen, H. S., 141
Ruhs, M., 44
Runkle, D. E., 130
Ruppert, E., 61
Rutledge, J. E., 4

Sachs, J. D., 6, 28, 33, 35
Sala-i-Martin, X., 25, 26, 31, 32, 33, 35, 73
Salas, V., 138
Sarel, M., 33
Saudi Arabia 1, 2, 5–6, 8–11, 167, 171–2
  financial markets 149–61, 163–5
  fiscal policy 87, 89, 93–4, 100–5, 109–10
  long-term growth 13–29, 34, 36–7
  migration 40–50
  monetary policy 113–17, 133–34
  loans/stability 134–6, 139, 146
  spending, subsidies, and efficiency 65–68, 70–3, 78–9, 82
Saurina, J., 138
Scharler, J., 117
schooling 24–5, 28, 170
segmentation 41–2, 45, 49
Sellon, Jr, G., 117
Senhadji, A. 26, 34, 86, 134
Setser, B., 8
Shendy, R., 176
Shin, Y., 58, 59
Shrieves, R., 139
Siegel, D., 86
Sims, C., 122, 130
Smith, R., 56
Solow, R. M., 15, 31, 32
Sorge, M., 138
sovereign wealth fund 8, 9, 65, 152
Spatareanu, M., 170
Spilimbergo, A., 91
spillover 10–11, 71–2, 88, 132, 150, 152, 158, 160–1, 163–5, 166, 174–5
spending 4, 8, 17, 54, 56–8, 60–1, 65–8, 70, 74, 77–8, 83, 87–94, 95, 100–6, 108–10, 114, 130, 132–3, 141
  boom 60–1
  capital 90, 95, 109, 114
  government/fiscal 4, 8, 56–60, 65–84, 88–95, 100–9, 123, 132–3
  elasticity of 100–3, 131–3
stability 4, 9, 10, 31, 33–4, 67, 86–110, 132, 134–45, 159, 161, 163, 165, 170
stock market 7, 9–10, 115, 135, 139, 149, 150–3, 155
stress test 135, 137–8
structural 1, 4–7, 33, 42, 56, 61, 65, 91–2, 105, 122, 135, 153, 156, 166, 176
subsidies 7, 21, 51, 65, 67, 70–83, 114, 176
Sundaresan, S., 138
Summers, H. A. R., 16, 19
Swan, T. W., 31
Systemic 9–10, 138, 143, 149–50, 158–9, 162–5

taxes 17, 57, 67, 73–6, 78, 80, 83, 88–9, 91, 108–9
Tibshirani, R. J., 119
total factor productivity 15, 25, 27, 29–37, 69
trade 2–3, 11, 22, 29–32, 34–5, 37, 41, 51–6, 59, 61, 106, 114, 139, 142–3, 166–71, 177
  international 2–3, 139, 142–3, 166–70, 175–6
  non-traded goods 52–6, 61
  openness 29, 32, 33, 35, 56
  terms of 31–2, 34–5, 37, 56
transmission 7, 117, 121–2, 134, 152, 168, 176
Trinidade, V., 168

Ugur, M., 36
Uhlig, H., 92
Ulubasoglu, M. H., 36
unemployment 13, 41–2, 46, 47–50, 66, 79–84, 91, 138, 139
UAE, *see* United Arab Emirates
United Arab Emirates 1, 2, 5, 6, 9–11, 167, 170–3
  financial markets 149–165
  fiscal policy 87, 89, 93–4, 100–4, 106
  long-term growth 13–14, 16, 18–30, 32, 36–7
  migration 40, 43–5, 48, 50–2
  monetary policy 113–17, 123, 133–4
  loans/stability 134–6, 146
  spending, subsidies, and efficiency 65–6, 69–71, 73–4
United Nations 13, 14, 16–19, 43–4
United Kingdom 28, 57, 65, 116, 160–1
United States 15, 115–16, 158, 160–1 169

VAR 8, 88–9, 91–2, 95, 100–2, 104–5, 108–10, 113, 116–18, 120–6, 131–3, 144–5
  Annual data panel VAR 123–5
  Quarterly data panel VAR 131
vector auto-regression, *see* VAR
Végh, C., 90, 92, 95, 109
Venables, A. J., 4, 56
volatility 9, 32, 34, 86–7, 104, 106, 110, 134, 150, 152–3, 156, 172

wage 26, 42–3, 45–9 , 53–5, 65, 67, 70, 73–5, 78–83, 88, 90
  disparities 42, 45–7, 78
Wang, Q., 89

Warner, A. M., 6, 28, 33, 35
Weil, D. N., 31
welfare 52, 54, 65–6, 76–7
Wijnbergen, S. van, 41, 57
Williams, O., 116, 152
Wilson, D. J., 29, 30
windfall 4, 40–1, 53–6, 58, 60–1, 64, 80, 83, 166
Woodford, M., 89, 90
workforce 43–4, 50, 170
World Bank 16, 25, 40, 66, 70, 167–8

Zanna, L.-F., 4
Zha, T., 130
Zicchino, L., 145
Ziemba, R., 8